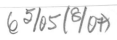

THE GENTLE TAMERS:

WOMEN OF THE OLD WILD WEST

THE
Gentle Tamers:

WOMEN OF THE OLD WILD WEST

DEE BROWN

UNIVERSITY OF NEBRASKA PRESS
LINCOLN AND LONDON

First Bison Book printing: 1968; reissued, 1981
Most recent printing indicated by first digit below:
5   6   7   8   9   10

Library of Congress Cataloging in Publication Data

Brown, Dee Alexander.
  The gentle tamers.

  Originally published: New York : Putnam, 1958.
  Includes bibliographical references and index.
  1. West (U.S.)—Social life and customs. 2. Women—West
(U.S.)—History. 3. Frontier and pioneer life—West (U.S.) I. Ti-
tle. II. Title: Women of the Old Wild West.
F591.B87   1981   978'.0088042   81-3428
ISBN 0-8032-5025-8 (pbk.)   AACR2

Reprinted by arrangement with the author

For A.E.C., L.C.B., and L.L.B.,
gentle tamers—past, present and future.

CONTENTS

Illustrations will be found following page 160

THE GENTLE TAMERS:

WOMEN OF THE OLD WILD WEST

The Sunbonnet Myth

WHO was the western woman? What was she like, this gentle yet persistent tamer of the wild land that was the American West?

Emerson Hough saw her as a woman in a sunbonnet and saluted her with eloquence: "The chief figure of the American West, the figure of the ages, is not the long-haired, fringed-legging man riding a rawboned pony, but the gaunt and sad-faced woman sitting on the front seat of the wagon, following her lord where he might lead, her face hidden in the same ragged sunbonnet which had crossed the Appalachians and the Missouri long before. That was America, my brethren! There was the seed of America's wealth. There was the great romance of all America—the woman in the sunbonnet; and not, after all, the hero with the rifle across his saddle horn. Who has written her story? Who has painted her picture?" [1]

Other evidence supports this stereotype of the woman in the sunbonnet. In a letter written from Kansas in 1857, Julia Lovejoy described such a traveler riding on the high seat of an ox-drawn wagon with household goods packed all around and above her head, "a basket of potatoes to rest her feet upon, in her arms a child not quite two years old, in one hand an umbrella to screen her throbbing head from the oppressive

11

heat of the sun, and in the other a bundle of sundries that could find no place secure from falling overboard, from the rocking to and fro of the ponderous vehicle."[2] And a Californian, describing the appearance of women at the end of a plains journey, said: "The poor women arrive looking as haggard as so many Endorian witches, burnt to the color of hazelnut, with their hair cut short, and its gloss entirely destroyed by the alkali, whole plains of which they are compelled to cross on the way."[3]

But the western woman was more by far than a face hidden in a ragged sunbonnet. Often her bonnet was gay with color and ornamented with flowers; sometimes she wore French millinery, the latest styles from Paris, small round hats contrasting with the enormity of her voluminous built-out skirts. Her petticoats were rainbow-colored. Her feet *might* be shod in rough work clods, but more than likely they were in high boots of finest kid, or high button shoes.

Whatever her dress, she had endurance, she had courage, sometimes she was wilder than the land she tamed.

Why did she venture there, into that vast and violent world of plains, mountains and sky, where danger and death waited —mocking her womanhood, crouching always outside the rings of her campfires, even at her hearthside?

Who was she, what was her name?

It might be Josephine Meeker, twenty-year-old Oberlin College graduate, who wanted to educate the Colorado Indians but was captured by a Ute who taught her the facts of life and then fell in love with her.

Or Frances Grummond, the sheltered Tennessee girl who married a Yankee soldier and learned to cook for him in the wilds of Wyoming; her heart was broken when he died in the Fetterman Massacre.

Or Margaret Irvin Carrington, who tried to soothe the grief

of Frances Grummond, never dreaming that within a short time this young southern girl would be married to her own husband.

And thirteen-year-old Virginia Reed, her young mother Margaret Reed, and Grandmother Keyes—all of Springfield, Illinois—who started to California one fine spring morning with twenty-nine others, including two brothers named Donner.

Esther Morris, a dignified lady of fifty-five, whose famous tea party in South Pass City, Wyoming, set in motion the machinery that brought women the right to vote for the first time anywhere on earth.

Julia Bulette of Virginia City, the prototype of all the fancy women in western literature, who wore sable muffs and silk scarves and would have blushed if any man ever caught her wearing a ragged sunbonnet.

Elizabeth Farnham, who sometimes wore bloomers; she tried to organize a party of New York women to journey to the California gold fields for the good of the female-starved miners.

And Flora Pearson Engle, who did join an expedition of prospective brides for Washington Territory's lonely bachelors and proudly told her story.

Eliza Hart Spalding and Narcissa Whitman, two gentle missionaries who rode sidesaddle most of the way from Independence, Missouri, to Oregon; they would have appreciated riding in the front seat of a covered wagon but they would not have worn ragged sunbonnets.

Dame Shirley, a gay young bride in the California gold rush, who read Shakespeare and Shelley and was amused by the hell-roaring life surrounding her.

Jane Barnes, a blond barmaid of Portsmouth, England, who traveled all the way to Astoria in Oregon with a "gentleman friend" and was the first white woman to set foot on the Northwest coast. Her fine bonnets so impressed a Chinook chieftain that he proposed marriage.

Elizabeth Custer, one half of a mutual admiration society consisting of herself and husband George—who died at the Little Big Horn.

Martha Summerhayes, who followed her Army husband into the wilds of Apache-ridden Arizona; both of them managed to survive.

And another Army follower, Annie Blanche Sokalski. She wore wolfskin riding habits, traveled with thirteen hunting dogs, and counseled her husband during his court-martial at Fort Kearney.

Ann Eliza Young, one of Brigham's wives, a female subversive among the Saints.

Janette Riker, who lived through a Montana winter alone in a covered wagon.

Lotta Crabtree, actress, adored by every western male; she smoked cigarets and showed her legs but still convinced her admirers that it was all in a spirit of childish innocence.

Susan Shelby Magoffin, the first white woman to travel the Santa Fe Trail. She did it in style, with silk sheets, counterpanes, a dressing bureau, and a maid. She was the antithesis of the gaunt-faced woman in the sunbonnet.

Loreta Janeta Velasquez, who fought through the Civil War disguised as a male, then went west dressed in frilly furbelows to catch herself a husband. She did, a rich one.

But most of their names are now forgotten, with only brief fragments of their lives preserved in a simple diary, a letter home, a notice in a contemporary newspaper. Schoolmarms, loving wives, eligible daughters, hopeful old maids, camp followers, adventuresses, missionaries, suffragettes, travel-book authoresses, actresses, reformers, calico cats.

They traveled westward not only in covered wagons but on

river boats, in army ambulances, in jolting railway cars, aboard sailing ships to Panama and by muleback across the Isthmus, or around Cape Horn to San Francisco, and some of them even walked, pushing handcarts before them.

The impulses that moved them were as diverse as the women themselves. Said the wife of a Pennsylvania carpenter who had pulled up stakes and headed toward the setting sun: "Oh, we had heard of the west, where everyone is sure to get rich, and so we came." Susanna Moodie put the answer even more frankly: "By what stern necessity were we driven forth to seek a new home amid the western wilds? We were not compelled to emigrate. Bound to England by a thousand holy and endearing ties, surrounded by a circle of chosen friends, and happy in each other's love, we possessed all that the world can bestow of goods—but *wealth*." [4]

The very poor, however, seldom were found in the westward moving caravans. A certain amount of *wealth* was required to outfit a wagon with supplies that must last the average five months required for a westward crossing. The Reed family who were with the Donner party were quite well to do, and so were most of their neighbors who were in the same company. Eliza Hart Spalding and Narcissa Whitman and their husbands were living comfortable lives in the East when they were struck with a compulsion to Christianize the northwestern Indians. On February 20, 1836, Eliza Spalding wrote in her diary: "Today we met Dr. Whitman who has been laboring for some time to obtain associates to accompany him west of the Rocky Mountains to establish a mission." [5] Two months later, in spite of her poor health, Eliza was on her way to Oregon, fortified by a burning missionary fervor.

Certainly the desire for an easier and more plentiful living was foremost among the reasons why women were willing to accompany their men upon the hazardous western venture, but there was also the lure of the unknown, and an intense spirit which historians usually describe as "manifest destiny."

The fact that so many women kept diaries of their journeys indicates their awareness of being involved in events bigger than themselves. In simple artless words they would make the first of their daily entries: "Early in the morning of May 15, 1855, we began yoking the oxen. There were twenty head and two cows, and only one pair had ever been yoked before. It was a great undertaking and it was four o'clock in the afternoon before it was done." [6] Or: "We started for California on the 14th day of April, with five yoke of cattle, one pony & sidesaddle." [7]

During the early periods of western migration—the 1840's and early 1850's—women were in an extreme minority. Among the members of the largest wagon company journeying to the Pacific Coast in 1841, there was but one woman; and only two were included among a similar party in 1844 traveling from the Missouri River to California. [8]

In the first sea journeys—of late 1848 and early 1849— around Cape Horn to the California gold rush, there were almost no women, yet several thousand joined their husbands and fathers in the numerous and more perilous land crossings of the latter year. "It seemed a pity," commented the historian Hubert Howe Bancroft, "to drag so many women and their charges from comfortable homes to face the dangers and hardship of such a journey." [9]

One estimate of the number of women who traveled westward in 1849 is 10 per cent of a total number of 50,000 emigrants—roughly 5,000 women, 2,500 children, 42,500 men. [10]

Even ten years later, when the town of Denver was founded, only five women were among a population of almost a thousand. (One of these women, incidentally, was the wife of Count Murat, descendant of the King of Naples. The countess washed the Colorado miners' laundry, her husband trimmed their hair and shaved their beards.) [11]

Rigid customs and nineteenth-century modesty in dress made overland travel difficult for the fairer sex. Recognizing this, one who had made the journey advised: "Side-saddles should be discarded—women should wear hunting frocks, loose pantaloons, men's hats and shoes, and ride the same as men." [12] Another woman, after reaching California in 1850, wrote back frankly to a friend in the east: "I would not say to any person Come for fear that they would not succeed as there will be hewers of wood and drawers of water everywhere but I do say if any of my friends or acquaintances are coming tell them not to bring females . . ." [13] But the females kept coming, and long before the first transcontinental railroads cut the journey from months to days, the numbers of the two sexes were reaching a more felicitous balance.

And whether she wore a sunbonnet or not, whatever her mode of dress, the pioneer western female was certainly a woman of tenacity and quiet force. She may have lived in dread of Indians and wild animals, she may have fled from rattlesnakes and tarantulas, but she contrived to create a home for her family and managed so that most of her brood survived without benefit of doctors or medicines.

Not all the brave women endured, of course, for they too were mere mortals. While journeying along the Platte route in 1866, Colonel James Meline noted a grave some distance off the road upon a solitary hillside, the marker evidently made from a portion of a wagon. "The inscription," he wrote, "was more remarkable than any I ever saw, and was touching and beautiful in its simplicity." [14]

The carved letters spelled out one word:

WOMAN

▌▌

"Peril Lay at Every Hand"

1

UPON reaching California after a hazardous journey in 1847, one young girl wrote: "We suffered vastly more from fear of the Indians before starting than we did on the plains." [1] This was a sound observation, for all the Indian tribes combined were far less of a peril to western emigrants than one raging epidemic of disease.

To the average woman, however, there was nothing more alarming than a threat of Indian attack. Death they learned to live with, but not the dread of captivity by male savages. In the present age of Freudianism, there is probably a ready explanation for the shivering ache of vulnerability that one finds expressed in letters and diaries of frontier women exposed to raiding Indians, and the often curiously unconcealed admiration for their half-naked bodies . . . "the best looking Indians I ever saw . . . tall, strongly made . . . light copper color, cleanly in appearance . . . the glare of the fire fell on the bare, brawny arms & naked bodies; having nothing on the upper part of the body but their loose blankets & as they move their arms about when speaking, their bodies are half naked most of the time . . . Chief Bowl boasted that the pretty ladies in Houston had danced with him, kissed him, and given him rings." [2]

From the time of the earliest settlement of America, women suffered Indian captivities, sometimes long and tortuous, and the more literate of the survivors began writing and publishing their experiences as early as the seventeenth century. By the time women began venturing into the Far West, there was a sizable literature of captivities, or "horrors and atrocities," as they were often called in the subtitles. The authors omitted nothing of such details as starvation, physical danger, and arduous marches, but in that age of reticence concerning sexual matters they rarely went any further in describing their "fates worse than death." Readers were supposed to read between the lines.

These horror books sold widely and were read as avidly by other women for vicarious thrills as their descendants now read sexy historical melodramas. The authors in many cases must have made enough money to compensate them for their miseries as captives. Mary Rowlandson's *Narrative* went through six or more editions, Fanny Kelly's story through four in nine years, and Abbie Gardner's book was reprinted time after time throughout her life.

Even Elizabeth Custer, who omitted most of the raw edges of frontier life from her several books, once took a side glance at the problem of female captives. "History," she said, "traces many wars to women; and women certainly bore a large though unconscious part in inciting our people to take up arms in attempts to rescue them, and to inflict such punishments upon their savage captors as would teach the Indians a needed lesson." [3]

It is easy to understand the settlers' compulsion for violent retribution when one reads such a contemporary account as that of Matilda Lockhart, returned from Comanche captivity in 1840, "her head, arms and face full of bruises, and sores, and her nose actually burnt off to the bone—all the fleshy end gone, and a great scab formed on the end of the bone. Both nostrils were wide open and denuded of flesh. She told a piteous tale of how dreadfully the Indians had beaten her, and how they would wake her from sleep by sticking a chunk of fire to her flesh, especially to her nose, and how they would shout and laugh like fiends when she cried." [4]

In the opinion of Colonel James Meline, a woman captive was fortunate to be made the mistress of one Indian rather than become the prostitute of the tribe. He cited the case of a Mrs. White, captured near Santa Fe in 1851; her husband was slain and she was raped by twenty-one members of the Apache band who made the attack. She then watched helplessly while an Apache knocked out her dead husband's teeth and made them into a necklace for the warrior's adornment.[5]

Women who had not read any accounts of Indian captivities certainly must have heard of some of them, for they were a part of the national legend. So, it is doubtful if any woman living in the West, or starting across Indian country, did not have a rather clear idea of what to expect if she were seized and carried off by a dusky, paint-smeared warrior. For example, a woman made captive by the Sioux in the Minnesota uprisings of 1862 was so terrified at the moment of her seizure that she "felt just like singing, so near did I in my excitement border on insanity. I have thought since many times that had I given up to the impulse and sung, it would have been a wild song and I should have certainly crossed the border of insanity and entered its confines." [6]

The philosophic Colonel Meline was somewhat puzzled by the failure of women captives to tell the whole truth after they were rescued. According to Meline, the truth was that when a woman was captured, the Indians almost always "passed her over the prairie." That was their jocular way of saying that she had been successively raped by all the Indians present. "It might as well be understood that this is the lot awaiting the female made captive by any Indians west of the Mississippi. It is invariable, and the mere statement of outrage and violation is but a meagre indication of such a woman's sad fate."

In many cases, Meline ironically observed, rescued women had caught venereal disease from the Indians, who had themselves gotten the disease from their women who had been "violated" by white men. "There is one singular feature attending all such cases," he continued, "which I leave the philosopher, the casuist, or the theologian to explain or justify. Whenever the poor creatures so captured and outraged are recovered, they invariably deny anything beyond mere hardship and privation. They are scarcely ever known to admit anything more." [7]

Not until 1879 was this screen of delicacy entirely torn aside. By that date the tribes had been subdued and confined to reservations, and any violation of the peace was subject to legalities, sworn testimony, and stenographic recordings. In that year, the last celebrated captivity of white women occurred, the case involving Josephine Meeker, who was taken by Utes after an uprising at the White River Agency in Colorado. Rather complete and detailed records were made of Miss Meeker's experiences.

In July 1878, Josephine Meeker, twenty years old and recently graduated from Oberlin College, arrived at the White River Agency, fired with ideals and ambitions for the improvement of the Ute Indians. Her father, Nathan Cook Meeker, and her mother Arvella had preceded her there by two months, the father having been appointed Indian agent in May.

Born in Ohio, Nathan Meeker had gone through college, become a newspaper reporter, and then joined Horace Greeley's *Tribune* as a Civil War correspondent. When Meeker went west after the war to write a series of stories on the Mormons, he was so impressed by the climate and scenery of Colorado that he decided to move his family there. With Greeley's backing, he founded an agricultural colony near what is now the city of Greeley, Colorado. After the publisher's death, however, Meeker's fortunes declined, and when the chance came in 1878 to become an Indian agent, he readily accepted the job.

Josephine was a tall, slender girl, intelligent, assured and alert, a true representative of the emancipated western woman. She wore her dark blond hair cut short at the shoulders, and her photographs reveal her as being pleasantly attractive. Welcomed as an assistant by her earnest-minded father, she was listed on the agency rolls as a teacher and physician. She immediately established a school for the Ute children, but was acutely disappointed because she could persuade only three to become her pupils.

In spite of the limited number of pupils, construction of a schoolhouse was begun in June 1879, but even before the building was completed two children were withdrawn from Josephine's classes as part of a tribal protest against the policies of Nathan Meeker.

From the very first weeks of Meeker's occupancy of the agency, the Utes had not been co-operative. They especially disliked his plans for converting them to farmers. In the first place it went against their superstitions to plow land, and in the second place they preferred hunting food to the tedious task of growing it. But Meeker went doggedly ahead with his plans. He employed several white men to work the farm and construct buildings, including a large house for his family, a granary, a bunkhouse for the employees, two storehouses and a hay corral.

When the Utes protested, Meeker clamped the agency regulations tighter. He issued a ruling that rations would be issued only once a week and required the head of each family to be present for the drawings. This kept the male Utes close by the agency, making it impossible for them to take long hunting trips.

Day by day the plowed fields and fences extended farther and farther out over the Utes' favored horse pastures. From their teepee village nearby, the Indians watched all these changes with growing suspicion and anger. "The most serious pursuit of these Indians," Meeker wrote in one of his reports to Washington, "is horse breeding and racing, and only those young men who have no horses will work." [8]

His continuous hints that the Utes' fine horses must go finally led to a mild revolt. The first indication of it came early in September 1879 when one of the employed plowmen was fired upon by an unknown assailant. On September 10, the revolt became more overt. One of the Ute leaders named Johnson entered Meeker's house; Johnson owned 150 horses and had no intention of giving any of them up. He quarreled with Meeker and forced the agent outside the house, tripping him to the ground. Fortunately for Meeker, agency employees working on nearby buildings rushed to his aid.

Alarmed by this show of violence, Meeker sent off a message to Rawlins, Wyoming, 170 miles to the north, asking for soldiers to guard the agency. On September 21, Major Thomas Thornburg left Fort Steele with 190 men; within a few days he was on Deer Creek, in striking distance of the agency. Thornburg wanted to avoid a fight; the Indian Wars were supposed to be ended and the War Department opposed any move that might revive old animosities. The column made camp, and Thornburg sent a message to Meeker, suggesting that the agent bring up the Ute leaders for a peaceful conference.

Meeker thought the matter over and decided to take Douglas, the friendliest of the Ute chieftains. But even Douglas was not reliable; only the day before he had removed his young son Frederick from Josephine's school, leaving her with no pupils at all. Douglas, however, had shown no outward sign of anger; in fact, he had raised the United States flag over his teepee in what appeared to be a gesture of loyalty. "Things are peaceful," Meeker replied to Thornburg. "We have been on guard three nights and shall be tonight, not because we know there is danger, but because there might be." [9] Meeker handed the message to an agency employee to deliver, a man named Harry Dresser. But Dresser never delivered it; he was killed by Utes twelve miles from the agency.

The morning of September 29 was bright and warm, with an autumn freshness in the air from the mountains. Sounds of busy hammers and saws came from the roof of an unfinished building which Meeker planned to use for storing crops. Some of the workmen were sleepy from dividing night watches over the past four nights, but there was no unusual activity in the Ute camps that morning. A few Utes were gathered around Douglas' teepee, smoking and talking, the United States flag flapping from its tall pole above the chief's lodge.

A little later in the morning Douglas walked up to the agency house and told Nathan Meeker he did not want the soldiers to come. Meeker replied: "Let them come if they want to; they will not harm a hair of your head. When the soldiers come they will sit down, and we will have a good long talk over all this matter and set it right." [10]

Douglas went away, apparently satisfied, but at noon he was back at the house with several other Utes. He was in the habit of appearing about lunchtime, the Meekers often offering him a plate of food. This time, bread and meat were handed out, and the Indians and the Meekers were laughing and talking as if nothing unusual was about to happen. Josephine afterward said she had never seen Douglas in better spirits.

"When are you going to bring Freddy back to school?" Josephine asked him. He said: "This afternoon," and went on to explain that he had taken the boy from school because he was afraid the soldiers from the north were coming in and there might be a fight.

"You had better bring him back," Josephine said, and Douglas replied: "I will." Then both of them laughed, and a minute or so later Douglas left the house.[11]

Josephine turned to her mother and said that she would wash the dinner dishes if Mrs. Meeker would dry them. As they began attending to the dishes, Nathan Meeker appeared just outside the kitchen door and asked Josephine for the key that unlocked the room where the government guns were kept. She gave her father the key, and he went away. That was the last time his daughter and wife saw him alive.

While Josephine continued washing dishes, an Indian came in to borrow matches. "I gave him some," she recalled afterwards, "and he laughed and said, 'Me now going to smoke.' He excited my suspicions because he said he was going to smoke, and he had such a sneaking laugh. I said to mother, 'I'll warrant he will set something on fire.' . . . He went on, and I heard several guns go off, and I looked out the window and I saw them shooting at Frank Dresser, and he was running. A dozen or more of them were there firing. One of the employees was on the roof and some on the ground, and the Indians were shooting at them." [12]

Mrs. S. F. Price, wife of one of the employees, had been washing clothes in the yard outside. She took cover in the Meeker residence, and a minute or so later Frank Dresser staggered in at the kitchen door. He was bleeding from a slight wound in the side of his head. As soon as Dresser obtained a rifle, he warned the women to stay away from the windows, then went back outside to join in the fighting. The three women went into Josephine's bedroom and hid under the bed, but they did not feel secure there. After a few moments Josephine said, "It's not safe here; let's go to the milk house." [13]

The milk house was only thirty yards from the agency residence, and they dashed across in a matter of seconds. As soon as they were inside they locked and bolted the door and sat down on the floor, their terror so great now they were afraid to look outside. After a while Frank Dresser knocked on the door, identifying himself. He had been hit again, this time a slight flesh wound in the thigh. Dresser went to the north window, studying the grounds outside, but he could see little of what was happening. He began stacking bread jars and cans in the windows so the Indians could not see inside. There was nothing they could do now but wait.

"We sat there all the afternoon," Josephine remembered afterward. "At intervals it would be perfectly quiet, and then again the firing would break out with say half a dozen or perhaps a dozen gun-shots at once. Then it would be quiet again. Then the guns would break out again. It kept up that way until about five o'clock." [14]

Shortly after five o'clock, Dresser and the women discovered that the milk house and agency residence were both on fire. In a few minutes smoke was so thick they began to choke, and in a sort of panic they decided to make a run for it.

For some reason they ran first into the burning residence. "The Indians were so busy carrying off blankets and goods they did not see us," said Josephine. "We ran into father's room. Everything was just as he left it; a book lay open on the desk where he had been reading; nothing was disturbed." [15]

Mrs. Price afterward recalled that they thought of secreting themselves under Nathan Meeker's bed, even though the building was on fire. "We looked out toward the north. The blinds were open. The Indians were busy taking out goods; they were taking the blankets, shirts, and everything else they could. I said, 'Let's try and escape to the north, in the sage-brush; it will not do to stay here; they will be in here in a minute.' Frank said, 'Let's go while they are so busy,' and we went. I ran outside of the fence; Josie, Mrs. Meeker, and Frank opened the gate and went into the field, and I crossed over through the wire fence. They then saw us; we had not got more than ten or fifteen steps from the corner of the fence north before they saw us and fired. They came running, on foot and ponies, and fired at all of us, and hit Mrs. Meeker. The bullets whizzed by my head and hit beside me. They shot at Frank Dresser, and as he would take a step the dust would fly. The last I saw of him he was about a quarter of a mile from the agency, in the field, still running." [16]

Because of a lame leg, Arvella Meeker could not run very fast, and Josephine stayed back with her. The Indians called out to them to stop, but they kept going. A moment later Mrs. Meeker was hit, but not seriously; it was only a slight flesh wound.

One of the Utes, a young man named Persune, called out to Josephine: "Come to me; no shoot you."

"Going to shoot?" the girl asked, hardly able to believe him. "No."

"Better not," she said, forcing calmness into her voice.

"Come to me," Persune commanded. And there was nothing else Josephine could do but obey. When she looked back toward the burning agency, she saw that her mother and Mrs. Price also had been captured.

Persune took her down to the bank of the river and told her to sit on a pile of stolen blankets which he had taken from the agency storehouse. She waited, helpless, while he packed his things on a government mule. When he finished packing, he ordered her to mount a horse, also government owned, and prepare to follow him.

Meanwhile Douglas had followed them down to the river,

and the two Utes began arguing; it was soon evident to Josephine that Douglas wanted her for himself. Persune, however, refused to yield his captive to the chief; nor would he give her up at any time then or afterward during the three weeks of her captivity. In his primitive way, Persune already had fallen in love with Josephine Meeker.

2

Not until October 21 was Josephine Meeker rescued from the Utes, by Charles Adams, a general of the Colorado militia. Acting under special authority given him by Secretary of the Interior Carl Schurz, General Adams searched out the location of the hostile Ute camp. With only three men and some friendly Utes, he entered the camp around ten o'clock in the morning. "There were only about ten or fifteen lodges there," Adams said in relating the circumstances of the rescue. "A boy that we met about a quarter of a mile away told me that the prisoners were scattered—that is, one woman was in one lodge at the lower end of the camp; another one in the center, and another above. I went to the lower end first, and I saw Miss Meeker peeping out of a tent. I dismounted and asked her who she was, not knowing her personally at that time, and told her that I had come to release her." [17]

In recalling the moment of her rescue, Josephine said there had been a rumor in the camp the day before that white men would be coming the next morning. "About eleven o'clock I saw them coming over the hills, and as they passed near where I was, a squaw tried to cover me up with a blanket and keep me in the tent. She made so much fuss, however, that it attracted their attention and they halted. I pushed the squaw aside and went out, when General Adams dismounted, shook hands with me and said he had come to take me back if I would go." [18]

General Adams appears to have been a thorough, almost

humorless man, bent on following the letter and form of the law down to the smallest detail. He wanted to make certain the guilty Utes were punished, yet at the same time he had no desire to draw in any innocent tribesmen. Adams decided to ask all living witnesses of the outbreak at White River Agency to make sworn statements in reply to questions which he would pose, the questions being directed toward learning the identities of the guilty participants and the degree of their guilt.

On November 4 at Greeley, Colorado, Josephine Meeker was sworn by General Adams to tell the truth, the whole truth, and nothing but the truth. It is from her testimony, probably the only stenographically recorded report of a young white girl's Indian captivity, that we may learn what happened after Persune took her away from the White River Agency in the fading twilight of that late September day in 1879:

ADAMS: How long did Persune keep you?
JOSEPHINE: All the time.
ADAMS: He had you all the time?
JOSEPHINE: Yes, sir; all the time.
ADAMS: Did he at any time feel willing to let you go back?
JOSEPHINE: Well, he often told me that maybe we would go to Uncompahgre and see white man. "Maybe so go; maybe so no go"; he did not know.
ADAMS: Did Persune treat you well while you were with him?
JOSEPHINE: Well, I do not know. No better than what I expected when I was first captured, because I knew the Utes and know their natures pretty well.
ADAMS: This of course is an official investigation and I must get at all the facts. It is not to be published in the newspapers or anything of that kind. I wish to hear the full truth in regard to the matter. Just consider yourself on the

witness stand. It is a matter of life and death with some of those Utes. The government will punish them if guilty and we must know the truth.

JOSEPHINE: Of course we were insulted a good many times; we expected to be.

ADAMS: What do you mean by insult, and what did it consist of?

JOSEPHINE: Of outrageous treatment at night.

ADAMS: Am I to understand that they outraged you several times at night?

JOSEPHINE: Yes, sir.

ADAMS: Forced you against your will?

JOSEPHINE: Yes, sir.

ADAMS: Did they threaten to kill you if you did not comply?

JOSEPHINE: He did not threaten to kill—Persune did not—only on one occasion. I asked him if he wanted to kill me. He said, "Yes." I said, "Get up and shoot me, and let me alone." He turned over, and did not say anything more that night.

ADAMS: Was it a constant thing?

JOSEPHINE: No, not all the time. He was away twice, making, altogether, a week.

ADAMS: He was the one who did it first?

JOSEPHINE: Yes, sir.

ADAMS: How long after the capture?

JOSEPHINE: The same night—Monday. Of course they were drunk, and we dared not refuse them to any great extent. A good many times I pushed him off, and made a fuss, and raised a difficulty.

ADAMS: Was it done while his own squaws were in the tent?

JOSEPHINE: Yes, sir.

ADAMS: And they knew about it?

JOSEPHINE: Yes, sir.

ADAMS: Did any others do the same thing?

JOSEPHINE: No, sir; not to me. He took me as his squaw, and of course the rest dared not come around.

ADAMS: While he was present no one tried to?

JOSEPHINE: No, sir.

ADAMS: Nobody even came near you?

JOSEPHINE: No, sir.

ADAMS: Did he say anything when he finally released you?

JOSEPHINE: The day you came?

ADAMS: Yes. Did he say that you must not tell?

JOSEPHINE: He asked me the day before what I was going to tell about the Utes. He said, "You go back and tell them that they are no good." I said no, I should not.

ADAMS: Have you told this to anybody besides your mother?

JOSEPHINE: Yes, sir; Mr. Pollock interviewed us. And I believe, also, Dr. Avery of Denver. She is a lady physician in Denver; of course we don't want the newspapers to get hold of it.

ADAMS: Did you tell Mrs. Avery that she must not make it known?

JOSEPHINE: She will not. But the Indians delight in telling such things. It is generally talked around at the camp.

ADAMS: They have not seen any white people, so far?

JOSEPHINE: But some of the Utes will in the course of time. They can all talk English, you know. You know how low they are.

ADAMS: They kept it from me very strictly.

JOSEPHINE: Of course they would not tell you.

ADAMS: Did they not seem to think it was very wrong?

JOSEPHINE: No; they thought it was a pretty good thing to have a white squaw. Persune's squaw told me I must not make a fuss about it; it was pretty good. I do not think she dared to do anything. I think she felt sorry for me, but she did not dare do anything for me.

ADAMS: Did Douglas ever offer you any insult?

JOSEPHINE: No, he did not to me, but he did on one occasion to mother. I think that is what made a good deal of the trouble —his squaws were jealous; they did not want her there.

ADAMS: Where did they take you to camp that first night?

JOSEPHINE: About twelve miles. It took us until one or two o'clock to get in, but we stopped on the way.

ADAMS: You remarked once or twice about the Indians having whisky?

JOSEPHINE: Yes, sir.

ADAMS: Where did they get it?

JOSEPHINE: They must have bought it at the stores, some of them. There are a good many stores at the agency—all of them outside—trading stores on the Bear and Snake Rivers. I think it did not come from the medicine supplies, because that comes in these round bottles and is labeled.

ADAMS: Did you see it?

JOSEPHINE: It was in flat whisky-flasks.

ADAMS: Did they have several bottles?

JOSEPHINE: What I saw—the bottle was about half full. They took two or three drinks and passed it around while taking me to the river. Douglas had whisky. Mother said a good many of them had. I smelt their breath.

ADAMS: Did you ever see your father's clothes in anybody's possession?

JOSEPHINE: One Indian had father's shoes on; I forget what his name was; I know him well enough.

ADAMS: Did you see his coat?

JOSEPHINE: No; but I saw his pants; I do not know who had them.

ADAMS: Did you hear them say who killed your father?

JOSEPHINE: No, sir.

ADAMS: Did you hear any one say who killed any of the other men?

JOSEPHINE: No, I do not think any one knew who killed them.

They would see a man, and half a dozen would fire at once and keep firing until they killed him. When they came across another man they would do the same thing.[19]

3

Josephine Meeker's story, of course, was only one part of a larger drama that had begun that bright September noon, outside the kitchen window of the agency residence. Her mother's experience as a captive varied slightly—was perhaps more painful because of her age, perhaps less painful because she had lived long enough to know how to accept fate.

When Arvella Meeker was hit by a bullet as she ran across the field toward the sagebrush, she lay quietly on the ground, pretending to be worse injured than she was. One of the Utes found her and told her he was sorry, "heap much sorry." He took her to Douglas, who was up by the burning residence. Douglas asked her if there was any money in the house. "Very little," she said.

"Go in and get money," Douglas ordered her.

Arvella replied firmly, "You go in and get it."

But on the chief's insistence she went inside, returning with thirty dollars in greenbacks and silver. She also brought out her husband's copy of Bunyan's *Pilgrim's Progress.*

As she came outside, she saw her husband lying dead on the ground, stripped of everything but his shirt. "Blood was running from his mouth," she testified afterward. "His head was leaning back, and he was lying very straight, as if laid out; with his hands right down beside him, just as if laid out . . . The Indian was ahead of me, and as I stooped to kiss my husband's face the Indian turned around and looked at me. I thought it would not do, and I started on and did not say a word to him or he to me. Douglas was half drunk and his breath smelt of liquor. All of them with us had liquor and drank it. They had, I should think, pint bottles at least, and they tipped it up, would look at it, take a drink, and pass it on to the next. We rode four or five miles and then stopped. It was a little canyon with high rocks all around except where we went in. They had us dismount and lay down, and this time they put the gun to Josie's head. They pointed the gun at me, but I was so tired that I just laid down and did not mind it."

When General Adams asked Arvella the inevitable question, she answered him directly: "It was made known to me that if I did not submit I would be killed or subjected to something of that kind, and after I gave up, nothing was said about it. Douglas I had connection with once, and no more. I was afraid he had disease." [20]

4

The full story of the White River Ute uprising cannot be told here; it had too many ramifications—an ambush, a bloody battle with Major Thornburg's troops in which the major was killed, government hearings that lasted for months. All the white men at the agency were slain, and the scene that met the eyes of the first soldiers to reach the place was horrible in the extreme. A chain was around Nathan Meeker's neck (he had been dragged about the grounds), his head was smashed in, an iron tent stake was driven through his mouth and neck. Frank Dresser's body was badly mutilated and burned. Mrs. Price's husband was found stripped and filled with bullet holes.

As General Adams summed up the case at the end of testimony taken from both friendly and hostile Utes, the uprising was "more the action of a lot of crazy and hot-headed young men than the result of a preconcerted plan." A final hearing on the affair was held in Washington in 1880. Of the participants in the revolt, only Douglas came in voluntarily to make the trip to Washington; the others had vanished in the wilderness of northwestern Colorado. Douglas said that he came in because he had always wanted to go to Washington where the great men lived. But Douglas was never to see Washington. At Kansas City, he was taken from the railroad train by a military escort and locked up in Leavenworth Prison. Long afterward he was declared insane, released, and sent back to his people.

Persune, it was said, never overcame his love for Josephine Meeker. He had promised her that she would not have to work if she would stay with him as his squaw. He offered her all his possessions; he wept when she rejected him and went away with General Adams. As for Josephine, she left Colorado soon after her rescue. She worked for a time as a copyist for the Office of Indian Affairs in Washington, then became secretary for Colorado's Senator Henry Moore Teller. She gave lectures on the Indians in several eastern cities. When she died, quite young, of a pulmonary infection, the Utes heard about it. They said Persune should paint his face black in mourning for her, but whether or not he did is not in the record.[21]

5

Few female captives were as lucky as Josephine Meeker. Some survivors became, in their minds, so degraded by the time they were rescued, that they had little desire to leave the Indians. After five years with the Apaches, 1851 to 1856, Olive Oatman appeared indifferent to being returned to civilization. Her rescuers found her "sitting on the ground, her face covered by her hands, so completely disguised by long exposure to the sun, by paint, tattooing and costume, that we could not believe she was a white woman." [22] Miss Oatman would make no response to the questions of the rescuing party, and not until several days after her arrival at Fort Yuma did she utter a word.

Josiah Gregg, on one of his trading expeditions in the Southwest, encountered a captive woman among the Comanches. "She had been married to a Comanche since her captivity," Gregg reported. "She did not entertain the least desire of returning to her own people." [23] Gregg also cited the case of another girl whose father had offered a large reward for her return. The girl refused to leave, sending word to her father that the Indians had disfigured her by tattooing, that she was pregnant, and that she would be more unhappy to return to her father than to remain where she was.

6

Less feared by women, but more deadly by far than the marauding Indian, was disease—the big killers being cholera, smallpox, and malaria, followed by such vague ailments as ague and bilious fever. In the first years of far-western migration, however, there were few deaths from any causes. Most of the travelers were young and healthy, and the land was so empty of human beings that there were no sources of contamination.

"Nobody took dying into consideration out there in those days," Elizabeth Custer said in describing a cholera epidemic at Fort Harker. "All were well and able-bodied, and almost everyone was young, who ventured into that new country, so no lumber had been provided for coffins. For a time the rudest receptacles were hammered together made out of hard-tack boxes." [24]

1849 was the year of the first serious cholera epidemic in the West. The disease followed the emigrants from the Atlantic seaboard up the Mississippi River, striking the wagon trains in the spring about the time of departures from staging points at St. Joseph and Independence, and pursuing them as far as the mountains west of Fort Laramie. An estimated 5,000 died almost before they knew what affected them.

As one traveler said, "there was one feature mixed with all this terror that afforded some degree of relief, and that was that there was no case of lingering suffering. When attacked, a single day ordinarily ended the strife in death or recovery." [25]

Sarah Royce, a member of one of the harassed California expeditions, told of driving through a storm filled with thunder, lightning, and fierce wind that threatened to tear the canvas covering from her wagon, but her fear of the elements receded before the dread of cholera; a victim lay stretched dead behind her in the wagon, awaiting a suitable place of burial.[26]

Women and children suffered both directly and indirectly from such epidemics. When they survived they were often left without husbands or fathers, stranded in the midst of plains or mountains, dependent upon others. Such a surviving family, a woman and five children, was vividly described by an overland traveler of 1852. "A more desolate looking group would be hard to find. An open, bleak prairie, the cold wind howling overhead, bearing with it the mournful tones of that deserted woman; a new made grave, a woman and three children sitting near by; a girl of fourteen summers walking round and round in a circle, wringing her hands and calling upon her dead parent; a boy of twelve sitting upon the wagon tongue, sobbing aloud; a strange man placing a rude headboard at the head of the grave; the oxen feeding nearby . . . We stopped to look upon the scene and asked the woman if we could be of any service. 'I need nothing,' she replied, 'but advice—whether I shall pursue my journey or go back to my old home in Illinois." [27]

Death on the trail was always poignant, occurring far from
familiar places and in the absence of friendly neighbors and
relatives back home. The same traveler reported the burial of
a child en route: "We had an empty cracker box which we
made answer for a coffin, dug a grave in the middle of the
road and deposited the dead child therein . . . We filled the
grave with stones and dirt, and when we rolled out drove
over it. Perhaps we had cheated the wolf by so doing—perhaps not." [28]

Susan Magoffin was profoundly impressed by such protective burials on the plains; she told of how stones were placed
over the dead in their deep graves, the earth tamped down,
the sod replaced. "Often the corral is made over it, to make
the earth still more firm, by the tromping of the stock." [29]

Common to virtually all diary records of the western crossings is mention of marked graves along the trails; in some
years the authors seem almost morbid in their meticulous citing of numbers and locations. "Saw a fresh made grave, a
feather bed lying upon it, we afterwards learned that a
man & his wife had both died a few days before, they left
2 small children, which were sent back to St. Joseph by an
indian chief." [30] Another emigrant wrote: "This afternoon
passed a grave; no name or sex; a fresh grave surrounded by
the green prairie . . . Were it not for the sick and dying, that
everywhere meet our eye, and the vast number of graves along
the road, the journey would be a pleasant one . . . there are
about 80 graves to the 100 miles so far; that is, new ones. The
old ones are nearly obliterated and their places no longer
known to man." [31] And Mrs. Lodisa Frizzell told of a man sick
with cholera, whose partner remained behind waiting for him
to die; the partner had already dug a grave beside the tent.

Nor did the dying stop at the end of the trail. In the places
of settlement, as a Kansas woman noted gloomily, "the grave-
yard is one of the first apportionments and the soonest to be

thickly inhabited." [32] An Army wife stationed at Camp Date Creek, Arizona, reminds us that Indians also helped fill burying grounds: "Our miserable little cemetery out on that lonely plain, had not one grave whose quiet occupant was more than 23 years of age, and none had died a natural death." [33]

Injuries were more common to men than to women on the western frontier, but a foot split by an ax, a broken leg, a severed artery, a frozen hand or foot could be and often was fatal to either sex—especially when no physician or surgeon could be called in to give aid.

Some accidents had their humorous aspects, and were often reported in lively fashion by early newspapers. The Minneapolis (Kansas) *Messenger* thus told of the perils of living in a dugout: "Sam White's cattle broke out and one of the steers weighing about sixteen hundred pounds wandered onto the roof of the Woody family's dugout. When directly over the bed occupied by Mr. and Mrs. Woody the steer broke through, falling across the head board of the bed. Mr. Woody finally got the steer off the bed and looked after the injuries of his wife and child. This is a great country, where cattle wander on top of the houses and fall in on people while they are asleep." [34]

But there was nothing humorous about being lost in the western wilds, as several women have attested. One of Frances Grummond's most harrowing experiences during her journey to Fort Phil Kearney in 1867 occurred when she was almost left stranded by the Army's wagon train in the midst of hostile Sioux country. To answer a call of nature she had walked a short distance away from the ambulance in which she was riding, only to find when she returned that the column had marched on without her. "When I returned to the road I found to my dismay that they had covered quite a distance. In my haste to reach the road, or trail, I had the dreadful misfortune to run into a cactus clump. My cloth slippers were instantly punctured with innumerable needles. There was no time to stop even for an initial attempt to extricate them, as fear of some unseen enemy possessed my mind as cactus needles possessed my feet. A realizing sense of the distance between myself and my escort was one of torture . . . With limping step, increasing the pain every moment, and without sufficient voice left to be heard I ran nearly a mile . . . The team stopped as I neared it. Thoroughly exhausted, I fell prostrate. On being lifted into the ambulance, I was unable to stir or explain my dilemma, for sensations are felt not expressed at the time of their occurrence." [35]

Janette Riker's experience in Montana was much more desperate, as she was left alone for an entire winter. She was traveling with her father and two brothers in 1849, headed for Oregon. Late in September they camped for three days in a grassed valley to rest the oxen, and on the last day the father and the two brothers went out to hunt for buffalo. When they failed to return at nightfall, Janette crawled into the Conestoga wagon, armed herself, and waited out the night. At dawn she started to follow the hunters' tracks, but lost all trace of them and had to return to camp.

For a week she waited, staring helplessly at the mountains that towered on all sides of the valley, gradually losing hope. She prayed for death, then decided she would try to survive. She knew she could not cross the mountains before another spring because the peaks were already growing white with early snows. Taking an ax and a spade from the wagon, she began building a rude shelter of poles and small logs. She stuffed the cracks with dried grass, banked earth around the walls, and stretched wagon canvas over the top for a roof, fastening it securely to stakes driven in the ground. Into this weathertight shelter she moved the tiny wagon stove, all the blankets, and the food stocks. As there was no meat among the provisions, she knew she must kill one of the oxen, which were growing fat off the grass in the valley. She shot the fattest one, cut up the carcass, salted it, and packed it away as she had seen her father do. She then began chopping dry logs and tree limbs for fuel.

Winter struck suddenly, a blizzard almost burying her shelter. For three months snow was packed to the eaves, but she kept a smoke hole clear. Every night wolves and mountain lions prowled around the shelter, howling, whining, and sniffing at the entrance. But Janette Riker endured until spring. The first thaw flooded her out, and she was forced to shift quarters to the wagon, living on uncooked cornmeal and raw ox meat until April.

Late in that month, with only a few days' supply of food left, she was found by an Indian hunting party. They were so astonished to find her there alone in the valley and so admired her hardihood, that they took her on to the fort at Walla Walla. She never learned what happened to her father and brothers.[36]

Fortunately, most of the women who dared the perils of the early West were resilient creatures, who for the most part rejected their afflictions and looked cheerfully to the future. An Oregon-bound woman whose husband died en route, leaving her with seven children, wrote to a friend back east in 1850: "I will not attempt to describe my troubles since I saw you. Suffice it is to say, I was left a widow in a foreign land without one solitary friend, as one might say, in the land of the living . . . I became as poor as a snake, yet I was in good health, and never was so nimble since I was a child." [37]

Faith in God was a mighty force, always at hand to strengthen the pioneer woman in her sorrows and her struggles against adversities. We find in almost every personal written record a daily prayer of thanks to God. "Thus the Lord provides, and smoothes all our ways for us, giving us strength." [38] And a phrase often repeated in the diaries of the period is this manifest witness to woman's need for religion in that time of stress: *The sustaining hand of God.*

The Army Girls

WOMEN have always accompanied men to wars—as wives, nurses, laundresses, or plain camp followers—and the women of the Indian-fighting army were no exception. In many cases the transition from the civilized East to the raw frontier was a rude shock, especially for wives of young officers just out of West Point. Those who recorded their emotions at the time often began with a note of exasperation at having to give up the comforts of the "States" for the far distant territories. But almost invariably at the end of their tours of duty in those isolated military posts, they had learned to love the life, and were eager to return to the West.

The wife of Lieutenant Orsemus Boyd learned on the second day of her honeymoon that the young man she loved had been ordered to an Army post in Nevada. "I considered New York the only habitable place on the globe," Mrs. Boyd declared, but then she bravely arranged to board a steamship so that she could meet him in San Francisco.[1]

The vehicle most commonly used for transporting officers' wives overland in the West was the mule-drawn Army ambulance, undoubtedly the most uncomfortable means ever devised for transporting wounded men or gentle females. Fitted up somewhat like a cowboy's chuck wagon, the ambulance carried a bucket suspended under the front axle for feeding and watering the mules, and a water keg for driver and passengers under the rear axle. A chain-supported platform at the back for storing baggage was called a "boot," as on stagecoaches.

Sometimes, if circumstances permitted, the vehicle was especially fitted up for long passenger hauls. Frances Roe's husband arranged to have one padded with straw and canvas on the sides and bottom, with a high canvas top drawn over the bows. A tent was folded to form a seat and placed in the back, "upon which I can sit and look out through the round opening and gossip with the mules that will be attached to the wagon back of me." [2]

On another journey, Mrs. Roe was not so fortunate. She had to ride with the commanding officer's wife and family, a total of six passengers. "There will be seats for only four, as the middle seat has been taken out to make room for a comfortable rocking chair that will be for Mrs. Phillips' exclusive use." [3] Rank prevailed even in a jolting ambulance.

In 1874, Martha Summerhayes crossed the Mohave Desert in a Dougherty wagon, "a large carriage, sometimes referred to as an ambulance." The vehicle had a good-sized body, with two seats facing each other and a seat outside for the driver. The inside could be closed, if desired, by canvas sides and ends which rolled up and down, affording a degree of privacy for the female passengers. Mrs. Summerhayes vividly described this desert crossing, "the massive blue army wagons, heavily loaded, the laundresses and enlisted men's wives and children in them." The order of march put the main body of troops in advance, followed by the ambulances, then the blue Studebaker wagons, the baggage wagons, and a small rear guard. A hot wind blew constantly; everything was filled with dust. Because of the heat she discarded her hat, and her head became a mass of fine white dust.

This being her first experience in the Southwest, she complained bitterly. Most of all she wanted a bath. A veteran Army wife scolded her, reminded her she was an "Army girl" now, and must not mind such minor adversities. Mrs. Summerhayes philosophically transferred her inward pity to outward pity for the Army mules, a feeling which soon grew into admiration for those much maligned beasts. "Each mule got its share of dreadful curses. I had never heard or conceived of any oaths like those. They made my blood fairly curdle, and I am not speaking figuratively. The shivers ran up and down my back, and I half expected to see those teamsters struck down by the hand of the Almighty." Her husband explained that the swearing was necessary, and after a while she accepted that theory and was constantly amazed at the feats performed by the mules and the skillful, profane Army teamsters.[4]

Upon arriving at whatever Army post their husbands were assigned, neophyte Army wives quickly learned the value of rank in obtaining desirable quarters. Second lieutenants were at the bottom of the ladder, of course, outranking only other second lieutenants whose commissions were of a later date.

When Martha Summerhayes discovered that she and her husband had forced another family out of quarters at Fort Russell, Wyoming, she was so remorseful she went to the commanding officer. "They'll hate you for doing it," the commander told her, "but if you don't do it, they'll not respect you. After you've been turned out once yourself, you will not mind turning others out."[5] During one five-year period at Fort Clark, Texas, in the 1870's, at least fifty general moves were necessary "because some officer arrived who in selecting quarters would cause a dozen other officers below him in rank to move, for each in turn chose the one then occupied by the next lower in rank." This system was called "bumping" or "bricks falling," an annoyance usually endured without complaint except when a bachelor officer would take over large, comfortable quarters, forcing a junior officer with a family into one small room.

After one series of "bumpings" at Fort Clark, a young lieutenant and his bride, fresh from luxurious eastern homes, found themselves quartered in a hallway between two other families. The wife accepted her lot gracefully, but no sooner had she fixed the place up comfortably than her husband was notified that a superior officer wanted his hall. This was the final blow; the young lieutenant resigned in a huff and left the Army forever.[6]

Many posts could offer new arrivals nothing better than tents, and even at large establishments such as Fort Lincoln during the Sioux-wars period, the detached frame houses for junior officers' families were so poorly constructed that the wind blew through the crevices. A lieutenant's wife, describing the interior of one of these Fort Lincoln structures, said the walls were hung with old canvas tenting to help keep out the cold. A sheet-iron stove in the middle of the room radiated heat for only two or three feet. The furniture included a few campstools and unpainted chairs and a dining table composed of three wooden planks stretched across two carpenter's horses (this also served as an ironing board, or as an overnight bed for unexpected visitors). The dressing table was a packing box turned on its side with shelves nailed in. Upon it stood a tin pitcher, a tin basin, and a crude mirror. A fur rug or two and some gray government blankets served as floor coverings. Curtains were unbleached cotton sheeting, sometimes dyed with beet juice for coloration. A kerosene lamp and candles furnished light after dark.[7]

During a stay at Fort Leavenworth, Elizabeth Custer lived

in similar surroundings, though she attempted to beautify her rough furnishings by covering packing boxes with cretonne, by tacking calico over shelves, fastening chromos on the walls to relieve the bareness, and decorating the windows with pressed ferns brought from the States. She also brought wild flowers in from her horseback rides and replanted them in the yard.

One of the worst posts for living quarters was Fort Rice in Dakota Territory. The family of the commanding officer, Colonel Frederick Benteen of Custer fame, had to keep the floor cracks of their house packed with strips of gunny sacking. Originally the walls had been papered with old copies of the *Army and Navy Journal* and *Harper's Weekly,* but the Benteen children, possibly intrigued by the illustrations, soon tore off large strips here and there.

Northern plains posts were generally disliked by Army wives because of the intense cold and complete isolation during long winters. Some of the hazards and discomforts of living in an Army tent during a Wyoming winter were listed by Margaret Carrington: "The snapping of a tent-pole at midnight under three feet of snow; the blaze of the canvas, as it touched the red-hot stove pipe; the snowdrifts that slip through the closely drawn entrance and sprinkle one's bed; frozen water buckets." [8]

Forts in Arizona and southwest Texas were equally disliked because of the hot summers. An oft-told tale around Yuma was that of the wicked soldier who ventured out in the middle of a July day and never returned; diligent research discovered only a grease spot and a pile of bones on the parade ground. Soon afterward his ghost was seen, searching for blankets because hell was not warm enough for one accustomed to Fort Yuma's climate. Camp McDowell also was notorious for hot nights. One wife told of having to sleep on the

parade ground there with ants crawling up the cot supports
and swarming over her bed—until she learned to put tin cans
of water underneath each cot leg.[9]

Housekeeping was a continual trial under almost any Western Army post's conditions. Wood for the cookstove was frequently damp; on the plains it was usually soft cottonwood
which would not burn at all if wet and burned too quickly if
dry. Indoor sinks were unheard of, and the contents of dish-
pans and garbage pails had to be flung outside. Drinking
water was kept in barrels outside the kitchen door, the lids
weighted down with stones to keep the wind from blowing
them off. The plains wind also was a great annoyance when
clothes were hung on outside lines, whipping sheets and tablecloths into ribbons or blowing them across the prairie.

"Sometimes we saw no eggs all summer long," Elizabeth
Custer complained. "The cook books were maddening to us."
The recipes always called for eggs, butter, and cream, all un-
obtainable most of the time, and she prayed that some clever
Army woman would prepare a little cooking manual for the
use of housekeepers stranded on the frontier.[10]

At a Fort Lincoln luncheon in the 1870's, the menu included tea, toasted hardtack, tart jelly made from buffalo ber-
ries, pie from chokecherries, and lemonade made with citric-
acid crystals.[11] Fresh milk was a great luxury. One Army wife
told of her excitement upon arriving at a new post where
cows were kept. The first thing she and her husband asked
for was milk. "We drank and drank again, and carried a
jugful to our bedside." [12]

As most forts were in areas of plentiful game, the meat supply was no problem. After a deer hunt, the meat was usually divided among the families on the post. Prairie chickens
or grouse, buffalo rump steak and tongue were common fare
in the plains country.

A surprising number of Army wives confessed afterward

that they knew nothing of cooking or housekeeping before marrying their young officers and journeying into the Wild West. Frances Grummond was typical of these gentle souls. Yet her adventures in Wyoming—a compound of excitement, romance, danger, personal tragedy, and a final desperate hegira across the plains in a blizzard—is one of the great epics of western women.

Frances Grummond's story properly begins with Army orders of 1866 which sent Colonel Henry B. Carrington and 700 soldiers up the Bozeman Trail into northern Wyoming Territory. There they were to build Fort Phil Kearney in the midst of hostile Sioux country and keep the trail open into Montana. With the first detachment of troops, Colonel Carrington marched north from Fort Laramie in the summer, taking his wife, Margaret, and a long wagon train loaded with mowing machines, shingle- and brick-making machines, doors, sashes, glass, nails, locks, rocking chairs, sewing chairs, churns, and washing machines. There were also boxes of canned fruits, live turkeys and chickens, even a brace of swine. One wagon was filled with the instruments belonging to a forty-piece band. Colonel Carrington evidently intended to spend a comfortable and peaceful winter at the then unconstructed Fort Phil Kearney.

While all these preparations were in the planning stages, George W. Grummond and his wife, Frances, were in Tennessee awaiting Army orders. George Grummond, a brevet lieutenant colonel of Volunteers during the Civil War, had only recently married Frances Courtney of Franklin, Tennessee. And he had also recently been commissioned lieutenant in the Regular Army, assigned to the 18th Infantry under command of Colonel Carrington.

The Grummonds arrived at Fort Laramie in the summer and, as Frances had had practically no experience as a cook, George arranged for both of them to dine with the officers' mess. The officers, according to Frances, "were most courteous and obliging to the only woman at their board." [13]

In September, George and Frances left Laramie with a second detachment, bound for Fort Phil Kearney, Frances already suspecting that she was pregnant. When they arrived, they found the fort under construction. Temporarily their quarters would be two "A" tents set up and drawn together, "the front one for trunks, two rather dilapidated campstools and a disfigured mess chest, the other for two hospital bunks which filled nearly all the space, a small heating stove opposite, leaving a narrow passageway to a tarpaulin beyond, under which was a cook stove placed ready for the preparation of next morning's breakfast."

During their first night in the tents, snow fell, drifting in and covering Frances' face; it was melting and trickling down her cheeks when she awakened. The pillows, bedding, and even the stove were also covered with snow. She shook snow out of her stockings and shoes and set about preparing her first breakfast in the wilds of Wyoming.

She managed to cook some fair bacon and coffee, but the biscuits were not of the sort she had known in Tennessee. Made from flour, salt, and water, they were as hard as stones. "No hatchet chanced to be conveniently near to aid in separating them in halves . . . impulsively I seized the butcher knife, but in the endeavor to do hatchet-work with it, the blade slipped and almost severed my thumb, mingling both blood and tears." [14]

Luckily, Frances Grummond had an understanding husband, and they lived an idyllic existence through that long exciting autumn of 1866. By December the fort was completed, ready for winter, but the ever present Sioux outside the stockade seemed to grow in numbers. The Grummonds did not give much thought to the Indians, however, for now they knew that sometime in the spring their first child would be born.

Early on the morning of December 21, a wood train moved out of the fort as usual. The day turned bright and sunny, warm enough by midmorning for the men to work without overcoats. About eleven o'clock, pickets on a nearby hill signaled a warning: "Indians approaching. Many Indians!" Colonel Carrington was notified, and he went up to the watchtower above his headquarters. A few minutes later, the signalmen informed the colonel the wood train had been attacked.

Carrington immediately ordered two companies assembled, twenty-seven mounted men, fifty on foot. Lieutenant George Grummond volunteered to lead the cavalry; the entire command was assigned to Captain William J. Fetterman. Aware of Fetterman's impulsiveness, Carrington made a point of warning him: "Under no circumstances pursue the Indians over Lodge Trail Ridge. Ride direct to the wood train, relieve it, and report back to me."

Meanwhile one of Grummond's close friends, Lieutenant A. H. Wands, walked out to the side of the cavalry leader's mount. Wands gave Grummond a friendly warning to avoid any rash action, reminded him of his wife's pregnancy, and wished him good luck.

Frances Grummond was standing in front of her quarters, watching and listening. "I was filled with dread," she said afterward. As soon as the column moved out through the open gate, Carrington leaped up to the sentry walk and ordered Fetterman to halt outside. "Under no circumstances, Captain," he repeated in a loud voice, "must you cross Lodge Trail Ridge." [15]

The story of the Fetterman Massacre is a classic example of Indian military deception, of the white soldiers' overconfidence. Decoyed by a young Sioux warrior, Crazy Horse, Captain Fetterman led his men up the slope of Lodge Trail Ridge into a cleverly concealed trap. Too late, Fetterman realized his blunder. As he turned to wave his troops back, hundreds of Sioux, Cheyenne, and Arapaho swarmed out of the brush and boulders. The fight was over in a matter of minutes.

Back in Fort Phil Kearney, Frances Grummond waited in her snug little log house nearby the colonel's headquarters, her heart "filled with strange forebodings." Some of the women of the post came in to cheer her, to assure her that all would be well. "Suddenly out of silence so intense as to be torture . . . a few shots were heard, followed up by increasing rapidity . . . Then followed a few quick volleys, then scattering shots, and then, dead silence. Less than half an hour had passed, and the silence was dreadful." [16]

When Colonel Carrington heard the rapid firing from the ambushed soldiers, he sent a second force to Fetterman's aid, but the captain commanding held up below the ridge when he saw literally thousands of Indians moving across the valley below. As the day died away, the temperature began dropping sharply, the sky darkening, the air smelling of snow. The relief force waited prudently until the Indians disappeared, then moved up to the battlefield. There were no survivors of Fetterman's force. The relief party brought in forty-eight of the dead, reaching the fort after dark.

George Grummond's body was not among the forty-eight, but Colonel Carrington knew after listening to the relief captain's report that there was no possibility the young lieutenant still lived. He asked his wife, Margaret, to go next door and inform Frances Grummond that her husband would not be returning. [17]

Frances Grummond described the scene in one sentence:

"Mrs. Carrington tenderly took me to her arms and to her home where in silence we awaited the unfolding of this deadly sorrow. Henceforth my home was with Mrs. Carrington." The irony of this moment was that in less than five years, Frances Grummond herself would be Mrs. Carrington.

Throughout that night, Colonel Carrington maintained double guard on the fort. At dawn he held a council of his officers and announced he would lead a strong force to the battlefield and bring back the remaining bodies; it would not do to let the Indians believe the fort's defenders were so weak they could not recover their dead.

Immediately before departing, Carrington went in to inform his wife and Frances Grummond of what he intended to do. "Mrs. Carrington was sitting near the window," Frances wrote afterward. "I was lying down. When the door opened we sprang trembling to our feet." As soon as the colonel spoke to his wife, he turned to Frances. "Mrs. Grummond, I shall go in person, and will bring back to you the remains of your husband."

"They are beyond all suffering now," she replied. "You must not imperil other precious lives and make other women as miserable as myself."

But the colonel was determined to go. He marched out with eighty men and several wagons, leaving secret instructions to the officer of the day: "If in my absence, Indians in overwhelming numbers attack, put the women and children in the powder magazine with supplies of water, bread, crackers, and other supplies that seem best, and, in the event of a last desperate struggle, destroy all together, rather than have any captured alive." [18]

The two women—Margaret Carrington and the future Frances Carrington—sat waiting through the long day. They wondered at all the activity around the powder magazine, the movement of barrels and boxes of food into the building. At last they heard the slow rumble of the wagons returning, the wagons bearing the remaining dead.

Colonel Carrington had found George Grummond some yards beyond the others, where he had evidently been covering the retreat. The lieutenant's head was almost severed; he had been scalped, his fingers removed, his body filled with arrows and bullets. Most of the other dead were so mutilated, "we could not tell the cavalrymen from the infantrymen." [19]

The first act of the colonel when he returned to the fort was a sentimental gesture, typical of the nineteenth-century attitude toward death. He visited Frances Grummond, handing her a sealed envelope, then left her to a moment of private grief. "I opened the envelope," she wrote afterward, "with eager but trembling hands. It contained a lock of my husband's hair." She suddenly recalled, then, another memento, an encased portrait of herself which her husband had always worn, and she wondered sadly what Indian warrior carried it in his possession as a trophy of the battle.

"And then the horrors of the following days, the making of coffins and digging in the hard, frozen earth for a burial place, when the cold was so intense that the men worked in fifteen-minute reliefs, and a guard was constantly on the alert lest Indians should interrupt . . . One half of the headquarters building, which was my temporary home, was unfinished, and this part was utilized by carpenters for making pine cases for the dead. I knew that my husband's coffin was being made, and the sound of hammers and the grating of saws was torture . . ." [20]

The dead in their numbered pine cases were solemnly buried in a pit fifty feet long by seven feet wide. And Christmas dawned, a day of gloom.

2

As news of the massacre trickled out across the West and on to Army headquarters in Washington, Colonel Carrington bore the brunt of public and military condemnation. Fetterman had disobeyed orders, but he was dead, and the fort's commander had to serve as the whipping boy.

Up from Fort Laramie, Brigadier General H. W. Wessels came marching with orders to assume command of Fort Phil Kearney. At the same time, Colonel Carrington and his detachment, with wives and children, were ordered to Fort McPherson, the journey to be made in the midst of a howling Wyoming winter. And because she no longer had a husband in the Army, Frances Grummond also must go.

She was swollen with child and insisted adamantly that her dead husband must go with her. Carrington gave in to her request and arranged for George Grummond's pine box to be disinterred and placed in one of the wagons. Then, in order that she might have sufficient funds for the long journey home to Tennessee, the few women who were to remain in the fort arranged to purchase her furniture and dishes, "paying double their value," she said afterward.

In preparation for the journey, covers on the wagons were doubled and the sides and ends of the wagon beds were walled up, leaving only a tiny window at each end. A hinged door was placed at the back of each vehicle for entry, and near the door was a small sheet-iron stove made from a stovepipe, with a smoke vent through the wagon cover. Pine knots and short blocks of wood for fuel were packed in one corner. Women and children were bundled into cloaks, shawls, beaver hoods, buffalo boots, and all the furs they owned or could borrow.

Departure date on the orders was January 23, 1867. Snowstorms and blizzards had been raging for a month, and Wyoming Territory was a drifted sheet of ice, the trail to Laramie blurred out. Snow was falling at 1:30 P.M. when Carrington gave the order to march. The women in the wagons waved farewells to the replacements from Laramie, already occupying the warm log quarters they had just abandoned.

That first afternoon and on into the dark night, the column struggled against the storm and the blocked road. A pioneer corps was formed and sent in advance to shovel out the deepest drifts. By ten o'clock that night, they had made only six miles. Carrington ordered the train corralled on a summit for defensive reasons, leaving them open to fierce gusts of wind which almost swept the sentries off their feet.

At one o'clock in the morning the moon rose, casting a cold blue light across the frozen land. Carrington ordered the bugle sounded, and by three o'clock they were moving again. The sky was clear, the stars brilliant, the aurora borealis dancing weirdly behind them in the north sky. The thermometer in Margaret Carrington's wagon dropped to thirteen below zero.

On through the moonlit night the column crawled, the wheels creaking, the cold intense. When Frances Grummond looked out her peephole window at dawn, she saw hundreds of buffalo wallowing in the snow. All that day the column was surrounded by buffalo, twenty-five miles of buffalo, a cheering sight, for it indicated lack of Indians in the vicinity.

At duskfall they halted on Crazy Woman's Fork and formed a corral in a grove beside the stream. Pickets were stationed on an adjoining bluff. The men dug wood out of the snow for night fires; as the wood burned the snow melted, then turned to ice, forming a crystal ring around each fire. They had to use axes to break their bread; coffee taken from the fires formed into frozen slush before it could be swallowed. From each little wagon pipe, white smoke poured in plumes, but Margaret Carrington's children were crying from the cold. The turkey she had cooked before leaving the fort was frozen so hard she had to chop pieces from it with a hatchet, then soften them over her little stove before they could be eaten.

Reveille again was at one o'clock in the morning. As the moon rose, the half-frozen men began shoveling snow off the river, broke through the ice for water to refill the kegs. A cavalryman had to be lifted from the saddle, his legs frozen from toes to knees. To keep other mounted men from suffering a similar fate, Carrington ordered their legs lashed with whips to start the circulation going.

Inside the wagons, the women wrapped themselves in buffalo skins and beaver hoods and sat with their feet to the tiny red-hot stoves. Margaret Carrington's thermometer dropped to forty below; then the mercury congealed in the bulb.

As soon as the teams were hitched, the column crossed the river, moved forward to a sixty-foot bluff, and began a slow ascent. Only one wagon could go up at a time, details of men tugging at the wheels, others pulling with ropes.

"When my turn came," Frances Grummond said, "I rolled over on my bed, clung for dear life to the sides of the wagon, with eyes shut and jaws clamped, to assist or ignore the situation, both being equally ineffective, for it all depended upon those mules . . . Of all rides I ever had taken in army life or out of it, this one in an army wagon without springs, with mules on a gallop over such a road, or no road, exceeded all in utter misery. One learns something from such an experience and I had learned to seize the sideboards of the wagon firmly, half reclining on the mattress with pillows compactly adjusted, and holding my breath abide the result." [21]

Dawn was breaking when the last wagon rolled over the crest of the bluff. Fort Reno and temporary security lay twenty miles to the south. By midmorning the sun's glare was blinding and those who had goggles put them on. All day, buffalo herds moved alongside, occasionally coming in close as if seeking company, the bulls tearing at the snow to uncover grass. Carrington passed along an order forbidding drivers to crack their whips lest the buffalo become frightened and stampede the train. There was one false alarm of Indians attacking the rear wagons, and an hour was lost in preparing defenses.

At dusk the first wagon rolled through the gates at Fort Reno, ending a sixty-five-mile journey that had required almost three days' time. They were all thankful to be alive, even the men who must lose fingers and legs by amputation in the post's infirmary.

After three days' rest in the warm quarters of Reno, they took the trail again, this time to Fort Casper, a march that was without perilous incident until the final day. As they neared the fort, Frances Grummond noted that her wagon was moving with increasing speed, and looking out her window she discovered the whole train at a trot, in column of six wagons front, moving all in mass. Indians had approached the column, stealing some of the led horses, but they ran off without a fight.

In March 1867, Frances Grummond and the pine-board box that carried the remains of her husband at last arrived home in Tennessee. A few weeks later, George Grummond's son was born.

Not long afterward, Frances Grummond read an announcement of the death of Margaret Carrington, and she sent a sympathetic letter to the man who had brought back from the battlefield a lock of her dead husband's hair. The correspondence which followed resulted in the marriage of Henry B. Carrington and Frances Grummond in 1871.

3

When Frances Grummond was making her long sorrowful journey home to Tennessee, one of her overnight stops was at Fort Sedgwick. Because of a shortage of quarters, she was told she must share her bedroom with another Army widow, the wife of the late Captain George Oscar Sokalski. Annie Sokalski "flourished into the room with her two favorite dogs, Romeo and Juliet. She unbuckled her belt from which two revolvers were suspended and handed them to a lieutenant who had escorted her to the door, giving him these laconic instructions: 'Have these pistols repaired at once, and see to it that the same are returned, for if exchanged or otherwise appropriated I can identify them anywhere in the United States.'"

As soon as she was settled in the room, Mrs. Sokalski arranged for a mattress to be placed on the floor for her use, explaining that her dogs always slept with her, and she did not wish to annoy Mrs. Grummond with their presence in the regular bed.

It is understatement to say that Annie Blanche Sokalski attracted attention wherever she went. In addition to Romeo and Juliet, she owned eleven other dogs for a total of thirteen—"the exact number of stripes in the American flag," she liked to say. She was a sure-shot markswoman and could outride the average cavalryman. She usually wore a wolfskin riding habit with wolf tails sweeping the ground at the bottom of the skirt, and a fur hat from which floated another cluster of wolf tails. The first time General Sherman saw her, she was galloping across the parade ground at Fort Kearney. As she swept past the general, he raised his hands in astonishment. "What the devil of a creature is that?" he cried. "Wild woman, Pawnee, Sioux, or what?" [22]

The court-martial of Captain George Sokalski and the part played in it by his wife is an almost forgotten episode of western military history. At the time of its occurrence, however, the case created considerable stir throughout the Indian-fighting army, involving as it did the bitter postwar friction between nonprofessional Volunteer officers and the professional career men from West Point. And because an Army wife counseled her husband in his defense, it attracted even more attention.

George Sokalski was a hot-blooded young West Pointer assigned to duty at Post Cottonwood (later renamed Fort McPherson) immediately following the Civil War. Both he and his wife were extreme individualists, almost eccentrics, and from the first Sokalski got along very badly with his associates. He scorned amateur, politically appointed officers, and was particularly resentful of his immediate superiors, all of whom were Volunteers of temporary ranks.

It should be remembered, before judging the actions of the accusers and the accused in this case, that all concerned had endured a long civil war and then without respite had been sent on active duty against the warring Indian tribes. Some of the Volunteer officers wanted out of the Army as soon as possible; others were maneuvering for permanent commissions in the Regular Army. Almost all of these men were very young, between twenty and twenty-five years; they had been soldiers all their adult lives. By modern terms they were neurotic, war-weary. They had had little opportunity to learn peacetime military procedures and military laws.

George Sokalski's troubles began early in January 1866, when he refused to obey an order to take his cavalry troop on a routine scout along the Republican River. He pleaded illness, and later testimony from a surgeon showed that his external ear had been frostbitten and that he was suffering from a painful infection of the inner ear. But Sokalski refused to bother with furnishing a surgeon's certificate of his condition, and when ordered to provide one he replied that "an officer's word for being sick was enough." He also appended an endorsement reflecting upon the competence and honesty of his subdistrict commander, Brevet Brigadier General Herman Heath of the Iowa Volunteers. This led to Sokalski's arrest for disobedience of orders, but no formal charges were brought against him at this time and he was soon released to duty.

During the next several weeks, aided and abetted by his wife, he carried on a vitriolic verbal warfare with the Volunteer officers of Nebraska Territory's Army Department, mainly because a sergeant had been posted as guard at the door of his quarters during his period of arrest.

In February, General Heath sent Lieutenant Seneca H. Norton to Post Cottonwood under the title of Especial Inspector, ostensibly to look into irregularities in the accounts of the quartermaster and the commissary. Sokalski soon suspected that Norton had been sent to gather evidence against him that would lead to his dismissal from the service.

If Norton hoped to connect Sokalski with the shortages and financial irregularities at Cottonwood, he was disappointed. The fact that the lieutenant soon dropped this line of investigation and began attempting to ferret out secrets in the private lives of the Sokalskis lends some credence to the captain's belief that Norton was sent to Cottonwood to manufacture a set of charges against him. At any rate, Lieutenant Norton secretly interviewed two enlisted men who worked as servants for the Sokalskis, asking among other questions if it was true that Sokalski regularly beat his wife and was cruel to her in other ways.

If the captain did beat his wife, she must have loved him for it, because no sooner had one of the enlisted men told the Sokalskis of Lieutenant Norton's questioning than she stormed down officers' row to the lieutenant's quarters and proceeded to give him a tongue-lashing he would never forget. She was calling Norton a "dirty little snipe" when her husband caught up with her.

"Your wife has just insulted me," Norton declared when he saw Captain Sokalski enter.

"He's preferred a set of charges against you," Annie Sokalski said to her husband, "accusing you of conduct unbecoming an officer and a gentleman." She turned back to Norton. "Why do you bring these charges?"

"I decline to—"

"Hold your tongue!" Sokalski cried angrily. "Don't speak to my wife in that tone. If you have been insulted, consider that *I* am responsible for whatever she said to you."

At this point, Norton's roommate appears to have interfered and calmed the quarrel. But a few days later it broke out anew. One of Annie Sokalski's unusual forms of recreation was to go down to the post's rifle range alone and blaze away for hours at the targets. While she was thus engaged one day, Lieutenant Norton and another officer chanced by. Norton watched her for a time with visible amusement. "By God," he then cried, loud enough for her to overhear, "when women go to shooting at targets, it's time for men to stop soldiering!"

When George Sokalski learned of this remark, his quick temper boiled over. He felt that his wife had been grossly insulted; he decided he must have satisfaction by dueling—if Norton would accept the challenge.

On April 17, Sokalski encountered Norton on the parade ground at Fort Kearney, stepped in front of him, called him "a damned dirty little pup," and slapped him on the chest.

"God damn you," Norton shouted. "I'll dismiss you from the service for this!"

Sokalski wanted to fight a duel; he was doubly angered now because Norton refused to accept his challenge. "Accept my

challenge," he roared. "If you bring charges against me instead, I'll blow your damn brains out!"

By this time, other officers arrived to break up the quarrel.
George Sokalski was ordered to appear for court-martial on
May 1. He refused to ask another officer to defend him, certainly not one of the despised Volunteer officers. He would
plead his own case with his wife's assistance. Armed with a
copy of Stephen V. Benét's *Treatise on Military Law*, the
Sokalskis began planning George's defense.

They composed a plea to the court: "The army is my profession; I entered it when a boy, it is my only means of livelihood; my time and what talent I possess have been devoted
to that profession . . . I do not ask for mercy at your hands,
but justice . . ."

Whether he received either justice or mercy is doubtful.
The court which tried George Sokalski consisted of one Regular Army infantry officer and eight cavalry officers of Volunteer regiments from the states of Nebraska, West Virginia,
Iowa, and Ohio. None of them knew very much about court-
martial procedures.

Sokalski's first defensive move was to object, one by one, to
the presence of the Volunteers on the court. "He is not my
peer, being a Volunteer officer," he said of each one. Then he
objected to the West Point infantry officer on the grounds that
the officer was prejudiced in his (Sokalski's) favor!

The court overruled his objections, as he must have known
it would, and the trial commenced. Charges and specifications
included his refusal to submit a surgeon's certificate for illness,
his "disrespectful and unofficerlike" endorsement of the order,
his assault and threats upon Lieutenant Norton, and an obviously drummed-up charge of unauthorized collection of
monies due a post sutler.

For eight days the trial dragged on, the Sokalskis carefully
studying Benét's *Treatise* and planning their strategy. Then

on the ninth day they decided the time had come to bring up the strongest defensive witness. That would be Annie Sokalski herself.

But when the captain asked the court's permission to call his wife, the judge advocate objected that "Mrs. Sokalski was incompetent to give evidence in this case." To the Sokalskis' dismay, the objection was sustained. Annie Sokalski had been confident that her appearance and testimony could turn the case in her husband's favor and against Lieutenant Norton.

From that moment on to the end of the trial, three days later, she knew her husband had lost his battle. However objective they might be, the eight Volunteers on the court were George Sokalski's enemies. They found him guilty on all counts except the specification that he had collected monies without authorization.

On July 10, the Adjutant General's office in Washington ordered Captain George Sokalski "dishonorably dismissed from the service of the United States."

It was a bitter blow for a professional cavalryman whose sole purpose in life was an honorable career in a service he loved—and that his wife loved, too. Very likely with his wife's help, George composed for the Adjutant General a long statement of his side of the affair, asking that his dishonorable dismissal be revoked. On August 27, the reply came: "Upon revision of the papers by the Judge Advocate General, he expresses the opinion that the statement does not contain any facts calling for a modification of the sentence."

After this, George seems to have lost heart; his ear ailment grew worse, and he was ill much of the time. But his wife refused to give up. She fought his case by every means at her command, and she was a stubborn woman. On October 26, 1866, George Sokalski was reinstated as an officer of the United States Cavalry. But ironically he had not long to enjoy this repudiation of his enemies. He died a few weeks later, at Fort Laramie.

And the night late in February that his loyal wife met Frances Grummond at Fort Sedgwick, she was on her way east, an Army widow without a home, like her husband "dismissed from the service of the United States."[23]

4

Even in an age when women's rights were yet to be won, the status of an Army officer's wife in the Old West may have seemed at times lower than the lowliest. No special provisions were made, no conveniences provided, for women to accompany their husbands to frontier posts; although such generals as William T. Sherman always urged that they do so. As we have seen in the cases of George Grummond and George Sokalski, when an officer died—in bed or with his boots on —his wife was robbed of both husband and home.

The constant moves from post to post created an enormous economic disadvantage for Army families; in the words of Martha Summerhayes, "the heavy outlay incurred in traveling and getting settled anew kept us always poor."[24]

Another wife stationed with her husband on the Pacific Coast complained that the Army always paid in greenbacks, which had to be converted to gold or silver before goods could be purchased in that region. The conversion premium was 50 per cent, or half the pay, and "that added to frontier prices kept us poor and hungry for years."[25]

If an officer and his wife wished to visit the States, they went on half pay, traveling at their own expense. "A cavalry officer was deprived of almost every opportunity of visiting home and relatives in the East, and when permitted to do so on leave was compelled to plunge in debt." Lieutenant Orsemus Boyd and his wife spent $1,300 on such a trip, a large outlay for an officer earning only $130 per month.[26]

Yet the Army wives managed to make life tolerable, with an unswerving loyalty to the service and a close cameraderie among themselves. As Frances Grummond discovered, the women's world revolved in a very small space. "With a coterie of five ladies at the post, each had four places to visit, and the most was made of it in comparing notes upon the important matters of cooking, sewing, and our various steps of advancement in the different arts."[27]

If a newcomer arrived with all her dishes broken, as was not unusual, the other women contributed new supplies. They banded together against their common enemy, the quartermaster, who dealt out supplies in niggardly fashion. "He seems to think that every nail and tack is his own personal property and for his exclusive use."[28]

In times of great trouble they comforted one another, as at Fort Lincoln when news came of the Custer Massacre. All the wives stayed together the first night, waiting for morning. Most of them lay on the floor with a pillow, sleepless, exchanging only a word or two, and springing up at every distant sound, thinking it might be a courier with messages.[29]

As hard as western service was on Army wives, however, most of them learned to love the wild land their husbands had come to pacify. On returning to western duty after a year's assignment in the East, a lieutenant's wife eloquently expressed what was probably in the hearts of most such women: "It all seemed so good to me. I was happy to see the soldiers again, the drivers and teamsters, and even the sleek government mules. The old blue uniforms made my heart glad. Every sound was familiar, even the rattling of the harness with its ivory rings and the harsh sound of the heavy brakes reinforced with old leather soles . . . I was back again in the army. I had cast my lot with a soldier, and where he was, was home to me."[30]

IV

Beau Sabreur and His Lady Fair

UNDOUBTEDLY the most romantic husband and wife on the Indian-fighting frontier were the Custers, George and Elizabeth. Together they formed a mutual admiration society that places them in the company of the world's great lovers, although George had a roving eye and there is documentary evidence in plenty that other women adored him. After George was killed at the Little Big Horn, Elizabeth devoted the remainder of her life to writing books extolling his admirable qualities.

While they were stationed at their last post, Fort Lincoln, Elizabeth was described as being slim, girlish-looking, with quiet, intelligent eyes. Her skin was soft and smooth, with character written on her face. Like other wives on the frontier, she usually dressed in slightly out-of-date frocks, favoring light colors. She kept up her French and German, carrying dictionaries and grammars of these languages with her wherever George might be stationed; she read frequently in the classics.

As for George, his most memorable physical features were, of course, his long golden curls, his keen blue eyes, and the tawny mustache which bordered his mouth. His face was thin and florid. Elizabeth once described his favorite dress as a broad hat, a navy-blue shirt with a wide collar, and a red necktie. He also favored fringed buckskin jackets.

The Custers seldom called each other by their first names. For the first few months after she married him, Elizabeth always referred to Custer by his middle name, Armstrong. This was soon shortened to "Autie." George began by calling his wife "Libby," but this was soon changed to "Old Lady," a name she did not care for but had to endure until the sudden end of her married career.

Among the constant trials of Elizabeth's life were Custer's dogs, a canine army which overran their quarters, ate all the meat in the larder, and often made sleep impossible. Legend has it that when Custer arrived at West Point in 1857 to enter the Military Academy he was accompanied by a dog, but the record shows he did not begin collecting his canine troupe in earnest until he was assigned to duty in Texas immediately following the Civil War. Many of these dogs were gifts from Texans, and when he was reassigned to Kansas he could not bear to part with any of them. He transported his pets by boat across the Gulf of Mexico to New Orleans, up the Mississippi, and on to Kansas, gathering additional members for the barking pack as he went. Elizabeth Custer learned early in her married life to control her feelings when her husband periodically brought in new litters of puppies and heaped them on her clean counterpanes.

"A crescent of dogs always hung about the kitchen door," she wrote. To feed them, she kept ready a huge kettle of mush boiled with meat, bones and grease, "but they preferred dainties from the family table."[1] Custer once took a quarter of venison to one of the neighboring officers; while visiting with the neighbors in their front room, he heard a tremendous scuffle from the kitchen. Nine of his dogs had followed him in and were busily eating the venison.

A female admirer of the curly-haired general described him as "a human island entirely surrounded by his crowding, panting dogs . . . he could halt his dogs with a sweep of his hand, locking them into a state of complete inertia."[2]

When on the march, however, the dogs were under rather loose control. Elizabeth complained that it was impossible to eat in the field "without being surrounded by a collection of canines of all ages . . . In order to save the buffalo meat from their tremendous leaps, it had to be strung far up in a tree, and let down by ropes when the meat for dinner was to be cut off."[3] Even then they had to be beaten away with sticks.

Custer also acquired a pet wolf, a female, which was assigned to the care of an enlisted man, who must have lived an unenviable life. On the post the wolf would chew tablecloths and sheets off the lines, and during one of Custer's outdoor excursions the animal came in heat, attracting so many male wolves that the enlisted man's field tent was entirely surrounded and overrun.

When he was campaigning against the Indians, Custer's numerous letters to "Libby" usually included more information about his dogs than anything else. For example: "We passed through Junction City without difficulty, the dogs behaving admirably." He later wrote her of how he had loaned one of his dogs to a fellow officer as a sleeping partner one cold night, gleefully adding that he had deliberately picked out the loudest-snoring member of his pack.[4]

By nature, George Custer was a practical joker, and as with most practical jokers there was often a trace of cruelty in his dramatized humor. Elizabeth, however, tolerated his jokes with better grace than she tolerated his dogs and described a number of his pranks in her books.

When Custer's father visited George and Elizabeth in Texas, George would tie firecrackers to the old gentleman's chair

while he was asleep and then light them. He also liked to drop
cartridges into the fireplace, laughing uproariously when his
father reacted by jumping halfway across the room.[5]

Once on a hunting trip in Kansas with some civilian guests,
George noticed that one of the men had fallen asleep on the
ground while resting after lunch. George placed a crockery
crate over the sleeping hunter, fastening it down with picket
pins and ropes. When the man awoke, he kicked wildly, bucking like a horse as he tried to throw the crate off. This antic
sent both George and Elizabeth into screams of laughter.[6]

Another joke that amused Elizabeth was the time George
told his Negro servant to launder his collars, handing him a
box of paper collars. The servant, of course, had never seen
paper collars, and when they came to pieces in the water
Custer roared and shouted in mock anger.[7]

On one occasion Custer terrified a young lady who had
accompanied his party to watch a buffalo hunt. After the buffalo was slain, he suddenly picked the girl up and sat her
down on the carcass. She cried out in panic, but Custer held
her firmly, gave her a knife, and ordered her to cut a tuft of
hair from the buffalo's head. The girl was so frightened she
could not move, so George's brother, Tom, gallantly stepped
forward and performed the task for her.[8]

Tom Custer also was quite a jokester. One of his hobbies
was collecting live rattlesnakes which he carried with him
even on field campaigns, caged in hardtack boxes. He loved
to frighten Elizabeth with these snakes.

When the two brothers were together rowdyism ran ram-
pant. One night George and Elizabeth were staying in the only
hotel in Ellsworth, Kansas, and because of crowded conditions
had to share their room with Tom, bedding him down on a
cot. Every time Tom would fall asleep, George would throw
shoes, brushes, and any other available missile at him to

frighten him awake. Elizabeth got very little sleep that night.[9]

A friend was amused by Custer's prankishness at a theatrical performance one night in Kansas City. Bored by the stage show, Custer entertained himself and his party by tossing crumpled programs at a bald-headed man in the orchestra seats below the General's box.

He always preferred to be center stage himself, enjoying dramatizing every situation, especially when women were present. One afternoon, while riding with Elizabeth and several other women, he came across a coiled rattlesnake. Instead of shooting the snake, Custer dismounted, circled it on foot, grasped it with his hand behind the neck, dashed it to the ground and stamped its head off with the heel of his boot.

Well aware that women adored him and admired his golden curls, he was thoughtful enough on the rare occasions when he had his hair cut to generously distribute his curls among the women of the post.[10]

Vain as he was, George Custer worshiped Elizabeth and arranged that she accompany him everywhere, except on the more dangerous field campaigns. Their honeymoon journey into Texas was an idyllic procession, the young lovers riding ahead of the column, foraging at farms along the way, buying only the best butter, eggs, and poultry. They slept each night in an Army wagon piled high with fragrant hay, and he had a special tent erected for her to take her morning bath, in heated water.

Even after they had been long married, the Custers amused themselves in the evenings with what Elizabeth described as "wild games of romps." Once while living in a temporary barracks, with neighbors separated from them by only a thin wall, they romped, "tearing upstairs and down, using the furniture for temporary barricades against each other, the

dogs barking and racing around . . . the din was frightful
. . . Rumors spread around the post that the commanding
officer was beating his wife."[11]

As far as the records show, George Custer appears to have
enjoyed only one serious extramarital adventure, and that
was during a long winter campaign against the Cheyennes
in Indian Territory. Following an attack upon Black Kettle's
village on the Washita, Custer ordered that the captive women
and girls be marched with his column to Camp Supply. Among
the Indian girls was Monahseetah, daughter of a chief, not yet
twenty years old. Custer mentioned her admiringly in his *Life
on the Plains*; he kept her with him for four months as an "in-
terpreter," though she spoke no English at the time of her
capture. According to testimony of Indians, who were not
unbiased, she gave birth to a child after Custer left her at
Fort Hays. The papoose was male and was yellow-haired and
fair-skinned, the Indians said, and Monahseetah named him
Yellow Swallow.[12]

One of the legends concerning Monahseetah that will not
die is that she was present in the lodges of the Cheyennes on
the Little Big Horn that fateful June day in 1876. Custer
learned of her presence from a scout, the legend says, and this
was the reason for his reckless impatience the day he marched
to his doom. But no one can prove this romantic tale.

As for Elizabeth, she too was fond of Monahseetah, a name
she said meant Grass-that-Shoots-in-the-Spring. Elizabeth met
Monahseetah at Fort Hays, after Custer arrived there with
the captives. "She was young and attractive," Elizabeth declared, "the acknowledged belle among all the other Indian
maidens." Elizabeth also said that she saw the baby, "a cun-
ning little bundle of brown velvet with bright beadlike
eyes."[13]

If Elizabeth knew of the whispered relationship between

George and Monahseetah, she gave no inkling of such knowledge in her written recollections. As far as Elizabeth was concerned, "Autie" Custer could do no wrong. He was her beau sabreur, and she was his lady fair.

Some Ladies of Easy Virtue

1

LATE in the year 1813, a middle-aged Scot named Donald McTavish was living temporarily at a hotel in Portsmouth, England, awaiting embarkation on a long sea journey to the Columbia River in North America. McTavish was, as one of his acquaintances put it, "of an amorous temperament," with a preference for lively blondes.[1] He was also a very wealthy gentleman, being one of the proprietors of Britain's North West Fur Company, and he had come out of retirement only because of the War of 1812, a war that offered an excellent opportunity for his company to regain its power in the west. Already the North West Company had captured John Jacob Astor's trading post, Astoria, at the mouth of the river, renaming it Fort George.

McTavish was bound for Fort George to serve as governor of the company's American empire. He was a man who enjoyed fine wines, rich cheese, roast beef—and lively blondes. He had loaded his ship, the *Isaac Todd*, with plentiful stores of wine, cheese, and tinned beef, but there were no blondes aboard. McTavish reflected on this deficiency; the sea voyage would be a long one, and no fair women would be waiting at the end of it. He recalled his younger days as a fur trader, remembering with distaste the fish-eating Indian maidens along the Pacific coast. They might do for a younger man, but not for Donald McTavish who liked his women fair.

He had noticed in the taproom of his hotel a particularly vivacious barmaid. She was flaxen-haired, blue-eyed, and to his taste. Her name was Jane Barnes. Being a plain-spoken man, Mr. McTavish made Jane Barnes a business proposition. If she would accompany him to western North America, he would outfit her with an unlimited wardrobe of dresses and millinery, and upon their return to England he would assign her an annuity of an undisclosed sum. Marriage was not in Mr. McTavish's future plans.

One of Jane Barnes's admirers said that she "consented to become *le compagnon du voyage* of Mr. McTavish in a temporary fit of erratic enthusiasm."[2] But after all, the offer was a tempting one, and Jane Barnes may have relished the thought of becoming the first white woman to set foot on the northwest coast of North America—in addition to acquiring several trunks filled with fine clothing, and the prospect of a lifelong annuity after her return to England.

Details of the long sea voyage are lacking, but on Sunday morning, April 24, 1814, the *Isaac Todd* lay anchored in the Columbia River off Fort George. About eight o'clock a schooner from the fort came alongside. The schooner bore the name *Dolly* in honor of John Jacob Astor's wife; the British had not yet got around to rechristening the captured vessel.

Among those in the Fort George reception committee who boarded the *Isaac Todd* was Alexander Henry, a very proper, almost prudish young man. "McTavish was just up," Henry recorded tersely in his journal for that day. "He met me on deck, and we went into the cabin where I was introduced to Jane Barnes."[3] Henry had not the words to express his astonishment upon discovering a young white woman, and a courtesan at that, in the new Governor's cabin.

As was to be expected, the presence of the beauteous Jane delighted the entire male complement at Fort George. They agreed immediately that the schooner *Dolly* must be rechristened in honor of the Governor's mistress, the *Jane*. And it was only by using the *Jane* that the young fur traders could see the object of their admiration; there were no spare quarters in the rudely constructed fort, and McTavish preferred keeping Jane aboard the *Isaac Todd*, where he could spend his nights with her in splendid isolation.

On one of Alexander Henry's visits to the ship, he dined with McTavish, Jane, a Mr. McDougall, and the post's surgeon, Dr. Swan. They were served cheese, brown biscuit, and port wine. "A vile discourse took place," Henry later wrote, "in the hearing of Jane, on the subject of venereal disease and Chinook ladies."[4] Henry was already beginning to feel a close attachment to Jane. He had never liked the "Chinook ladies," was disgusted with their immodesty and sexual looseness. Jane Barnes, he felt, was different somehow,

A few days later, Alexander Henry offered Jane the use of his room in the fort. On May 8 she accepted, and Henry wrote in his journal: "The longboat came with Jane, bag and baggage . . . About sunset the jolly-boat took Mr. D. McTavish on board alone; Jane, of course, remained, having taken up her lodging in my room."[5] Why McTavish elected to return to the *Isaac Todd* is not explained. Perhaps he preferred his luxuriously furnished cabin to the crude comforts of the fort. Or perhaps he was tiring of Jane, or she of him.

During the next several weeks, Jane Barnes ruled Fort George like a queen. One day she would decorate her head with feathers and flowers, the next she would braid her hair and wear no bonnet, always displaying her figure advantageously to the delight of all observers. She was "the greatest curiosity that ever gratified the wondering eyes of the blubber-loving aboriginals of the northwest coast of America. The Indians daily thronged in numbers to our fort for the mere purpose of gazing on, and admiring the fair beauty."[6]

Cassakas, son of a Chinook chief, soon decided to put in his bid for the hand of the lovely Jane. One day he bedaubed his face with red paint, smeared his body with whale oil, and in full courting array appeared at the fort for audience with Miss Barnes. He promised her that if she would become his wife he would send one hundred sea otters to her relatives, that he would make her mistress over his other four wives, that he would never ask her to carry wood, draw water, dig for roots or hunt for provisions, that he would permit her to sit at ease from morning to night, smoking as many pipes of tobacco as she thought proper.

These tempting offers held no appeal for Jane. She replied firmly that she had no use for a husband with "a flat head, a half naked body, and copper-colored skin besmeared with whale oil."

Cassakas' pride was crushed by Jane's refusal. He informed her indignantly that "he would never come near the fort while she remained there." But shortly afterward, rumors reached Alexander Henry that Cassakas was planning with some of the daring young men of his tribe to capture her and carry her off while she was walking on the beach, which was her custom every evening. Warned of the danger, Jane discontinued her walks alone.[7]

As she settled into the life of the fort, Jane began holding daily salons. She had memorized a few literary quotations, sprinkling them into her conversations, and evidently desired to be admired for her wit as well as her beauty. In his book, *Adventures on the Columbia River,* Ross Cox told of how, during one of her salons, Jane lost the devotion of a certain Fort George clerk when she violently attacked the moral character of the Chinook women. The clerk replied that their conduct was no worse than that of many white women he had known, and then he glanced significantly toward Jane.

"Oh," said Jane, "I suppose you agree with *Shakespeare* that 'Every woman is at heart a rake'?"

"*Pope,* ma'am, if you please."

"Pope, Pope!" replied Jane. "Bless me, sir, you must be wrong, *rake* is certainly the word—I never heard of but one female Pope."

Then in order to terminate the argument, she pretended to read an old newspaper (she was holding it upside down, according to the clerk). The clerk left the room abruptly, and as he was coming out he met Ross Cox, who noted "a wicked and malicious grin ruffling his sunburnt features."

"Well," said Cox, "what's the matter? You seem annoyed."

"What do you think," the clerk replied hotly, "I have just had a conversation with that fine-looking damsel there, who looks down with contempt on our women, and may I be damned if the bitch understands B from buffalo!"[8]

Meanwhile, Governor Donald McTavish was completing his business affairs at Fort George; he decided the time had come for him to depart for Montreal, inspecting other posts along the way. Originally he had planned to take Jane Barnes with him on the long overland journey. Why his plans were changed is not clear. Possibly Jane refused to go; possibly McTavish realized the journey would be too arduous for a woman. At any rate, it was decided that Jane would return on the *Isaac Todd,* which would be sailing in a few weeks with a load of furs for England, by way of Canton.

During the interim between McTavish's departure and the ship's sailing, Jane was to be in the keeping of Alexander Henry. McTavish ordered it that way, young Henry recording the agreement in his journal: "Conferred with Mr. D. McTavish regarding Jane; his three stipulations were: first, her person: second, the table; and third, to cause no misunderstanding with the young gentlemen, etc. This was the sum total . . . My part is mainly to protect her from ill usage. Affection is out of the question; our acquaintance is too short, and she has placed her affections elsewhere. I shall, therefore, make it my duty to render her situation as comfortable as possible; not as a lover, but through humanity. I know the ground on which she stands, and the pros and cons of the whole situation."[9]

Fate intervened, however, and all the gentlemanly agreements between McTavish and Henry came to naught. A few days later, on the eve of McTavish's planned departure for Montreal, while the Governor and young Henry were attempting to cross the Columbia River from Fort George, their open boat capsized and both were drowned.

Left with no protector, Jane Barnes calmly rejected one more suitor—the fort's surgeon, Dr. Swan—and prepared to sail aboard the *Isaac Todd*. At last she was off for Canton, where she went ashore and immediately "captivated an English gentleman of great wealth connected with the East India Company." The gentleman offered her "a splendid establishment."

In comparison with the lady missionaries who arrived in Oregon some three decades later, Jane Barnes has been treated badly by historians. "A vain, dressy, loose-boned, ex-vestal of engaging address with an eye to the main chance," Elliot Coues described her.[10] This is harsh judgment on a true pioneer. Jane was merely ahead of her time; had she landed in San Francisco during the gold rush she would have more than made her mark.

What finally became of her? Records indicate that she appeared some years later in Montreal to claim from the North West Company the annuity she declared had been promised her by Donald McTavish. After that, she vanishes.

2

Almost a half-century after Jane Barnes sailed away from
Fort George, a young woman of similar talents was beginning
a legendary career in Virginia City, Nevada. Her name was
Julia Bulette. Brunette rather than blonde, she had the face
of a Creole beauty—rich creamy complexion, large dark eyes,
wide sensuous mouth.

Julia Bulette arrived in Virginia City soon after the discovery of the fabulous Comstock Lode in 1859. For some
weeks she was the only unattached female in the booming
community of hundreds of miners. The combination of her
beauty, the scarcity of her commodity, and the affluent condition of her customers explains the magnitude of the fortune
she accumulated during the next three years. At the height of
her fame, her fee was reputed to be one thousand dollars per
evening.

No one ever knew for certain where Julia Bulette came
from; some said she was French, some said English. More
than one Virginia City gentleman swore he had seen her in
New Orleans in earlier years, and one writer described her as
being "pure Gulf" in origin. But after her death, by violence,
the local newspapers reported she was born in Liverpool and
that her real name was Smith.[11]

Whatever her origins, Julia Bulette's sudden prosperity
enabled her to build the first magnificent structure in Virginia
City. Her house on D Street, with its rococo ornamentation,
was an oasis in a community of drab shacks and cheerless
rooming houses. Known as Julia's Palace, it was the only real
home the miners had, a well-appointed, well-regulated center
of social life. She allowed no disorderly conduct in the Palace;
visitors had to behave at all times as gentlemen, or out they
went. She taught her customers to appreciate imported
French wines as well as the more commonly available "taran-

tula juice." She served French cooking; she wore the latest styles from Paris. Elegance was the word for Julia Bulette and her Palace.

And to a man, the miners adored her. "Her skin may be scarlet," said one of them, "but her heart is white." A more imaginative admirer said that she "caressed Sun Mountain with a gentle touch of splendor." She inspired chivalry in these roughest, toughest men the West ever knew, and they accorded her the homage of a great lady.[12]

As Julia's earnings increased, she expanded her operations, importing only the most accomplished and refined girls from San Francisco. She appeared regularly in the streets of Virginia City driving a lacquered brougham which bore a painted escutcheon on the panel—four aces crowned by a lion couchant. She wore sable muffs and scarfs. Each day the Wells Fargo stage from California brought cut flowers for her Palace.

Her greatest delight, however, was her honorary membership in the Virginia City Fire Company. On July 4, 1861, the firemen elected Julia the Queen of the Independence Day parade. Crowned in a fireman's hat and carrying a brass fire trumpet filled with fresh roses, she rode Engine Company Number One's shiny new truck through the town, the red-shirted firemen marching behind. For the occasion she had designed a large banner which was mounted in front of the engine.

Julia took her membership in the fire company seriously and donated money regularly for new equipment. When the warning whistle shrilled, she would rush from her Palace to the scene of the fire. If the engine passed her, the driver would slow down and take her aboard, and she in turn would lend a hand at working a water pump. If the fire burned for some time, she would brew coffee and serve it to the toiling fire fighters.[13]

One of the more exciting events in Virginia City during the

reign of Julia Bulette was the so-called Piute War of 1860. The trouble started at nearby Williams Station, after some white men captured two young Piute girls, shut them up in a cellar, and raped them. The Indians responded by attacking the station and massacring every man there. As no troops were in the vicinity, a force of 105 volunteers was raised in Virginia City. They marched down the Carson River to deal out punishment to the Piutes for taking the law into their own hands. The Indians, however, set a clever trap in a narrow pass and wiped out a large part of the force.

When a lone horseman rode back with the startling news of disaster, Virginia City became panic-stricken, sure that an attack upon the town was imminent. The miners warned Julia to go to Carson City for safety. She replied that if the miners stayed, she also would stay and make soup for the defenders. They finally persuaded her to join the dozen or so other women who had moved into an unfinished stone hotel. Window openings were boarded up and walls barricaded, and guards were stationed to patrol the area. The miners were determined to protect their beloved Julia to the death.

A few days later, a second volunteer army was formed, 750 strong, and Julia cheered them out of the town. They met the Piutes this time at Pinnacle Mount and defeated them, ending any further danger to Virginia City from Indian attack.[14]

Julia always stood by her miners in times of danger and misfortune. When several hundred men became ill from drinking water impregnated with arsenic, she turned her Palace into a hospital and went on duty as a nurse, soothing and comforting, and bringing the patients back to health on a diet of warm soup and rice. And she showed her patriotism during the Civil War by making a speech before a mass meeting assembled to raise funds for President Lincoln's Sanitary Commission. She bid up the value of an auctioned sack of flour to a phenomenal sum, then turned it back to be auctioned again.[15]

Julia Bulette's power reached its zenith in 1863, the boom year when Virginia City's population was 30,000, the second largest city then west of Chicago, with "a red light district superior to any other from Denver to the Coast, both in size and in the variety and amiability of its inmates."[16]

Gradually the town's size and wealth turned it toward conservatism and respectability, and as the community matured Julia's position changed. For example, it had always been her custom when attending the local theater to sit in the audience with the rowdy miners. But when Adah Menken came to Virginia City in March 1864, Julia sat in a box behind half-drawn curtains, exiled because the town had become too respectable for her. She still wore her diamond earrings, her brilliant rubies, her costly sables, but she was no longer a part of the public show.

Julia Bulette, however, was not to drift into the drab obscurity that is the usual fate of her kind. She died as flamboyantly as she had lived. One winter's night, three men with coat collars turned up about their faces knocked on the door of the Palace. Some time later they left, unnoticed, their pockets filled with Julia's valuable collection of precious stones and jewels. Next morning, Julia's French maid found her dead, stretched partially nude across her expensive bed, her beautiful throat marked by a strangler's hands.

Every adult male in the area immediately went into mourning for Julia Bulette. The mines and mills shut down, the saloons hung out black wreaths, the fire company covered its engines with black streamers. When the forces of law failed to turn up the murderer, there was talk of organizing a vigilante committee to track him down.

On the day of her funeral, thousands formed a procession

of honor behind the black-plumed, glass-walled hearse, first the firemen in their blue, pearl-buttoned uniforms, then the Nevada militia band playing the funeral dirge. Every window along the respectable streets was shuttered, the respectable women shielding themselves from the passing spectacle. Julia was buried with pomp and dignity in unconsecrated ground, and then the procession turned back toward the town, the militia band playing, as it would have done for a dead soldier, the sprightly music of "The Girl I Left Behind Me."

Not until almost a year later was the murderer discovered. He was John Millain, and although he had some of Julia's stolen goods in his possession, he denied being guilty of murder, claiming that he was only an accomplice in the robbery. Nevertheless, he was sentenced to be hanged on April 24, 1868, and a gallows was built for him in a natural amphitheater north of town. While Millain awaited the day of his doom, the respectable women began a crusade to free him, some declaring him to be innocent, others lauding him for ridding Virginia City of such a wicked creature as Julia Bulette. They brought wines and fine delicacies to the prisoner in his cell but got nowhere with their cause.

On John Millain's hanging day, the mines, saloons, and schools all closed down, and the populace gathered around the gallows for a holiday. Shortly after noon, Millain and a priest arrived in a barouche, followed by the sheriff and other high officials, all wearing top hats. Millain mounted the gallows, kneeled for the blessing of the priest, bowed to the crowd, and began addressing a flattering speech of farewell to the respectable ladies of the town. His last words were a denial of guilt; then he was dropped through the trap on the end of a rope.[17]

There should have ended the legend of Julia Bulette. Yet somehow the town she had grown up with could not forget her. Even after Virginia City's fortunes declined through the following decades, her memory persisted. The Virginia & Truckee Railroad honored her by naming one of its richly furnished club coaches the *Julia Bulette*, a car which was purchased many years later by a motion-picture company for use in filming western movies. In at least two Virginia City saloons of today may be found paintings of the immortal Julia. And in his book, *Silver Kings*, Oscar Lewis says that she has been written about more than any other woman of the Comstock Lode. Certainly in the stylized literature of the American West, she seems permanently ensconced—not only under her own name, but as the prototype of all the fancy women of the Old West. If Bret Harte never met her, he certainly must have heard of her. Rex Beach renamed her Cherry Melotte and used her in his novel, *The Spoilers*. Other greater and lesser writers of serious literature and melodrama have used Julia Bulette as a model. She seems destined to endure forever, this harlot with a heart of gold.

3

In the years following the murder of Julia Bulette, the West passed through its violent period of the gunfighters, and the temperaments of its "calico queens" matched the land's reckless mood. Typical of the period was Kitty Le Roy, who started her career at the age of ten as a jig dancer in Dallas, Texas. Kitty soon turned her talents to dealing faro. In the booming 1870's she transferred her operations to Dakota's Black Hills, attracting considerable attention around Deadwood with her extravagant gypsylike attire.

"Kitty Le Roy was what a real man would call a starry beauty," an admiring newspaper correspondent wrote of her after her fifth husband shot her to death. "Her brown hair was thick and curling; she had five husbands, seven revolvers, a dozen bowie-knives, and always went armed to the teeth, which latter were like pearls set in coral. She was a terrific gambler, and wore in her ears immense diamonds, which shone almost like her glorious eyes. The magnetism about her marvelous beauty was such as to drive her lovers crazy; more men had been killed about her than all the other women in the hills combined, and it was only a question whether her lovers or herself had killed the most. She married her first husband because he was the only man of all her lovers who had the nerve to let her shoot an apple off his head while she rode by at full speed. On one occasion she disguised herself in male attire to fight a man who refused to combat a woman. He fell, and she then cried, and married him in time to be his widow."[18]

Kitty's gambling den in Deadwood was called the "Mint," and she used it to attract husbands as well as money. One of her victims was a German prospector who had struck a rich vein of ore. Kitty made a play for him, took him for eight thousand dollars in gold, and then, when his claim would yield no more, crowned him with a bottle and drove him from her door.

But the magnetic Kitty met her doom in the person of her fifth husband. He beat her to the draw, shot her dead at the early age of twenty-eight, and then dramatically killed himself.

4

The West's golden era for women of easy virtue was during the 1850's in California, a time and a place wherein men outnumbered women ten or more to one, a raw society without order, morality or sobriety. In her book, *Incidents of Land and Water*, Mrs. D. B. Bates devoted a chapter to what she called "the moral tone of society" as it existed in California in 1851 and 1852. "Well may it call a blush to the cheek of our own sex," she wrote, "when I assert that the immoral predominated as far as the female portion of the community were concerned." She related the story of Lillie Lee, whose mother innocently brought her to California to seek a home for both of them. "Better, far better," said Mrs. Bates, "had she immured herself and child in the catacombs of Rome than thus to have launched their frail bark upon the golden wave of a California sea," and she wonders why the mother could not have realized the danger incurred by placing a young, lovely, and attractive girl "in a country where virtue was regarded by the mass only as a name."

Needless to say, Lillie Lee was far too captivating to remain long in obscurity. Despite her mother's vigilance she succumbed to the wiles of a gambler and fled with him to one of the interior gold settlements. After a bit of soul searching, the mother armed herself with a Colt's revolver and started in pursuit. Arriving in the gold-field town, she wandered from one house of sin to the next, where "elegantly attired women within whose natures long since had expired the last flickering spark of feminine modesty, were seated, dealing cards at a game of Faro or Lansquenet, and by their winning smile and enticing manner, inducing hundreds of men to stake their all upon their tables."

At last the mother found the house where Lillie and the gambler were staying, and when the villain answered her knock upon the door of their room she leveled her revolver at his breast. But little Lillie sprang between them, and after the gambler promised marriage the mother spared his life.

The sequel to Lillie Lee's story is pure modern soap opera. The wicked gambler already was married to another woman, the wife was soon to arrive on a boat from the east, and Lillie supposedly was taught a bitter lesson.

But did she reform, repent of her sins? No, she rushed recklessly into the life of a scarlet woman. And Mrs. Bates makes

Lillie's career so attractive that one wonders what the effect of this story was upon sheltered young ladies reading the book a century ago.

On some days, "Lillie Lee would appear in a splendid Turkish costume which admirably displayed her tiny little foot encased in richly embroidered satin slippers. Thus she would promenade the thronged thorofares of the city, the observed of all observers." On other days she would mount her glossy, lithe-limbed race horse, "habited in a closely fitting riding-dress of black velvet, ornamented with a hundred and fifty gold buttons, a hat from which depended magnificent sable plumes, and over her face, a short white lace veil of the richest texture . . . the fire of passion flashing from the depths of her dark, lustrous eyes. She took all captive. Gold and diamonds were showered upon her." Such was the sad fate of Lillie Lee.[19]

A representative masculine observation of the place and period is that of Hiram Ferris, writing from Central Diggings in December 1850: "Vice and crime I believe abounds more in this country than any other civilized state on the globe. Gambling of every sort, drinking & hoaring are common in every city, town & village in California."[20] A young Frenchman described the popular Countess of Campora as "one of the most shameless of women. She was a pseudo Lola Montez, seated like a queen at the counter of her Café restaurant. She was the Flower Queen, whose beautiful efflorescence had been the joy and admiration of Chile for many years. But she had imposed on California her too ripe fruits which, although deteriorated, commanded fabulous prices. At that time, from 1849 to 1852, I never knew of a woman who could procure such a large income by abusing her sex."[21] Janos Xandus, a Hungarian visitor to San Francisco in 1857, wrote: "All night long there is dancing and music and whoring, as well as gambling at dice and cards; and at dawn all the community is again on foot."[22]

Even as late as 1877, the peripatetic Mrs. Frank Leslie noted that while in all other cities of the world prostitutes imitated the fashions of upper-class women, in San Francisco "the case is reversed, and the caprices of the former class are meekly copied by the latter."[23]

After two years of observing life in California mining towns, William Perkins concisely summed up his opinion of the situation: "If a woman is to stay pure in the licentious life of California, her virtue must indeed be very firm." In Sonora, he said, "the French women are monopolizing the business of the Lansquenet tables and the drinking saloons . . . there is no decent place to get a drink in which you will not see behind the counter a pretty and well-dressed Frenchwoman, which naturally attracts customers."[24]

Before law and order came to California, traffic in young women grew into a big business; they were brought in by hundreds from Mexico and transferred to bidders with whom the girls shared their earnings. Beauties from South America were eagerly sought for dancing salons. Frenchwomen were favored in gambling establishments. Ships brought in kidnaped girls from Pacific islands and from as far away as China. An organized system was arranged for supplying native Indian women to the mining camps. Viewing all this with alarm, the *Home Missionary* of San Francisco charged that half the women of California were of "the loose element."

Eleanore Dumont was one of the more notorious of the West Coast's "loose element." A plump, dark girl in her mid-twenties, with a French accent and an air of modesty, she made her start in Nevada City. She opened a gambling house, with free champagne for all, and soon convinced the miners it was a privilege to lose their gold at her tables. When Nevada City's boom collapsed, Eleanore began moving from one camp to another, her fortunes gradually declining. Her beauty faded, she drank too much, and a shadow of down began growing on her upper lip. Dubbed Madame Mustache by a disillusioned miner, she retained the sobriquet to the end of her life. She roamed across the West, following the new mining camps, to Idaho, the Black Hills, then dropped a degree in the scale and began offering her services in the construction camps along the route of the Union Pacific Railroad. In 1877 Madame Mustache was running a brothel in Eureka, Nevada; then two years later the Sacramento *Union* ran a brief dispatch from Bodie: "A woman named Eleanore Dumont was found dead today about one mile out of town, having committed suicide."[25]

5

Gold-rush California held no monopoly of western sirens. The girls swarmed into the Kansas trail towns from St. Louis, Memphis, and New Orleans, flashily dressed in ruffled skirts and rainbow petticoats, their kid boots adorned with tassels and shiny lone stars to attract the Texans. Many were armed with pistols or jeweled daggers concealed in their boot tops to keep the boisterous cowboys in line.

A respectable woman traveling through Colorado in 1868 was shocked by members of her sex seen in Julesburg: "Such a collection of fiends in human shape I hope never to see again. The women were, if anything, worse than the men, and I did not meet more than two of my own sex while I was there who made the most distant claims to even common decency or self-respect."[26]

In Montana almost every cow town and mining camp had its "line," imitative of the crib streets of New Orleans, a row of one-room wooden shacks rented to prostitutes at high prices. Here probably originated the old mining-camp ballad:

First came the miners to work in the mine
Then came the ladies who lived on the line.

The "ladies" lived in cell-like compartments, a bed in one corner, a coal stove in another, a small dresser with a washbowl and pitcher in another. It was the custom for each crib's occupant to have her name emblazoned upon the door. In towns such as Butte, the girls were paid off in silver dollars which they stuffed in their stockings. "Sometimes," said one male observer, "it was all they could do to navigate coming down the sidewalk. They'd have to use both hands to keep their stockings from dropping and spilling the silver dollars out on the street."[27]

Wyoming's tolerant attitude toward ladies of the evening is indicated in this newspaper story of 1884:

A few evenings since a couple of women of medium age arrived at Pine Bluffs. They were from Cheyenne. Both wore yellow hair and store complexions. The garments which they wore weren't very costly but they were rather variegated and colors bordering onto crimson predominated. Each had on a Leghorn hat, which was only less elevated than a steeple, and wore bangle bracelets and jewelry until you couldn't rest. The jewelry was of that character which is euphoniously termed "snide," but it shone like a tin pan on a milk house.

Why ladies so elaborately arrayed and apparently so wealthy should stop off at Pine Bluffs where the accommodations are so meager was not at first apparent. To add amazement to the wonder already existing, they camped on the depot platform. They seemed perfectly at home and allowed their feet to depend toward the track with considerable freedom. They didn't appear to be a very frivolous pair of girls, yet they were quite giddy. Without flattering them, neither could be said to possess classical beauty of face or form. A rich veneering of powder and paint rather completely cast into the shade the ordinary efforts of nature in the matter of complexion.

There were many cowboys in the vicinity, and finally one bolder than the rest, advanced toward the pair of females. He was received with ostentatious manifestations of kindness. One

of the women addressed him as "Pete" and he called her "Maud."
They seemed to be overjoyed to see each other. Other cowboys
soon appeared, and without the formality of an introduction,
immediately became intimately friendly. Then followed beer.
This was succeeded by more beer, which was succeeded by quite
a lot of beer. Then came beer.

For eight mortal hours the pale air was laden with disjointed
chunks of revelry. It was a scene of the wildest and most extravagant carousal set down in the quiet midst of the bleak prairie,
and one which would give life and reality to an early-day border
romance.

At noon the next day not a man in the settlement could have
worn less than a No. 12 hat.[28]

The social standing of prostitutes in the West varied from
place to place and from time to time, but in general the attitude of males was that there were two classes of women only
—they were either soiled doves or pure, and there was to be
no mingling of the two. According to the code, a "good"
woman's name was never to be mentioned in a saloon or
sporting house, and the very existence of sinful females was
to be kept secret from respectable ones. For example, when
the wives and daughters of General Custer's command were
driven through Hayes City during its wicked trail-town period, the curtains on the traveling carriages were strapped
down so the fancy women and other objectionable sights on
the streets could not be seen.[29]

The sentimental feelings of western males for prostitutes,
however, is shown in the nicknames they gave their favorites.
"Queen" and "Rose" were popular appellations—Wild Rose,
Texas Rose, Prairie Rose, Irish Queen, Spanish Queen—as
well as such descriptive sobriquets as Molly b'Damn, Little
Gold Dollar, Contrary Mary, Peg-Leg Annie and Velvet Ass
Rose. One of Calamity Jane's partners for a time in Wyoming
was Cotton Tail, who was of course a natural blonde.

When one considers the crudity of what was predominantly

a male society, it must be admitted that the scarlet representatives of the gentler sex played an important role in taming the West. As one old Montanan put it, "many's the miner who'd never wash his face or comb his hair, if it wasn't for thinkin' of the sportin' girls he might meet in the saloons."[30]

In the rough frontier camps, the saloon with its girls was the only real home the men knew. The brightly lit interiors contrasted sharply with the dismal hovels they had to live in. The glittering chandeliers, the costly mirrors wreathed with inspiring banners, the inviting arrays of decanters, the carved woods, the music, the striking though often lascivious paintings, the girls in their fine frilly clothes, lent a touch of gentility to an otherwise drab and harsh existence—altogether a civilizing influence whether the males were aware of it or not.

VI

"Many a Weary Mile"

1

ON a sun-filled April morning in 1846, a crowd began gathering in the small town of Springfield, Illinois, to bid farewell to thirty-one friends and neighbors who were that day starting a long overland journey to California. The organizer of the party was James Frazier Reed, and drawn up beside his house was an extraordinary covered wagon.

Reed's thirteen-year-old daughter, Virginia, had already christened it the "pioneer palace car," and it was indeed as palatial as an overland wagon could be made in that day. Heavy 12-inch boards extended over the wheels on each side, running the full length of the wagon to form a foundation for a roomy second story in which beds had been placed. The entrance was at the side, like a stagecoach; when one entered, it was like stepping into a cozy living room. At right and left were spring seats with comfortable high backs where the passengers could sit and ride with as much ease as on the seats of a Concord coach. For cold nights and mornings, a small sheet-iron stove had been braced in the center, the vent pipe running out the top through a circle of tin which prevented fire being set to the canvas roof.

Under the spring seats were compartments for storing work

baskets, a medicine chest, and spare clothing packed in canvas bags. A small mirror hung directly opposite the entrance. "Knowing that books were always scarce in a new country," Virginia afterward recalled, "we also took a good library of standard works."[1]

Three of the occupants of this wagon were James Reed's young wife, Margaret, his daughter Virginia, and his mother-in-law, known to all Springfield and her family as Grandma Keyes. Grandma Keyes was seventy-five years old, an invalid, and she had to be carried out of the house and placed on a large feather bed, propped up by pillows, in the second floor of the pioneer palace car. Her two sons, remaining behind, begged her to stay with them, but Grandma Keyes paid them no heed; she was determined to go to California.

James Reed was not leaving Springfield because he needed to better his fortunes. He owned a thriving furniture factory, was well off financially, was a close friend of two rising young politicians, Abraham Lincoln and Stephen A. Douglas. Reed burned with the "western fever"; his ambition was to become Indian agent for all the territory west of the Rocky Mountains, and his political friends had promised their aid in this undertaking. Reed had hoped that Lincoln, with whom he had soldiered in the Black Hawk War, would be in Springfield that morning to see him off, but the future President was away on circuit-court duties. Mary Todd Lincoln and her small son Robert were present to represent the family.

As Virginia later remembered that leave-taking, "we were all surrounded by loved ones, and there stood all my little schoolmates who had come to kiss me goodbye. My father with tears in his eyes tried to smile as one friend after another grasped his hand in a last farewell. Mama was overcome with grief. At last we were all in the wagons, the drivers cracked their whips, the oxen moved slowly forward and the long journey had begun."[2]

The eight oxen drawing Reed's two-story wagon were large Durham steers, the preferred draft animals for plains crossings. They were not bridled, but were yoked to the tongue of the wagon. Instead of riding, the drivers walked alongside with a stock or whip, controlling the oxen with a simple "whoa," "haw," or "gee."

Across Missouri and into Kansas the wagons rolled, the first weeks uneventful. "Our little home was so comfortable that mama could sit reading and chatting with the little ones [there were three children younger than Virginia] and almost forget that she was really crossing the plains."[3]

Death, which was to follow this wagon train all the way across the West, struck first near the Big Blue River in Kansas. On a day late in May, Grandma Keyes died quietly. James Reed hewed a coffin for her out of a cottonwood tree, carved her name on a stone, SARAH KEYES, BORN IN VIRGINIA, and they buried her under the shade of an oak, planting wild flowers in the sod.

At Independence Rock, little Virginia Reed wrote a letter about this to a cousin in Illinois, sending it back east by an obliging traveler on horseback. "Gramma died, she became speechless the day before she died. We buried her verry decent We made a nete coffin and buried her under a tree we had a head stone and had her name cut on it and the date and yere verry nice and at the head of the grave was a tree we cut some letters on it the young men soded it all ofer and put Flores on it We miss her verry much every time we come into the Wagon we look at the bed for her."

Early on the afternoon of July 4 the wagons rumbled into Fort Laramie, and Virginia wrote of the grand dinner and celebration: "Severel of the gentlemen in Springfield gave paw a botel of licker and said it shoulden be opend till the 4 day of July and paw was to look to the east and drink it and

thay was to look to the West and drink it at 12 o'clock paw
treted the company and we all had some lemminade."[4]

After leaving Fort Laramie, the Springfield train increased
considerably in size, many other wagons joining it for the
hard passage through the Rockies. During a stopover at Fort
Bridger, the leaders debated whether or not they should take
the long trail by way of Fort Hall, or a shorter route known as
the "Hastings Cut-off," said to be 200 miles shorter. Disagree-
ment followed, and the train divided into two sections, one
group heading for Fort Hall, the other taking the shorter
route. James Reed decided to go with the "Hastings Cut-off"
party. Before leaving Fort Bridger, this group elected a new
captain. His name was George Donner. The Reeds were riding with death for certain now, the ill-fated Donner Party.

As they drove toward Great Salt Lake, they found the cut-
off was no road at all, not even a trail. Heavy underbrush
blocked the way, so thick it had to be cut down and used for
a roadbed. A month was spent in reaching the lake, and the
oxen were unfit for the long desert crossing that lay ahead.
"It was a dreary, desolate alkali waste; not a living thing could
be seen; it seemed as though the hand of death had been laid
upon the country."[5]

They were now into September and time was running out
for the crossing of the high snowy Sierras. The oxen began
dying for lack of water. Hoping to save his Durhams, Reed
unhitched them from the palace car and sent them ahead
with two of his drivers in search of a water hole. Somehow,
along the way the oxen panicked, escaping from the drivers
in the night. A week was wasted in search of them, but they
could not be found. Now the Reeds were stranded on the desert, still many miles from California. The wagon company
voted to let them have four oxen, but the fine palace car had
to be abandoned, and they moved into a smaller vehicle.

On October 5th "the hand of death" showed itself again. During a quarrel with a man named John Snyder, James Reed was forced to defend himself; he killed Snyder with a knife. As soon as the deed was done, Reed's anger turned upon himself; he ran and hurled his knife into the Humboldt River.

That night the wagon company's members held council, voting to banish Reed from the train even though the murder was committed in self-defense. They agreed to care for his wife and children, provided he did not show himself again. He was given a horse and some food, but no rifle, and was told he could pay for his crime by going ahead to Fort Sutter and seeking help for the company in crossing the mountains.

As Reed was saying farewell to his wife, Virginia slipped a rifle and ammunition from their wagon and waited outside the camp in the darkness until her father rode out. He took the weapon and ammunition, gave her a silent hug, and rode westward alone into the desert.

For a day or so, Reed left messages along the way in the form of scattered feathers of birds he had killed for food, then there was no further trace of him. The oxen on Margaret Reed's wagon died; she had to ride muleback, one child in her lap. Virginia and her younger sister and brother shared another mount.

By the time they reached the Sierra approaches, autumn snows were falling. On the slopes the snow reached to their waists. The party broke into small sections, and soon they could go no farther, the Donner families camping near a lake, Margaret Reed joining a group that found an old cabin farther up the slope. They built more log shelters, killed all the surviving oxen, packed the meat in snow for preservation, and used the hides for roofing.

The snow continued falling, the days passed, the carefully rationed ox meat was all consumed. Margaret Reed recooked bones that she had thrown out; she cut strips of rawhide from her roof, boiled them into a sort of gluey paste. But on Christmas Day, she was able to give her children a special treat. She had hidden away a few dried apples, some beans, a bit of tripe, and a small piece of bacon. She said as they all sat down to Christmas dinner: "Children, eat slowly, for this one day you can have all you wish."[6]

But after Christmas nothing was left. She trapped field mice on the snow, she slit her dog's throat and fed him to her children. Despairing of rescue, she decided to start out with Virginia and cross the mountains to obtain food for the younger children. But neither she nor her daughter could climb through the high passes in the bitter cold. They returned, living out another seven weeks on boiled ox hides.

Down in the lake camp, more grisly events were occurring; some of the survivors were eating their frozen comrades. At last, after many died and hope was all but gone, on February 19, 1847, a relief party from Sutter's Fort arrived with food. James Reed had made his way across the Sierras and found help. "I can not describe the death-like look they all had," he wrote in his diary. "Bread Bread Bread was the begging of every child and grown person except my wife."[7]

From California a month later, Virginia Reed was writing again to her cousin in Illinois: "There was 3 died and the rest eat them, they was 10 days without anything to eat but the Dead." That was her only reference to the cannibalism always associated with the tragic Donner Party. The story of the others, of Lewis Keseberg and how he kept himself alive by cannibalism, gradually coming to prefer human flesh to that of animals, of how finally in his madness he slew the last of the Donner women for her flesh—that is a gruesome tale which can be pursued elsewhere.*

As for Virginia Reed, she lived a long and happy life in California. "She was a handsome young lady and was noted

* See Homer Croy's *Wheels West* (New York, 1955).

for her superior equestrianship, having obtained several first premiums at county fairs for her graceful riding." [8] She married an Army officer, John Murphy, who became one of the first real-estate operators in the state. When Murphy lost his eyesight, Virginia led him each day to and from his office, and after he died Virginia continued the business, becoming a pioneer as a real-estate saleswoman as she had been a pioneer in crossing the frozen Sierras.

2

Although Virginia Reed, her mother Margaret, and Grandma Keyes were representative of females from girlhood to old age who ventured across the early West, many others made the crossing at far less cost in hardship and anguish. Indeed, the first two women to travel overland to Oregon, Narcissa Whitman and Eliza Spalding in 1836, could look back upon their journey almost as a long summer's outing. Probably the greatest moment of danger to either was the day Mrs. Spalding's horse stepped into a hornet's nest and threw her from the sidesaddle with one foot still in stirrup, dragging her a short distance. She received no serious injury from the accident, which could have occurred anywhere, including her safe old home place back in Utica, New York.

During the decade between the pioneer journey of the Whitmans and Spaldings and that of the Reeds in 1846, westward emigration steadily increased. The summer of 1843 was known as the Great Emigration year, when 200 families in "120 wagons using 694 oxen and 773 loose cattle" made the long crossing to Oregon. 1847 was another important year, then for some reason the flood ebbed temporarily only to rise to phenomenal numbers following the California gold discoveries, and it did not slacken again until the Civil War.

In July 1852, a correspondent of the New York *Tribune* described one of these vast summer migrations: "We have been 18 days on the plains, amid the greatest show in the world. The train is estimated to be 700 miles long, composed of all kinds of people from all parts of the United States, and some of the rest of mankind, with lots of horses, mules, oxen, cows, steers and some of the feathered creation, moving along about 15 or 20 miles per day; all sorts of vehicles from a coach down to a wheelbarrow; ladies on horseback, dressed out in full-blown Bloomers; gents on mules, with their Kossuth hats and plumes, galloping over the prairies, making quite an equestrian troupe and a show ahead of anything Barnum ever got up." [9]

The early trails to the Far West originated at various staging points such as Independence, St. Joseph, or Council Bluffs, converging on the Platte River route to Fort Laramie, and continuing past Independence Rock through South Pass to Fort Bridger and Fort Hall. Then if the travelers were going to Oregon they followed the Snake River, if bound for California they moved down the Humboldt and through the Sierras to the junction of the American fork and the Sacramento Rivers.

By 1855, so many wagons had followed the Platte route that the trail was a hundred feet wide. "The grass had been killed by travel, but along it for nearly a hundred miles was the most beautiful bed of flowers, portulaca in bunches four feet high, and a great variety of other flowers." [10]

Women perhaps more than men were fascinated by the landmarks along the way, and it is a rare trail diary, if kept by a woman, that does not mention all of them. After weeks on the flat plains of Nebraska, Chimney Rock stood out like a welcoming beacon. "We were some weeks," one woman wrote, "in sight of that wonderful rock." [11] Fort Laramie was a symbol of safety, a sort of halfway haven for washing clothes, taking stock of supplies, and relaxing under the welcome protection of the United States Army. "This is quite a

place, several fine buildings, nestled here among the hills it
looks like a rose in the wilderness." [12]

Beyond Fort Laramie was the most mentioned landmark
of all, Independence Rock, resembling the shell of a huge tortoise. By 1852, thousands of names of passing travelers had
been marked upon its sides. "Independence Rock I call the
'bulletin board' of the Sweetwater Valley . . . It seemed that
every emigrant that had a tarbucket left his name and date
there." [13]

The first sight of Great Salt Lake was startling in its sud-
denness, the wagons coming out of narrow mountain gorges
and rough crooked turns, the road leading abruptly through
an opening like an immense doorway, with a view for many
miles across clear atmosphere. And none ever forgot that
stretch of trail along the Humboldt, the dust as fine as flour
enveloping the wagons in clouds so thick one could not see
ten feet ahead. Alkali in the dust blotched and blistered
women's tender skins, alkali in the water weakened and killed
oxen by thousands. A traveler approaching Carson River
counted an average of thirty abandoned wagons to the mile
for forty miles. "The dead animals will average about 100 to
the mile for 40 miles—4,000." [14]

Ox skulls or skeletons themselves became landmarks, the
dying cattle constant objects of pity. Lodisa Frizzell told of
"one old cow by the road with a paper pinned on her head,
it stated that she had been left to die, but if anyone chose,
they might have her, but requested that they would not abuse
her as she had been one of the best of cows, she looked so piti-
ful, & it called up so many associations in my mind that it
affected me to tears." [15]

The most impressive sight of all, however, was the ending
of the journey, whether it was the green valleys of Oregon, or
the first view of California from the summit of the Sierras,

"a soft haze, a warm rosy glow," the golden magic of the Sacramento Valley.

In those years women were also moving into other areas of the West—into Texas, the great Southwest, and the high plains. The same year that Eliza Spalding and Narcissa Whitman were riding sidesaddle to Oregon, Mary Ann Maverick was traveling from South Carolina to Texas in a horse-drawn carriage. The party included "ten Negro slaves, a big Kentucky wagon, three extra saddle horses, and one blooded filly." The wagon carried a tent, a supply of provisions and bedding, the cook, and the Maverick children. "We occasionally stopped in a good place to rest, to have washing done, and sometimes to give muddy roads time to dry." [16]

The first white woman to travel down the trail to Santa Fe was Susan Magoffin, on a honeymoon journey in 1846 when Susan was only eighteen years old. Her wealthy young husband outfitted a train of "fourteen big waggons with six yoke each, one baggage waggon with two yoke, one dearborn with two mules (this concern carries my maid) our own carriage with two more mules, and two men on mules driving the loose stock." [17]

On a trail journey, the interior of a covered wagon was a woman's province, and upon undertaking her duties as wagon housekeeper her first reaction was usually astonishment over how much a wagon could hold. A female observer describing a Conestoga remarked that it had "eight holes cut in the canvas on one side, and a child's face peeping out of every one of the holes. Besides the children, it contained cats, dogs, beds, cooking stove, tin pans and kettles." [18]

The major duties of a woman en route west by wagon were not much different from those for which she was responsible in the home she had left back east, although accomplished under much more difficult conditions. Food had to be cooked for her family, clothes mended and laundered, babies and children tended, and also guarded from dangers accompanying travel.

Most women readily adapted themselves to the problem of preparing meals in the open. Among Narcissa Whitman's duties during her journey west was that of baking bread regularly for ten persons. "It was difficult at first," she admitted, "as we did not understand working out-doors; but we became accustomed to it, so that it became quite easy." [19] Mountain man James Clyman was impressed by a young lady he saw at work beside a wagon train in 1844. He said she "showed herself worthy of the bravest undaunted pioneer of the west, for after having kneaded her dough she watched and nursed the fire and held an umbrella over the fire and her skillit with the greatest composure for near 2 hours and baked bread enough to give us a verry plentiful supper." [20]

One of the things they learned quickly was that stoves were of little use in outdoor cooking. Lodisa Frizzell reported finding a sheet-iron stove sitting beside the trail. "We took it along cooked in it that night, & then left it; for they are of very little account, unless you could have dry wood." [21] Women always welcomed a long encampment because cooking could be made easier by such devices as drawing two wagons together to shut off the wind and then digging a hole in the ground for a fireplace. In the wonderland of the West, they also discovered novel ways of cooking, such as Mrs. Whitman's experience while encamped near some hot springs: "Boiled a bit of dry salmon in one of them in five minutes." [22]

Meals were usually served in containers of pewter, tin or iron, with forks and spoons of the same materials. A commonly used dining cloth, spread upon the ground, was the India-rubber poncho designed for use by horsemen against the rain.

Women unused to the ways of the West had a tendency to

resist the use of buffalo chips as fuel for cooking. But when wood was no longer available on the treeless plains, there was no alternative. "We soon had a large pile of them, & set fire to them, when they immediately blazed up & burned like dry bark, it was laughable to see the boys jump around it. On saying that I feared the dust would get in the meat, as it was frying, George said he would as soon have his broiled as any way, so laughing, & jokeing we forgot our antipathies to the fire. Some said it had improved all the supper, even the coffee." [23]

Susan Magoffin, in her luxuriously fitted train bound for Santa Fe, had a maid and a cook, and could describe such dinners as "boiled chicken, soup, rice, and a dessert of wine and gooseberry tart." She and her maid had picked the gooseberries during a trail stop near the Arkansas River, and her provident husband had brought along a coop of live poultry. On another day, near Bent's Fort, she wrote: "So we have lain here in the hot sun with the tent windows raised, and eating roast-hare and drinking wine for dinner." [24]

Milk was an unobtainable luxury unless emigrants had the foresight to take along a few recently calved cows. Sometimes work cattle furnished a small supply, Mrs. Whitman recording that her husband carried a cup for milking tied to his saddle. "They [the oxen] supply us with sufficient milk for our tea and coffee, which is indeed a luxury." [25] Another woman advised that all travelers take a milk cow along on the trip. "Use the milk to make bread, for you can do very little with yeast, & the soda & cream tartar I do not like."

Buffalo meat was almost always a welcome addition to the monotonous fare. "We made some soup from the marrow bone, which I think an epicure would have called good, and eating this with boiled rice helped us very much." [26] After her first taste of buffalo, Mrs. Whitman could say: "I relish it very well and it agrees with me . . . So long as I have buffalo meat I do not wish anything else." However, after a steady two weeks' diet of nothing else, she complained: "Have been living on buffalo meat until I am cloyed with it." She had an even lower opinion of pemmican purchased from Indians. "It appears so filthy! I can scarcely eat it; but it keeps us alive, and we ought to be thankful for it." And of horse meat, she wrote frankly: "I do not prefer it, but can eat it very well when we have nothing else." [27]

After the experience of a trail journey, travelers often wrote home to relatives and friends preparing to follow them, advising what provisions they should bring along. A typical letter, from Sutter's Fort in 1850, suggested that "apple and peach fruit and rice are as useful articles of food as can possibly be taken on the road. To each man 80 pounds of rice, and three quarters of a bushel of apple or peach fruit, at least are necessary, being easily cooked, they are always convenient. Now, if the emigrant will use as little side bacon, and also very little hot lard and saleratus biscuit, and more of other articles, as above mentioned, I will warrant him to come through unscathed with scurvy." [28]

Because of its keeping qualities, rice became a popular staple for western crossings, as well as hard biscuits and dried fruits. Dried apples, used against scurvy, were eaten so often that most travelers developed an acute dislike for them before the journey's end. One woman who had dutifully consumed her dried apples three times a day stated that when she finally reached Sacramento she paid $2.50 for a dinner and was served "bear steak, and—oh horrors—some *more* dried apples!" [29]

Although they could and did adjust to trail cooking, women were unable to solve the problem of keeping their families' clothing laundered. As most stops were only of overnight duration, time seldom permitted washed clothing to dry. Nor was there always a suitable supply of water at camping places, and it was not easy to heat enough to wash a big laundry. "This Gypsy life is anything but agreeable," one diarist complained. "It is impossible to keep anything clean." [30] Mrs. Whitman, for example, was able to put out but three washings from the time she left New York until the end of her six-month journey. One of the favored laundering places along the Oregon Trail was Soda Springs, where, as Jesse Applegate observed, "some of the women improved the opportunity offered by plenty of hot water here at the springs to wash a few things." [31]

Lack of opportunities for laundering and bathing was especially discomforting for babies and young children. Towels were frequently used for diapers, and one woman told of washing the towels out each night in cold water and then making her husband stand holding them before the campfire until they were dry.

Babies also suffered from being bathed in the unfamiliar alkali water which inflamed and blistered their delicate skins. Travelers with young children soon learned to take along a supply of glycerine to soothe the skin of infants exposed to strong water and sunlight or chafed from lack of any baths at all.

Because of the long time required for crossing the plains and mountains, births en route were quite common, several being listed during the Great Emigration of 1843. On a journey to California in 1855, a woman told of how the wagon train had to be halted all one afternoon for the birth of a baby. Indians had been threatening the column during the morning, and several warriors rode in close when the wagons stopped. One of the company leaders was quick-witted enough to make the sign for smallpox, and the Indians withdrew in a hurry. "The mother of the woman who was confined cried and cried, fearing her daughter would die. Then the others followed suit, and so, as usual when there was trouble,

I had to boss the job. We laid over one day, and then moved on. The mother and child did well, could not have done better anywhere else." [32] But not all childbirths on the trail went so smoothly. Susan Magoffin spent her nineteenth birthday at Bent's Fort, ill from pregnancy. She lost her child a week later and wrote sadly in her journal: "In a few short months I should have been a happy mother . . . but the ruling hand of a mighty Providence has interposed and by an abortion deprived us of the hope, the fond hope of mortals!" [33]

Transporting infants and small children across the West was a complicated business, left to the management of efficient mothers, of course. In California during the 1850's, some ingenious female discovered that the abundant supply of champagne baskets imported from abroad made ideal baby carriers, and they were generally adopted for that purpose. A cavalry officer's wife transported her month-old infant from Los Angeles across the desert to Arizona in a champagne basket strapped to a wagon seat. She said the wagon acted as a perpetual lullaby and the baby slept soundly except when progress ceased.

Oftentimes, however, over rough stretches of trail, mothers had to walk, carrying babies in their arms for hours. Or as Sarah Royce did, riding horseback with her baby in her lap, the infant's necessities suspended from the pommel, canteen and diapers in a saddlebag on one side, a little pail on the other, the weight of the child on one arm, she clinging with the other to the pommel of the saddle.

One method devised for transporting children by horseback was a special packsaddle constructed with fifteen-inch arms around which rawhide strands were woven to make a sort of basket. "Two children could be placed in one of these pack saddles without any danger of their falling out," said Benjamin F. Bonney of Oregon, who claimed that even a bucking horse could not spill out the occupants.[34]

Because morning starts had to be made early on the trail—usually by sunrise—mothers soon learned that in order not to delay the train it was best to allow smaller children to sleep in the wagons until after several hours of travel. "Our caravan had a good many women and children and although we were probably longer on the journey owing to their presence —they exerted a good influence, as the men did not take such risks with Indians and thereby avoided conflict; were more alert about the care of the teams and seldom had accidents; more attention was paid to cleanliness and sanitation, and lastly but not of less importance, the meals were more regular and better cooked thus preventing much sickness and there was less waste of food." [35]

In addition to the usual tasks of the gentler sex, wives and older daughters occasionally had to lend a hand at men's work, such as hitching oxen, driving teams, and on some occasions assisting at shoeing oxen and horses. Blacksmith work was usually done by the men at such stops as Fort Laramie, but sometimes a horse or an ox would need attention along the route. Lydia Waters told of how she and her husband shod an ox out on the Wyoming plain. They dug a trench the length of the animal and the width and depth of their spade. "The animal was then thrown and rolled over so that its backbone lay in the trench and all four of its legs were up in the air. In this position it was helpless and the shoes were nailed on readily." Mrs. Waters neglected to describe how the animal was set upright again.

For such rough work, women had to dress roughly and, following the advice of trail veterans at the staging towns, they would purchase specially made men's boots of smaller sizes for use during the crossing. They also outfitted themselves with knickerbockers that reached to their boot tops, although they modestly concealed this outlandish garb with knee-length skirts. Any woman starting west in a silk dress was immediately suspected of being a prostitute; a respectable woman was supposed to wear working clothes, at least until she completed the journey.

3

One of the recurrent phrases on almost every lip during America's period of western expansion was "seeing the elephant." The phrase had various shades of meaning—to see the sights, to gain experience of life—but in the main, seeing the elephant meant going west with one's eyes wide open, expecting to find marvels and wondrous fortunes only to be monstrously defrauded in the end. It meant hard travel, exotic adventure along the way, discomfort from the elements, chicanery from traders, trickery by the Indians.

Women no less than men expected to see the elephant when they started westward, and often wrote back home, both wryly and proudly, that they had done so.

Indians were the most exciting "elephants" to be seen in the West, some tribes threatening attack, others operating various schemes designed to swindle or mulct the gullible passersby. Women in particular resented such devices as the Indians' tax on each head of cattle driven across their territory or on each tree cut down for fuel on their tribal holdings. At river crossings, Indians sometimes built crude little bridges, charging fifty cents or a dollar for any wagon using it. At wide crossings, they would offer the use of their canoes or bullboats to ferry the women, taking payment in money or goods. "Anybody preparing to come to this country," one woman wrote, "should make up some calico shirts to trade to the Indians in case of necessity. You will have to hire them to pilot you across rivers . . . My folks were about stripped of shirts, trousers, jackets, and 'wampuses.'" [36] Another woman told of her first encounter with the Sioux, who wanted to trade buffalo robes for bridles, clothing and food. One old chief stopped the wagons by standing in the middle of the road and brandishing a rusty cavalry saber. When the wagons halted, he threw a blanket down by the roadside, demanding that presents be thrown into it in exchange for buffalo skins.

The first women travelers into the West were as much a marvel for the Indians as the Indians were for the women. After meeting some Pawnees along the Platte River, Mrs. Whitman observed that "they seemed to be very much surprised and pleased to see white females . . . We ladies were such a curiosity to them. They would come and stand around our tent, peep in, and grin in their astonishment to see such looking objects." [37]

Plains Indians were the most dangerous of the tribes, not only because they were more warlike, but because the travelers grew accustomed to friendly treatment from tribes such as the Sacs, Foxes, and Pawnees, before they reached the Great Plains, and so tended to discount the Plains Indians' deadly intentions. During the period following the Civil War, Indians attacked so many carelessly armed trains that the military command at Fort Kearney was given authority by the government to stop all wagons at that point unless they were properly manned and armed. A train too weak to protect itself was required to wait until it could join another train strong enough to furnish the minimum defensive force required by the military order.

Second to the Indians in interest to travelers were the shaggy buffalo, described in every trail diary but seldom seen at such close range as the herd that came charging up to Lydia Waters' camp, veering away at the last moment except for five belligerent members that "would have run over the tents had the women not shaken their aprons and sunbonnets, and shouted at them." [38] Prairie dogs also were sights to see. "They kept up a wonderful barking, & running from house to house, but disappeared on our approach & kept perfectly still, until we got a little passed, when they would jump up, & stand as straight & bark with all their little might." And the mirages, seen on the deserts and the high dry plains, wondrous colored visions of beautiful streams bordered with green trees, or small cool lakes, "and once on looking back, we saw several men in the road, who looked to be 15 ft. tall."

The women learned to take the bad with the good, as they knew anyone going to see the elephant must—the dangerous river crossings, the dust, the flies, mosquitoes, illnesses, excessive heat and cold, rain, wind, and thunderstorms.

River crossings were always a special adventure. "I felt a little nervous when we were about to cross, for the river here is all of one mile & a half wide, & a more foaming madening river I never saw, & its banks being very low, & the water the color of soapsuds you cannot see the bottom where it is not more than six inches deep, consequently looks as deep as the Missouri, & the many islands and bars which obstruct this swift current makes an awful noise, you cannot make a person hear you, when you are in the river, at 5 yds. distant; and I call this one of the greatest adventures on the whole route." [39] This was the Platte in 1852.

An Oregon-bound woman told of riding in a wagon mounted on a raft going down the Columbia River in November 1848: "The icicles are hanging from our wagon beds to the water . . . we women and children did not attempt to get out of our wagons tonight."

Dusty trails were also an abomination. "You in the States know nothing about dust. It will fly so that you can hardly see the horns of your tongue yoke of oxen. It often seems that the cattle must die for the want of breath, and then in our wagons, such a spectacle—beds, clothes, victuals, and children, all completely covered."

And it was a rare family that escaped that common ailment of far travelers—dysentery. "Dysentery prevails in our company," a woman recorded, then added shortly afterward: "Saw the ground covered in many places with epsom salts, but so shallow and thin on the ground that we could not collect it, and indeed, having no expectation of ever needing it any more, we left it there." [40]

Yet, in spite of all, there were hours of pleasant relaxation, moments of sheer delight, for women engaged upon a trail journey. The nooning hour, when all travel stopped, was a favorite time of day for resting. "Husband knew how to provide shade even on the open prairie. Spread a saddle blanket upon some sticks placed in the ground, made a rude sofa from saddles, fishamores and other blankets." [41] Susan Magoffin told how "after dinner to get rid of the hot sun, we spread out a buffalo robe in the little shade made by the carriage, and took a short siesta of a few minutes." [42]

At free times during the day's onward progress, women visited from wagon to wagon, sometimes spending an hour walking with others of their sex, reminiscing about their lives back in the States, voicing hopes for their future in the Far West, and exchanging gossip. "High teas were not popular, but tatting, knitting, crochetting, exchanging receipts for cooking beans or dried apples or swopping food for the sake of variety kept us in practices of feminine occupations and diversions. We did not keep late hours but when not too engrossed with fear of the red enemy or dread of impending danger we enjoyed the hour around the campfire. The menfolk lolling and smoking their pipes and guessing, or maybe betting, how many miles we had covered during the day. We listened to readings, story-telling, music and songs and the day often ended in laughter and merrymaking." [43]

The evening campfire was the center of gaiety, of fiddling and dancing, thus romantically described by Jesse Applegate: "Before a tent near the river a violin makes lively music, and some youths and maidens have improvised a dance upon the green; in another quarter a flute gives its mellow and melancholy notes to the still air, which as they float away over the quiet river seem a lament for the past rather than a hope for the future . . . But time passes; the watch is set up for the night, the council of old men has broken up and each has returned to his own quarter. The flute has whispered its last lament to the deeping night, the violin is silent and the dancers have dispersed. Enamored youths have whispered a tender 'good night' in the ears of blushing maidens, or stolen a kiss from the lips of some future bride—for Cupid here as elsewhere has been busy bringing together congenial hearts and among those simple people he alone is consulted in forming the marriage tie." 44

Crossing the West by wagon train was an experience never forgotten, a collection of high adventures, both tragic and comic, to be told and retold to the third and fourth generations. Lydia Waters expressed what must have been the feelings of most of her sisters involved in the great migrations: "For six months and three days we lived in our wagons and traveled many a weary mile," she wrote, and then concluded her account with this casual second thought: "But there were many things to laugh about." 45

<h2 style="text-align:center">4</h2>

Although most women settlers of the West journeyed there in covered wagons, some went all or part of the way in stagecoaches, others in river boats (up the Missouri), and a few by ocean vessels around Cape Horn or via the Panama Isthmus land crossing. A goodly number of women were among the Mormon handcart pioneers who crossed the plains on foot, pushing or pulling carts filled with their clothing and bedding. In later years, of course, railroads replaced other means of long-distance travel.

Stagecoaching, except for short journeys, was a miserable

substitute for the roomy covered wagons. "There was a front and back seat and between the two a middle one, which faced the back which we occupied," a woman traveler wrote of a journey across pioneer Nevada. "Whenever in the course of the succeeding five days and nights it was needful to move even our feet, we could only do so by asking our *vis-a-vis* to move his at the same time, as there was not one inch of space unoccupied . . . The rough frontiersmen who were our fellow-passengers tried in every way to make our situation more endurable. After we had sat bolt upright for two days and nights, vainly trying to snatch a few moments' sleep, which the constant lurching of the stage rendered impossible, the two men directly facing us proposed, with many apologies, that we should allow them to lay folded blankets on their laps, when, by leaning forward and laying our heads on the rests thus provided, our weary brains might find some relief. We gratefully assented, only to find, however, that the unnatural position rendered sleep impossible, so decided to bear our hardships as best we could until released by time." [46]

Another woman traveling across Kansas about this same time told of riding in a makeshift coach, a sort of cart covered with a sailcloth top that was not quite high enough to allow the passengers to sit upright. The journey was a wretched one, the vehicle's "sailcloth covering knocking against our bonnets at every jolt; its plank seats without backs; its cramped, uncomfortable crowdedness of people, of children, of baskets, of carpet-bags, of cloaks and shawls; its sickening odor of crumbled gingerbread, of bread and butter, of cheese and dried beef." [47]

Not only was western stagecoach travel uncomfortable, it was dangerous, coaches occasionally turning somersaults off the rough and narrow mountain roads. "In mountainous sections," declared Mrs. D. B. Bates, "passengers are obliged to alight and push behind the vehicle, to assist the horses up every hill, and when they arrive at the summit, chain the wheels, all get in, and ride to the base of the next mountain, in danger every moment of being overturned and having their necks broken. For thus working their passages, they have to pay exorbitant fares." [48] One stagecoach road across the southern California mountains was so rugged the line always scheduled its coaches to cross during the night so the female passengers would not be stampeded by fear; a special driver had been trained with a blindfold to handle the reins over this route.

Additional objections women found to western stagecoach travel were the unsavory fellow passengers, who were sometimes other women, as noted in this account of a trip from Julesburg, Colorado, to Cheyenne, Wyoming, in 1868: "The men were tolerably full when we started, and we were scarcely off before they produced a bottle, and after taking some of the fearful smelling whiskey which it contained, passed it around. I begged to be excused from partaking, but tho other female passenger was not so fastidious, and she took a good drink every time it was handed to her. Her whiskey-drinking capacity was great, equal to that of any of the men. The language the woman used was frightful, and she seemed to be unable to open her lips without uttering some blasphemous or obscene expression. Finally having taken eight or nine big drinks from the bottle, she became stupidly drunk; and then, to vary the monotony of her proceedings, she produced a filthy pipe which she filled with the blackest plug tobacco, and commenced to smoke. Arriving at the Cheyenne House, the men were almost forced to lift her out, to prevent her from falling flat on the ground." [49]

By all accounts, early railroad travel in the West was little improvement over stagecoaching. After describing her first train ride into San Francisco seated on a rough bench over a roadbed that jolted her severely, an Army lieutenant's wife concluded that a stage ride would have been preferable. Trains usually ran hours late, the prime cause of delay being hotboxes, or overheated axles. If the weather was pleasant, passengers did not mind these short half-hour interruptions; they had a chance to stretch their legs, the men gathering around the crew working on the hotbox, the women and children picking wild flowers or sunning themselves.

Women traveling on trains learned to wear linen dusters as protective covering against the coal dust which continually sifted through the loose, rattly windows. There were no dining cars; at mealtime the train would halt at an eating station, usually a crude wooden shack on the plains. Like the meal stop of a present-day bus line, time was quite limited, and the passengers all rushed madly for a sandwich and a tin cup of coffee. The food was monotonous, being almost invariably a piece of steak thrust between a soggy biscuit bitter from too much baking soda.

But even before the rail lines reached across the continent, westbound travelers began using the railroads. In 1867, many women and children rode the Union Pacific as far west as North Platte, Nebraska, and waited for their men to arrive with the wagons. Recalling this journey, a Montana woman said they rode on backless benches, in springless cars that rattled and jolted them over the newly built roadway. "I got tired and wished to sleep," she said, "so I stretched out on the floor under the seats. I remember the conductor kicking my feet, which were sprawled out into the aisle." [50]

Train travel through buffalo country was an exciting experience, according to Elizabeth Custer. "When the sharp shrieks of the train whistle announced a herd of buffaloes the rifles were snatched, and in the struggle to twist around for a good aim out of the narrow window the barrel or muzzle of the firearm passed dangerously near the ear of any scared woman who had the temerity to travel in those tempestuous days . . . It was the greatest wonder that more people were not killed, as the wild rush for the windows, and the reckless discharge of rifles and pistols, put every passenger's life in jeopardy." [51] If the buffalo herd was a large one, sometimes the train would stop for an hour or so, the conductor, engineer, and entire crew joining the passengers in the sport.

An indication of the obstacles hindering westbound rail travelers during the Civil War is a Kansas woman's account of her troubles in crossing the turbulent border state of Missouri in 1862: "At Quincy [Illinois] our trunks were opened and searched, our carpet-sacks examined, and not even one you carried in your hand but must be examined and sealed with Uncle Sam's insignia ere you pass into the land of Secesh, lest some documents may be concealed, or something found to brand you as spies. Every part of our luggage was sealed with sealing wax, stamped with 'U. S.,' and a bit of red tape, about six inches in length, sealed across the mouth of the carpet-sack. This is to prevent spies from passing in rebeldom and conveying important intelligence to Secesh." [52] From Quincy to the end of the line at St. Joseph, she rode at fourteen miles an hour through roadblocks of troops, and no bridge could be crossed until it was carefully examined for sabotage.

During the decade following the Civil War, railroads made startling progress in the West, and by 1876 a visiting Englishman could write this waspish impression of train travel across Nevada, a paragraph which has a rather modern flavor: "A lot of children were in the car who raced about from end to end, knocking over books and incessantly disturbing one's papers. Occasionally they varied the amusement by howling loudly, while their mothers looked complacently on without endeavouring to stop them, evidently well pleased with the healthy condition of the disagreeable little animals' lungs. I certainly did pine for the ease and quiet of an English first-class carriage, in which, thank Heaven, such bores can be avoided." [53]

One of the more exciting routes by which women reached the Far West was the journey by ocean vessel to Panama, then across the Isthmus by muleback, and on to California aboard another ship. As there was no Panama port, vessels anchored offshore and the passengers were rowed to shallow water in small boats. The shallows being half a mile from shore, some Panama natives went into the business of carrying women on their backs to dry land, for a fee of ten cents. "There was no alternative," a female traveler reported, "but to place ourselves upon the backs of these natives and ride post-back to the shore. Before placing ourselves in this rather unladylike position, there was much screaming, and laughing, and crying and scolding . . . some of the more corpulent ladies were afraid to trust their immense proportions on the back of a slender native, for fear of being dropped. This accident did happen to some of them; and it was ever accompanied with much laughing and joking at the sufferer's expense." [54]

After getting ashore, travelers learned that for the jungle crossing they must equip themselves against tropical sun and rain with a large sombrero, India-rubber boots, and, for locomotion, a mule. Standard price for a Panama mule was twenty dollars, the seller usually trotting along with the column until the journey ended and the mule had to be abandoned by its temporary owner. As there were no sidesaddles for the ladies, they had to ride astride, a situation that helped increase the popularity of bloomers in the 1850's. A gentleman making the crossing in 1854 noted that women suffered considerably from this unfamiliar mode of transport. "I got a bottle of sweet oil, for Mrs. Otingnon as well as her children were badly chafed." [55]

Among the more resolute females venturing into the West

were those who journeyed there on foot, in particular the members of the Mormon handcart migration of 1856. In that year thousands of new converts to the church arrived in this country from Europe, most of them too poor to provide funds for the land crossing to Utah. To solve the problem, Brigham Young devised a scheme for bringing them by rail from New York to an outfitting point near Iowa City. There they formed into companies of about five hundred members, every five persons being assigned a sixty-pound handcart to carry their supplies. Each emigrant was limited to seventeen pounds of clothing and bedding, with fifteen pounds additional allotted each cart for cooking utensils, a total of about one hundred pounds per cart. Provisions and tents were hauled in four or five ox-drawn wagons accompanying each party.

Three companies, departing in late spring, made the 1200-mile journey successfully, but two others were delayed for lack of carts and did not start until almost August. Axles and boxes on the latter carts were constructed entirely of wood, and soon began wearing out from friction. The travelers wrapped their axles with leather cut from their boots, or with tin obtained from kettles and buckets. For lubrication they sacrificed part of their already insufficient supply of bacon, and the women gave up their soap.

Averaging about fifteen miles per day, the handcart army reached Wyoming as cold weather struck. They marched bravely on toward Utah, the company leaders equalizing the strength of the parties by distributing the stronger men among different families. Even so, several carts had to be drawn entirely by women and young girls. Cold, hunger, fatigue, and dysentery began taking their tolls. The handcart song, set to the music of "A Little More Cider," was not sung as often or with as much conviction as they had sung it earlier on the journey:

Hurrah for the camp of Israel!
Hurrah for the handcart scheme!
Hurrah, hurrah, 'tis better far
Than the wagon and ox-team.

Snowstorms added to their misery, then the cutting, blinding wind off the Rockies. Women and children struggled through deep drifts, some freezing to death. When a person died, serviceable clothing was removed from the corpse and divided among needy survivors. At last, supplies from Salt Lake City reached the struggling emigrants, but not until two hundred of the one thousand pioneers had perished.

Occasional handcart parties crossed during the next few years, but none was permitted to start late in the season, and after the Civil War, crossings on foot were so rare they were considered worthy of newspaper stories in every community through which they passed. Much publicity, for example, was given a family which emigrated on foot in 1884 from New York City to a Dakota homestead, drawing a two-wheeled cart the entire distance.

Other modes of travel attracting much attention, but achieving little success, were the wind wagons built like sailboats. No record exists of anyone traveling very far across the plains in a wind-propelled wagon. But there were always individualists among the intrepid pioneers, as the St. Joseph (Missouri) *Herald* noted in 1866: "Yesterday morning a party of emigrants passed through and created some excitement, owing to the very novel conveyance made use of. In a 'dog cart' leisurely reclining upon a mattress, were an old woman and a young girl, both enjoying the luxury of a pipe; the old man and his youthful son being hard at work giving the necessary locomotion to the vehicle." [56]

VII

A Lodging for the Night

IN their pursuit of western emigration, women met with other adventures along the way, including some wryly humorous experiences at wayside stops. Those who traveled in covered wagons usually spent the nights inside, snug under canvas tops, but if families were large and wagons crowded with household goods the women would bed their children down in the wagons and then join their husbands on the ground. On pleasant summer nights they voluntarily slept outside under the stars, using India-rubber cloaks or buffalo robes to keep out the earth's dampness, adding a mattress for comfort, and rolling up in saddle blankets. In rattlesnake country most women would stretch a hair lariat around their beds to prevent intrusions by the reptiles, a custom whose efficacy seems never to have been satisfactorily proven or disproven.

Travelers expecting to make long stops en route, or Army wives journeying in cramped ambulances, usually had tents for night camps. As their experience increased, they learned to pitch them on high ground and to add a few boards to the baggage for use as flooring in rainy weather. Buffalo robes and other animal skins also made comfortable tent floors. Susan Magoffin's husband provided her with a luxurious tent, a roomy conical-shaped shelter with an iron pole support, for their honeymoon trip down the Santa Fe Trail. It was fitted up inside with a carpet of sailcloth, portable stools, a table fastened to the support pole, and a stand above the table that served as a dressing bureau. Elizabeth Custer spent much of her time in tents, but if opportunity offered she was inclined to desert them in favor of a snooze in an Army wagon filled with fragrant hay. During one of her nights in a hay wagon she had the peculiar experience of hearing a "munching and crunching" at her ear; an Army mule was quietly eating the pillow from under her head.

After stagecoach routes were opened, crude stage stops sprang up along the trails to provide hostelry service—if service it could be called during the early years. In the nomenclature of the times, such a place was known as a *ranche,* and indeed it often was an original ranch building. Colonel James Meline defined a ranche as "not a dwelling, nor a farmhouse, nor a store, nor a tavern, but all of these, and more. It is connected with a large corral, and capable of standing an Indian siege. You can procure entertainment at them . . . and they keep for sale liquors, canned fruit, knives, playing cards, saddlery, and *goggles*—both blue and green." The goggles, as Meline explained, were a prime necessity. "You will find them on sale at every ranche on the plains, north and south. The prevalent heat, dust, and glare make them almost indispensable." [1]

The typical ranche was earth-floored and candlelit, one room outfitted with plain plank counters loaded with everything from calico to nutmegs, saleratus and ready-made clothing. Another compartment served as a public dining hall where teamsters, stagedrivers, and passengers huddled around roughhewn tables to drink and dine. A loft served for sleeping quarters. Margaret Carrington told of stopping at French Pete's ranche on the Fort Reno road in 1866, the first enterprise of its kind in the hostile Sioux hunting country. Canned fruits, liquors, tobacco, beads, cheese, crackers, and a lodging for the night were available to any intrepid traveler. French Pete had a Sioux wife, but when the Indian hostilities began around Fort Phil Kearney the loyal wife could not stop her tribesmen from burning the ranche and killing her husband.

A well-known Kansas ranche was that of Paschal Fish, on the road between Kansas City and Lawrence. Fish was a Pawnee, shrewd enough to employ a New England Yankee as business manager and cook. A New England woman, stopping there one night in 1855, was not favorably impressed, however. "We dismount and enter at the only door into the first story of a large building, simply boarded and loosely floored. It is dimly lighted with poor tallow candles in Japan candlesticks, which bear evidence of having been the support of many candles before. There is a long table, and men, in whose faces there is absolutely no mouth to be seen, and only a gleam for eyes—an entire party of heads, covered with dirty, uncombed, unwashed hair. There were no more chairs. Our baggage was brought in, and we made seats of it. The men ate as though the intricacies from their plates to their mouths had become a perfect slight of hand with them. As they passed out of the room, the dishes were wiped out for us!" [2]

Another woman's experience at a ranche stop in Arizona was a bit more stimulating. All night long, she said, wild cats jumped in and out of the room, "first across the Bailey's bed, then over ours. The dogs caught the spirit of the chase, and added their noise to that of the cats. Both babies began to cry, and then up got Bailey and threw his heavy campaign boots at the cats, with some fitting remarks. A momentary silence reigned, and we tried again to sleep. Back came the cats, and then came Jack's turn with boots and traveling satchels. It was all of no avail, and we resigned ourselves. Cruelly tired, here we were, we two women, compelled to sit on hard boxes or the edge of a bed, to quiet our poor babies, all through that night." [3]

Spending a night in a sod-house inn also could offer certain novelties. "I had not been asleep long when I was awakened by something similar to fine hail falling on my face and hands. I called out: "Please get a light, there is something falling on my face and hands, and all over the bed.' This aroused the lady, and she remarked, 'It is only the dirt falling out of the sod which our house is made of, and when the wind blows, now it has become dry, it crumbles off, and we are so used to it that it does not disturb us.' But I could not sleep, for I was afraid every minute that the whole roof would fall in on us." [4]

A curious sort of hotel service was that offered to muleback travelers crossing Panama during the years of the California gold rush. Along this jungle route canvas shanties were erected by enterprising Americans, who lightheartedly christened their shabby hostelries with such names as St. Charles House, Revere House, and Astor House. Fruit and liquors formed the basic bill of fare at all these establishments, the owners charging prices worthy of the illustrious originals.

No woman ever seemed to have a kind word for the food served at western way stations, the common complaints being that too much saleratus was used in the biscuits, making them green in appearance and bitter to the taste. All meats were sodden in grease, deliberately done, some women believed, to disguise the natural flavor so that fastidious female diners would not know what animal of the prairie they were being served.

Crowded conditions brought forth similar indictments. A woman traveler never knew whether she could obtain a bed or be forced to sleep in a chair beside other luckless comrades drawn up around a fireplace. If a bed was available, chances were she would be required to share it with a stranger, as the universal rule of frontier hotels required that all double beds must be filled before customers could be turned away—provided the sexes of the occupants were the same, of course. A woman traveling in the Southwest with her infant told of sharing her bed with another woman and child. A cold wind blew in upon them through knotholes and cracks, resulting in a continual tug of war for the blanket. "It soon became a question of whether or not I, who occupied the side next the wall, should be shoved through it." [5]

During a journey in the West shortly before the Civil War, Sara Robinson spent a night with fifty other guests in a small mission inn. "I gave up my room to some of the new comers, and slept on comfortables and buffalo robes on the floor in the attic, and, with the exception of an occasional tug at my pillow, or nibble at my finger, from some stray mouse, I never slept better." [6]

This casual mention of mice and other vermin, found so often in women's accounts of experiences in frontier hotels, indicates that such annoyances must have been very common, considering the nineteenth-century reticence of females to mention household pests in polite society. In 1855, a discriminating young lady from New England penned this essay on the fleas of the Cincinnati Hotel of Lawrence, Kansas: "Mother, in the first place, did you ever see a FLEA? Don't consider the question impertinent . . . I ask for information; because I *have*. And on this night, when I imagined no enemy was near, they took sole possession of us all! I think I always had some respect for mosquitoes; they give warning always of their approach. Quite another sort of villain is this black, shambling, hydra-legged 'varmint'; using his legs only to lean with; never walking off, as though he had rights, but sneaking up from the floor just as one hopes to take possession of a bed, paid for, whisking in between the sheets in columns. Yet, put your finger on one of them if you can! Settle down and close your eyes . . . now they play 'hop scotch' along the extremities. You give a sudden brush with your hand; but you hit nothing. Now they commence a tramp, up, up, up! it is no longer endurable. Out of bed, off comes the night-dress, turned wrong-side-out. In the greatest apparent rage at the harmless piece of cotton, you thrash it most vigorously against imaginary chairs, get into it again, lift up the sheets and go through the same pantomime. Here they come like a herd of homeopathic buffaloes, as if by a preconcerted signal and set up anew their night's banquet at your expense." [7]

A strong effort to raise the standards of hotels in this very area was made in 1866 by none other than Mary Ann (Mother) Bickerdyke, the famed Civil War nurse. She decided that what Kansas needed was a clean, comfortable hotel that would appeal to women—white sheets, private washbowls, and delicious meals. But Mother Bickerdyke was ahead of her time; her hotel went bankrupt in short order.

A sociologist probably could make a good case for the proposition that the germinating point of women's rebellion against masculine authority was in the American frontier hotel. Here, for the first time in our history, thousands of women came to close quarters with thousands of strange males; they saw the dominant sex as he really was, learned his empty secrets through thin canvas walls, and viewed the nakedness of his body and soul. In that locale may have been born the American woman's first doubts of the male's superiority, of his right to claim mastery over the female, doubts that soon would lead to demands for the right to vote, and for complete social and legal equality.

Certainly there was no privacy in the first western hotels. "The partition walls of the best buildings were only of calico, or paper upon this; and though one could retire from sight, one could not from sound. In the public-houses you went to sleep with terrible oaths haunting your ears, and in the morning they were the first signs of human neighborhood." [8]

In many places, men and women slept in one large room, the women on one side, the men on the other. Relating her experiences in a single-room inn, Elizabeth Ellet said that when the bed was prepared the hostess turned to her husband with this casual remark: "Nicholas, the lady wishes to go to bed; turn your face to the wall." Nicholas, as if accustomed to this nightly drill, wheeled swiftly about and stood as still as if he had suddenly become one of the scanty articles of furniture, while Mrs. Ellet speedily undressed and crawled into bed. [9]

Another female traveler told of spending a night at a stage stop with fifteen men. There was only one bed, and curtains were strung around it to give her some privacy. "I tried to feel doubly protected, instead of embarrassed, by the vicinity of so many men; nor did I consider it necessary to peer about in an effort to learn how they disposed of themselves. I well knew it was too cold to admit of any sleeping outside. Being startled by some noise in the night, I drew back the curtains, and looked on a scene not soon to be forgotten. Not only were the men ranged in rows before me, but the number of sleepers had been augmented by at least six dogs, which had crept in for shelter." [10]

Some of the best descriptions of early western hotel interiors were recorded by women who endured the experience of being guests in them. After a close inspection of a typical California gold-rush hotel in 1851, Amelia Clappe had this to say of it: "You first enter a large apartment, level with the street, part of which is fitted up as a barroom, with that eternal crimson calico which flushes the whole social life of the Golden State with its everlasting red, in the center of a fluted mass of which gleams a really elegant mirror, set off by a background of decanters, cigar-vases, and jars of brandied fruit, the whole forming a *tout ensemble* of dazzling splendor. A table covered with green cloth—upon which lies a pack of monte-cards, a backgammon board, and a sickening pile of 'yallow-kivered' literature—with several uncomfortable-looking benches, complete the furniture." Adjoining this entrance room was the hotel's parlor, its floor covered with a straw carpet. Here, the ubiquitous red calico covered a long couch and hung from the windows as curtains. The 8-by-10-foot bedrooms also were curtained in red calico, but the color monotony was relieved by their purple calico walls and doors of blue drill cloth hung on leather hinges.[11]

In the booming towns of the western plains, the picture was much the same—hotel parlors furnished with rickety tables and chairs and with crude lounges made of unpeeled wooden frames over which were stretched calico coverings stuffed with prairie grass.

After stopping at the celebrated Cheyenne House in 1868, Loreta Velazquez described it as "the worst hotel I had ever met with in the course of my rather extensive travels." The bedrooms of this poorly constructed frame hostelry were the standard 8-by-10-foot size, separated by canvas partitions, so that any real privacy was impossible. The bunk beds were sized for two occupants. Mattresses and pillows—made of flour bags with the millers' brands still visible—were stuffed with straw. The gray Army blankets bore U. S. markings, probably "the plunder of some rascally quartermaster who had cheated the government." The hotel's entrance room was floored with rough pine boards exuding resin in sticky lumps. A pot-bellied stove heated to a glowing red was in the center, surrounded by a motley crowd of males, "smoking, chewing, spitting, and blaspheming." It was impossible, said Loreta, for a woman traveler to get near the stove. In the public washroom she found a dirty tin washbasin, a lump of home-made soap in an empty sardine tin, a tow towel on a roller, filthy and wet.

She shared her bed with a stranger, a half-drunken woman who slept in her clothing, snoring happily all night, blissfully unconscious of the active vermin. Next morning the sobered stranger took a six-shooter from under her pillow, buckled it around her waist, and inquired: "How did you sleep?"

"Not much," replied Loreta. "This kind of bed doesn't suit me."

"Well, I've slept too damned much," the stranger said. "I'm tired yet. I'd as soon sleep on a board or a rock as one of these damned old straw beds." [12]

Another unpopular sort of hotel during the early days of western railroads were those built along the right of way to serve coach passengers. Trains had no Pullman cars then, and at bedtime they scheduled sleep stops at such hell-roaring trail towns as Abilene, Ellsworth, or Hays City. The ground floors of these railroad hotels were usually bars, billiard rooms, or dance palaces, and most travelers would have preferred sleeping upright in a train coach to enduring the noisy revelry provided by cowboys whose frolicking kept the frame-and-canvas structures shaking most of the night.

For one reason or another many women emigrating to the West became operators or part owners of hotels and boarding-houses. Some of them, like Mother Bickerdyke, had a genuine desire to improve the service, especially for women travelers. Others looked upon hotelkeeping as merely a means of earn-ing a living, sometimes good, sometimes bad. One type of landlady was described by Elizabeth Farnham in California: "A young woman, quick, tidy, and self-respecting, with a re-serve in her countenance which shows that she has lived among people whom she has been obliged to repel." [13] Another sort was this hostess of a Nevada inn: "After we had partaken of the cheer set before us, she washed the dishes, turned round, and dashed the dish-water up in one corner of the apartment, wiped her hands upon her dirty apology for a dress, and sat down for a smoke." [14]

A nightmarish succession of experiences, which illustrates the adversities women travelers met with in finding lodgings for the night, was recorded by Julia Lovejoy, en route west to join her husband in 1855. For six weeks, while awaiting word of her husband's whereabouts, she and her two children suffered as guests of a Kansas City hotel. "Hundreds were almost constantly thronging the hotel," she wrote, "bringing various diseases with them, and seldom a boatload without more or less sick until the very air in the different rooms seemed impregnated with disease and death. Within a few feet of our own room, lay at one time four men, sick with lung fever. A little farther on, in the passage that led to our room, within a short time lay two dead bodies . . . We left the hotel and went to a private house to board, when our elder daughter was seized with pneumonia . . . and our younger became very ill, whilst we too were violently seized, and we feared the whole 'trio' would die, and not a human face we had ever seen before to express any human sympathy." Hearing from her husband at last, she escaped from Kansas City by boarding a boat bound up the Kaw River for Fort Riley. Unfortunately the boat grounded en route, sticking fast on a sand bar. Going ashore, Mrs. Lovejoy found a furnished log cabin unoccupied by human beings but filled with a nauseating odor. The source of the odor was a dead cat in a linen closet. She industriously set about cleaning up the place, but in a day or so the owners returned and she had to move into another cabin with a half-breed Indian woman. There she spent "an awful week with a drunken woman for a hostess, carrying scars upon her person received in drunken fights." [15] Mrs. Lovejoy's long ordeal ended when a passing wagon offered her a ride to the town where her worried husband was waiting impatiently for her.

VIII

Vanity Conquers All

1

AFTER reporting a windstorm that "sat down on its hind legs and howled and screeched and snorted," the Wichita (Kansas) *Eagle* of April 15, 1880, added a note of commiseration for the women of the community. "Weighted down with bar lead and trace-chains as their skirts are, their only protection from rude gaze is the dust, which fills up the eyes of the men so that they can't see a rod farther than a blind mule."

Women in the West who insisted on wearing the full-skirted modes of the nineteenth century—including the hoop-skirt, the bustle, and Mother Hubbards—fought a continual battle against a hostile environment. The fact that flowing yards of silk and satin eventually won out over buckskin and rawhide is only one more confirmation of the theory that woman's vanity can conquer all, any place and any time.

The problem of billowing skirts in windy plains country was no minor one, and though it was met and overcome, there is some evidence that the solution was the work of a male—none other than our old friend, George Armstrong Custer. When the Custers went to Fort Riley after the Civil War,

Elizabeth's dresses were all "five yards around, and gathered as full as could be into the waist-band." On her first walk across the windy parade ground, her skirt billowed like a balloon, flew out in front, then lifted over her head. His military dignity thus affronted, George immediately figured out a way to keep his wife's skirts at their proper level. He cut some lead bars into strips and ordered Elizabeth to sew them into the hems of her dresses. Thus weighted down she was able to outwit the elements while taking her constitutionals about the post. Other women followed her example, and a dozen years later all were wearing bar lead in their skirt hems on the windy western plains.

In rainy weather, a different effect was desirable, as skirts had to be lifted to keep hems out of the mud—an almost impossible operation when the cloth ran five or six yards around. To solve this problem, a practical inventor devised an apparatus called the "instant dress elevator." An advertisement which ran in the Leavenworth *Daily Times* during December 1874 made this claim: "You can raise your skirt while passing a muddy place and then let it fall, or you can keep it raised with the elevator. It keeps the skirt from filth. It can be changed from one dress to another in less than two minutes." The price of this marvelous invention was only seventy-five cents.[1]

If there was ever a dress style unsuited to the Wild West it was the hoopskirt, yet it was quite in vogue there during and immediately following the Civil War. In a land where almost every female had to ride horseback, sidesaddle or astride, the hoopskirt was an impediment of the first order. The only solution was for the lady to remove the hoop contraption and ride in her pantaloons, and we have testimony from the observant Colonel James Meline that he witnessed a young lady so riding with her lover in New Mexico. She sat in front of the saddle, the gentleman supporting her with one hand and carrying her hoopskirt in the other. Just who was holding the bridle, the colonel did not state.

When a Wyoming woman imported a hired girl from the East in 1867, the young lady arrived in a hoopskirt so wide she could not move freely about the narrow ranch kitchen. After some discussion between employer and employee concerning the suitability of hoops for western wear, the girl compromised by agreeing to hang her hoops on the kitchen wall while working there. One morning the hoops mysteriously disappeared, and a wild search ensued, the girl bitterly accusing her mistress of hiding them. The mystery was solved that evening when the squaws at a nearby Indian camp came out of their teepees to dance around the supper fires. One of them was attired in the stolen hoops, over which was draped a gay plaid shawl.[2]

In such ways and others, the hoopskirt soon vanished from the western scene, only to be succeeded a few years later by the preposterous bustle. No sensible female could have enjoyed wearing a bustle, but in the words of a plain-spoken Oregon woman, "as long as bustles were fashionable, they wore bustles. They breathed a sigh of relief when bustles were no longer necessary, although, having worn them so long, one might feel shamefully 'nekkid.' "[3] Western citizens who had the most fun with bustles were male newspaper editors, this being a sample comment: "A fashion paper says, 'Bustles are worn somewhat lower.' Such stuff is all nonsense. No paper can tell just how high from the ground a bustle should be worn. A tall girl wears hers where it will do the most good and a short one the same. Think of a tall giraffe-built girl wearing her bustle at the same height as a short beer-keg built girl. She could not move with grace at all and if the short girl gets hers at the same altitude as the tall girl's she would look humpbacked and disconsolate. No, a girl always wears her bustle where it will do the most good, and there are no rules as to the height."[4]

During the Mother Hubbard craze of the 1880's, a great public debate raged from Missouri to Oregon over the merits and drawbacks of that peculiarly unattractive costume. In Missouri, the *Sedalia Bazoo* proposed to organize a club for the purpose of buying belts for ladies who insisted upon wearing Mother Hubbards. The *Clinton Daily Advocate* supported the costume, however, and congratulated the ladies for their "good sense displayed in adopting an attire which if not graceful in itself can at least lay claim to airiness and comfort these hot days. Besides the looseness about the waist allows the wearer to do away with the foolish custom of wearing tight laced corsets." [5] The most extreme male action against Mother Hubbards was taken by the city fathers of Pendleton, Oregon, who claimed the voluminous swishing skirts were frightening horses on the streets and causing serious accidents. In 1885, they met and solemnly passed an ordinance outlawing Mother Hubbards unless worn tightly belted. Notices were posted, warning all females that they would be heavily fined if caught wearing costumes which might "scare horses, cause accidents, and ruin business."

Horses were not the only animals disturbed by outlandish feminine costumes, as a young eastern girl visiting a western ranch discovered when she went riding sidesaddle to view a roundup. "The bodice of my habit," she later recalled, "was buttoned tightly from throat to waist, but from there on it gave play to all the whims of the wind. With the wind blowing a will-o'-the-wisp gale, my riding skirt inflated like a balloon. The wild-eyed long-horn steers took one look at something they had never seen before, milled a minute and then stampeded. Immediately, I found my smart eastern togs were unpopular around the place."[6]

Western women were practical creatures or they would never have survived, and they learned that styles in dress had to be adapted to circumstances. If they saw that heavy high-topped shoes were suited to a given situation, they wore them cheerfully. If they could obtain no other head coverings but sunbonnets, they wore sunbonnets, making them from left-over bits of bright calico and fitting thin strips of wood into them for stays. They sewed most of their clothing by hand, the only sewing machines available in those days being hand-cranked contraptions fastened to tables, and very few of these were known in the West. In cold country, such as the Dakotas, they learned to wear three pairs of underdrawers and three pairs of socks at the same time, covering all this with cloth coats, buffalo coats, fur caps, shoes, and arctics.

Yet, being women, they always added some decorative touch, if only a gay slip of ribbon pinned about the throat. As one pioneer remarked in reminiscing about the styles of the early days, "no matter how ordinary her clothes or how rough her task, nearly every woman wore her bit of ribbon." [7] And although Elizabeth Custer boasted that she never worried about wearing out-of-date styles on remote Army posts, she confessed that when anyone was going to the States for a visit or for official reasons she always prepared a list of women's vanities to be purchased for her. "Shoes ordered by mail," she explained, "were usually sent separately because of postal regulations concerning bulk. We often waited a long time for the second shoe to arrive." [8]

Another Army wife told of her disappointing experiences in trying to order millinery by mail. Isolated at Fort Bayard, New Mexico, with no hat suitable for riding or driving, she ordered a "quiet little bonnet" from New York. "Instead I received a very gaudy, dashing piece of millinery that would have been suitable for the opera, but was altogether out of place on the frontier. The bonnet cost me twenty dollars and the express charges twenty-two." She had spent forty-two dollars, but still had no hat, for she never had the courage to wear that one.[9]

Because they moved about from post to post and back and forth from the States to the Territories, Army women were more style-conscious than others. A concise yet vivid description of women's wear on the Great Plains in 1865 was recorded by the observant daughter of an Army sergeant at Fort McPherson: "The ladies wore long skirts that touched the ground, and they had bustles and puffed sleeves, and short basques which made them look plump and full figured. Their bright shawls made them look very pretty. The wind blew hard, and caused them to reach for their bonnets, and it twirled their full skirts so we could see their high buttoned shoes. We girls wore Scotch plaid dresses made with gored skirts and short jackets buttoned in back. We had red topped boots made of cowhide and trimmed with brass tips. Mother had knitted our black wool stockings, and grandmother had spun and dyed the wool. Our little flat hats were covered with small flowers. We all wore red flannel underwear, of course."[10]

Few references to corsets are to be found in contemporary letters and diaries, perhaps because corsets were "unmentionables," but we do have the word of Mary Maverick that they were in occasional use in Texas as early as 1841: "A belle of the ball in San Antonio purchased a new silk dress that fit so tightly she had to wear corsets for the first time in her life. She was several times compelled to escape to her bedroom to take off the corset and 'catch her breath.'"[11] And a strange accident involving a corset was reported by a Kansas newspaper in 1880: "The lightning struck a Great Bend girl last week. She was not injured in the least, but her corset ribs were sadly demoralized, as was also the arm of a young man who was trying to keep them in place. When asked by his friends why he keeps his arm in a sling he explained that he 'didn't know she was loaded.' "[12]

Corsets, of course, were *de rigueur* in California, especially in San Francisco, which was a sort of Paris of the Wild West so far as women's styles were concerned. As early as 1851, San Francisco stores were advertising not only corsets but white satin and French-kid slippers, Jenny Lind ties, and polka boots for women. In July of that year the *Alta California* took note of a new style of ladies' dresses introduced into San Francisco. "Mrs. Cole, who has a ladies' dress store on Clay Street, has received the patterns and not only has a figure in the window with the dress on, but wears one herself in the store. It is really very pretty. Mrs. Cole's dress consists of green merino, fitting well to the figure above the waist and reaching below the knee some 3 or 4 inches. Below this are loose, flowing trowsers of pink satin, fastened below the ankle. Mrs. Cole already has received orders for three dresses and the ladies appear to like it but from its singularity scarcely dare adopt it at present."

The writer for the *Alta* apparently was unaware that the costume he was describing was the creation of Amelia Jenks Bloomer, ardent advocate of "a sensible costume for women," who had bravely introduced it a year or so earlier in her home town in New York State. Already these "flowing trowsers" were known in the east by the name of their creator, and very soon "Bloomers" would be as controversial in the West as they were in the east.

Either the same reporter, or one a bit more alert fashion-wise, used the word "Bloomer" in a later *Alta* story: "The city was taken quite by surprise yesterday afternoon by observing a woman in company with her male companion, crossing the lower side of the Plaza, dressed in a style a little beyond the Bloomer. She was magnificently arrayed in a black satin skirt, very short, with flowing red satin trousers, a splendid yellow crape shawl and a silk *turban à la Turque.* She really looked magnificent and was followed by a large retinue of men and boys, who appeared to be highly pleased with the style."[13]

The development of the bloomer costume came at an opportune time for the many skirt-handicapped women who were crossing the plains during the gold-rush period and the booming fifties. "Bloomerism has done wonders for Oregon," a gentleman wrote from there in 1853. "All the women emigrants who cross the plains dress in that style."[14]

Women traveling west by boat and the Panama Isthmus also wore bloomers. While Edward Sherman was boarding a Panama-bound vessel at Boston in August 1854, he noticed a commotion among the dockside crowd, then heard cheering, laughter, and an occasional bantering remark flung from the bystanders. "I observed a gentleman leading a little girl about twelve years old up the gang plank, followed by two ladies dressed in brown linen bloomers." The gentleman turned out to be John C. Frémont, the little girl his daughter Elizabeth, and the two females in bloomers were the Misses Mary Atkins and Sarah Pellet. Like most males of the time, Sherman thought bloomers were amusing, but he did admit they were also useful to the wearers while they were crossing the Isthmus on muleback. He "made bold to make acquaintance with the two ladies in bloomers," and discovered that Miss Atkins planned to start a female seminary in California, while Miss Pellet hoped to earn her living by delivering lectures on temperance. Sherman gave them the names of some influential Californians he thought might be interested in aiding them, then said bluntly: "If you want to succeed in California, discard at once your bloomer garb. You will find it difficult to succeed otherwise."

The young ladies thanked him for his friendly advice, and he had the satisfaction of recording later that Miss Atkins was quite successful as the operator of a female seminary at Benicia. Miss Pellet lectured on temperance for a while, then joined up as "aid or something to the filibusterer William Walker. What her career was after that, I am not informed."[15]

Among other Californians who disapproved of bloomers was Dame Shirley, who, after observing some women clad in them, posed this rhetorical question: "How can they so far forget the sweet shy coquetries of shrinking womanhood as to don those horrid bloomers? I pin my vestural faith with unflinching obstinacy to sweeping petticoats." Later, however, she conceded that bloomers were useful under certain conditions: "There is one thing for which the immigrants deserve high praise, and that is for having adopted the bloomer dress (frightful as it is on all other occasions) in crossing the plains. For such an excursion it is just the thing."[16]

And for a decade of western crossings, bloomers continued to be "just the thing." In a letter from the Platte Valley, June 5, 1860, Albert D. Richardson reported: "The bloomer costume is considerably in vogue, and appears peculiarly adapted to overland travel. We passed a bloomer, a day or two since, who apparently weighed about two hundred and fifty, and who, while her better half was soundly sleeping in the wagon, was walking and driving the oxen. Her huge dimensions gave her the appearance of an ambulatory cotton bale, or a peripatetic haystack."[17]

2

It was no easy thing for women to surround themselves with an aura of sex mystery in a raw land of derisive males and very little privacy anywhere. Gunpowder was far easier to come by than face powder, and all the red paint and rouge had been monopolized by wild Indians and harlots.

When a petticoat pioneer desired a beautifier, she used what was at hand—sour milk or buttermilk applied as skin bleaches at night, or complexion salves made of white wax, spermacetti, and sweet oil, scented with homemade rose or lavender water. Honey was an old reliable cosmetic, used by frontier women for everything from softening the teats of their milk cows to a base for beauty soap. A shiny nose could be concealed under a slight dusting of corn starch, or an entire weather-beaten face under a coating of flour paste.

Vogues for rouge and other skin reddeners varied from place to place, beet juice in season being commonly used. A young Norwegian traveling through the western border states in 1854 was so impressed by the "unspeakable amount of paint" used by young ladies that he wrote a long letter home about the custom. The "genuine article," he said, was too expensive for most young females to afford, but if they wanted "to be in the competition" they had to content themselves with a substitute which would not stick to the skin and in a warm room would melt and run down the wearers' cheeks, "which makes them look as if they were crying bloody tears over their own and the world's vanity. Still further down in society the women cannot even afford to buy the adulterated paint, so here they have to try the most desperate means, for red they must be. What do you think they do? I have not happened to see it, but it is generally said that they pinch their own cheeks, and if they can get away in private where no one sees or hears them—something that is not so very easy in America —rumor has it that they do not hesitate to box themselves on the ears, and by so doing produce the most natural blooming complexion you can imagine. These boxes on the ears are the most well deserved I have yet heard about. But despite these attempts to aid nature, there can be no doubt that the American ladies really do look like angels."[18]

In western communities where "red light" districts flourished, respectable women avoided use of facial cosmetics in public so as not to confuse the males. Anything red was suspect. In Cheyenne of the 1870's, the street women were known as "painted cats," readily identified by their "chalk-white faces, scarlet-painted lips and cheeks, sometimes with a red feather or red bow on their hats, and leading a little dog on a leash."[19] Respectable women of Cheyenne, therefore, disdained all such accoutrements as these. San Francisco women were less bigoted in their approach to rouge and red paint, travel writer Emily Faithfull reporting in 1884 that there was "more flagrant use of rouge and cosmetics in San Francisco than I ever encountered elsewhere."[20]

Care of the hair consisted mainly of keeping it washed, brushed, and combed. If rain water was not obtainable, well water was softened with borax for a rinse. A popular homemade shampoo was concocted of a mixture of castor oil and pure whisky scented with lavender. If a patented hair curler was lacking, resourceful females learned to use a slate pencil heated over a kerosene lamp chimney. Dark hair was considered slightly immoral for elderly ladies, but in the female code it was ethical to conceal premature grayness by touching it up with sage tea. False curls, chignons, buns, waterfalls, and other forms of artificial hair came and went ("dead women's hair" was the derisive male term for these adornments) but like hoopskirts they were never very practical in a wind-blown, horse-riding civilization.

The basic aid to feminine daintiness, a good soaking bath, ofttimes was one of the rarest luxuries, achieved only by the most determined of the sex. On an overland journey, or in new settlements where wells or springs were not handy, an outdoor stream usually served as the tub. Martha Summerhayes told of how she used the Colorado River. "Like Pharaoh's daughter of old, I went with my gentle handmaiden every morning to the river bank, and wading in about knee-deep in the thick red waters, we sat down and let the swift current flow by us. A clump of low mesquite trees afforded sufficient protection at that hour; we rubbed dry, slipped on a loose gown, and wended our way home."[21] When Lydia Waters reached Mohawk Valley, California, at the end of a long trail journey, she discovered that a settler had built a bathhouse nearby. Not having enjoyed a bath for several weeks, she asked permission to use it. "The water had an exhilarating effect," she wrote in her diary, "made one feel as lively as champagne."[22]

With assistance from husband George, the efficient Elizabeth Custer managed a daily bath even on a cavalry march. When reveille sounded, George would lift her out of their hay-wagon bed into a tent, "and by the light of a tallow candle I had my bath and got into my clothes, combing my hair straight back, as it was too dark to part it. Then, to keep my shoes from being soaked with the wet grass, I was carried to the dining-tent, and lifted upon my horse afterward." But when she reached a permanent Army post, she always found it a comfort to get out of bed onto a carpet and bathe and dress before a fire. She once wrote her mother: "Don't tell Armstrong I said so, as I never mentioned to him that dressing before day, my eyes streaming with tears from the campfire while I took my bath, was not the mode of serving my country that I would choose." [23]

Bathing in frontier hotels was as hard on women as sleeping or dining in those rough establishments. Bathrooms were almost unknown and water had to be brought to the bedrooms in tin basins. Western river water was, as Hannah Ropes described it in a letter to her mother, "precisely the color of dirty soapsuds." Before taking her first bath, she let the water settle until "the mud was not more than a finger deep at the bottom. I poured it off carefully as you would cream from a pan of milk, until the stir of the mud made me stop. You should have seen me, mother of mine, squatted on the floor at midnight, comparing those two bowls . . . What had been poured off was a poor edition of the rinsing water which old Rachel used to be so choice of in the tubs standing under the well-sweep."[24]

In 1864, the editor of an Idaho newspaper boldly faced up to the perplexing problem of preventing "body odor" in a country where bathtubs were in short supply. "The unpleasant odor produced by perspiration," he wrote, "is frequently the source of vexation to persons subject to it. Nothing is simpler than to remove this odor much more effectively than by the applications of such costly perfumes as are in use. It is only necessary to procure some compound spirits of ammonia and place about two tablespoonsful in a basin of water. Washing the face, arms and hands with this leaves the skin as clean, fresh and sweet as one could wish."[25]

His female readers undoubtedly knew a deal more about such matters than that Idaho editor. Using what they had—a washbowl and a pitcher or a tin basin, a broken piece of looking glass or a tin mirror, a tiny shelf of homemade toiletries, a dash of rose water, a bright sprig of ribbon—they managed to keep their sex appeal shining under the worst of conditions.

3

If any single group of western women deserves the most credit for conquering obstacles to vanity, that valiant band of females who settled Utah, the Mormon women, surely would be in the vanguard. President Brigham Young, who allowed his brilliant imagination to be concerned with everything his people did, made the mistake of setting himself up as a dress designer for the women of his colony. He had favored bloomers for trail crossings, but once the Mormons were established in Utah he decided the time had come to introduce a new costume. He called it the "Deseret Costume," a modification of Amelia Bloomer's design, covered over with a loose shapeless sacque. To this he added a hat eight inches high with a straight narrow brim. With all the eloquence and power at his command, he urged the sisters to wear the "Deseret Costume," but few of them ever adopted it with any enthusiasm.

Possibly this disaffection may have had something to do with the later breaking up of polygyny. Certainly the introduction of stylish and expensive clothing was a powerful economic force against multiple wives, at least as strong as the force of civil law. A traveler in Utah during the 1870's quoted a Mormon gentleman as saying regretfully that his wives were no longer content to dress as rustics. "Our women want new bonnets," he said, "they pine for silk pelisses and satin robes, and try to outshine each other. All this finery is costly; yet a man who loves his wives can hardly refuse to dress them as they see other ladies dress. To clothe one woman is as much as most men in America can afford. In the good old times, an extra wife cost a man little or nothing. She wore a calico sunshade, which she made herself. Now she must have a bonnet. A bonnet costs twenty dollars, and implies a shawl and gown to match. A bonnet to one wife, with shawl and gown to match, implies the like to every other wife." The man paused, shook his head ruefully and concluded: "This taste for female finery is breaking up our Mormon homes. Brigham Young may soon be the only man in Salt Lake City rich enough to clothe a dozen wives."[26]

IX

"A Little Light Diversion"

1

WHEN early westerners chose to relax they went about their recreation with as much verve as they put into more serious activities of life. Being extreme individualists, their methods of pleasuring themselves were as varied as the people and the land, but, judging from records left behind, dancing and party-going of all kinds surely were the most popular community entertainments. For solitary diversion, everybody read—everything from the classics to yellow-back novels, almanacs and mail-order catalogs. Because they spent more time at home women probably read more than men; at least, they mentioned reading more often in their diaries than men did.

But the women also were ardent participants in the more vigorous community affairs. After all, a dance was not a dance without petticoated partners, and hell and high water would not keep a high-spirited female from a proper hoedown. During the cold winter of 1871 in Washington Territory, a pretty young schoolmarm rode horseback one evening in freezing weather to a flooded stream, crossed in a canoe, rode a waiting horse to a ranch where she boarded a sled behind a span of mules, and managed to arrive on time for the dancing party.

"We were sure anxious to get a girl for that dance," said one of the males who assisted in this efficient transport operation. Another resourceful swain in the same area did not allow lack of a sled to keep him from delivering his partner to a dance over a snow-blocked road. He took a beef hide, put some stretchers across, attached whiffletrees, hitched the horses, wrapped himself and the girl in a blanket, and away they rode to the dance on the hide.[1]

In Wyoming, women thought nothing of riding horseback or in a buggy for forty miles to a dance. One ranch wife told of a series of dances given in 1874 by neighbors living twenty miles apart—each entertaining on successive evenings. When they were snowed in, they kept the conviviality going until dawn, then went home if they could. Even in high mountain country, the rough, dangerous roads were not enough to keep a determined female from a frolic. "The road there was the steepest I had ever been on. It felt like the mule was going up a flight of stairs. But it was the best party I'd ever been to, and at daylight we returned."[2]

Whether it was a gallop, shuffle, money musk, quadrille, or Virginia reel, pioneer women could dance anywhere, on rough puncheon or hard-packed earthen floors—although if on the latter, a sprinkling can had to be kept handy to lay the dust. Music was usually furnished by one or more fiddles, but whatever instruments were at hand were made to serve—cottage organs, jew's-harps, accordions, harmonicas, guitars, banjos.

In addition to troop dances and officers' balls, military posts frequently held public dances for civilians in the outlying areas. Spacious mess halls made excellent dancing places for large crowds. Walls were decorated with flags, wreaths, and evergreen garlands; ceilings were draped with colored tissue and bunting; and canvas was stretched tightly over the floors, transforming the usual barrenness into what must have seemed a fairyland to the early settlers. "Some of those affairs," recalled an officer's wife, "would have presented a strange picture to people in the East; but the very absurdity and variety of the costumes and conduct of frontiersmen and their wives, who were always invited, only added zest to our enjoyment, and the recollections amused us for days."[3]

One of the reasons frontier females favored dances was the opportunity afforded for showing off new frocks, there being few other public places for parading their finery. Indeed, it was customary in some localities for girls to change their dresses at midnight, thus giving them a chance to appear in two costumes at one dance. During the years immediately following the Civil War, calico was the universal party-dress fabric, costing fifteen or twenty cents per yard, and it was considered stylish to wear dance costumes consisting of a light-colored skirt and a dark-colored waist. One woman, remembering these dances, said that only quadrilles were danced in her neighborhood. "While two couples danced to each other, the opposite couples stood in the dim light with their arms around each other; when their time came the other couples rested in the same position."[4]

Some frontier people frowned upon dancing for moral or religious reasons, but they appear to have been in the minority. A Britisher living in Kansas during the 1870's noted that staid social gatherings often turned into dances "after the Methodists had gone home." He quoted his host at one of these affairs: " 'Jack,' says the host, 'just watch till you see the pious folk about to git, and then you ride off like the dickens for a fiddler, while I walk around and tell the girls that ain't too good that we're going to have a dance. You bet we'll have a high time yet.' And so they do, and keep it up till daylight."[5]

Other westerners, such as the editor of the White Cloud (Kansas) *Chief* in 1859, viewed dancing with alarm because of the hazards involved. "We understand that at the Iowa

Point Ball last week, several young gentlemen and ladies, in dancing a Schottische, tried which one could out-dance the others. One young man keeled over, and came very near 'kicking the bucket'; and, we understand, has been laid up ever since. How many deaths are caused by such foolishness in dancing?" [6]

One western religious group which actively supported dancing was the Mormon church. Grand balls were held frequently in Salt Lake City, led off by President Brigham Young, who conscientiously danced with each of his wives in turn. Not all the wives approved of these balls, however. "No matter how old and homely a man is," complained one of these disaffected women, "he thinks that he has as much right to flirt and dance with the girls as the youngest boy; for they all look upon themselves and each other as boys and single men, even if they have a dozen wives . . . They are always in the market." [7]

In many places, especially mining camps and cow camps, the supply of women was so limited that they had to be rationed among the male dancers, and when this would not satisfy the exuberant males they took turns wearing bandanna handkerchiefs around their arms to designate them as playing the parts of females. Writing of early days in the Washoe mining country, Dan De Quille recalled how every Saturday night a grand ball was given at Dutch Nick's saloon. "As there were but three white women in the town, it was necessary, in order to make up the set to take in Miss Sarah Winnemucca, the Piute Princess . . . all danced with ardor and filled the air with splinters from the puncheon floor."[8]

Similar affairs were held in the California mining country, Dame Shirley delightfully describing a typical one in a Rich Bar saloon where the ceilings were so low a tall man could not stand upright. Although everything was elegantly draped with red calico, "there was some danger of being swept away in a flood of tobacco-juice, but luckily the floor was uneven, and it lay around in puddles, which with care one could avoid, merely running the minor risk of falling prostrate upon the wet boards in the midst of a galopade."[9]

As the West matured, its dancing became more stylized, a less spontaneous expression of energetic release. Dancing schools opened for business as early as the 1850's in California, "teaching all the new and fashionable dances of the age, including the quadrille, waltzes, polkas, schottisches." A young Scandinavian traveling through the West observed that all frontier women seemed bent upon improving themselves, in season and out of season, even while dancing. Of one of his dancing partners he said: "It did not surprise me to learn that she danced because it was good for the digestion. And her dancing was what might have been expected; it was a conscientious exercise. At every bar of the music she emphasized the time with a jerk, as if she were trying to help me along."[10]

Whether the young Scandinavian's dancing partner was a representative specimen or not, and even if dancing did become a "social grace" in some of the more sophisticated settlements, the old hoedown survived and flourished in many places. Then there were always party games, candy pulls, and box suppers, where a female could act as natural as she pleased.

Saturday night socials were a most common form of frontier entertainment, neighbors gathering at one house by entire families—the term "baby sitter" being then unknown. As radio and television were also nonexistent, the evening was devoted to plain conversation about community events, the condition of the crops, books they had read. Because everybody in the community was usually present, personal gossip was an unlikely subject. At children's bedtime they were put upstairs and the social continued until midnight or dawn. Some of the women sewed or crocheted; the girls gathered in the kitchen and made molasses candy. In some years there were puzzle crazes, and young and old would compete for hours over intricate enigmas and riddles. Cribbage and Authors were popular card games. Midnight suppers were customary, and if the activities continued until dawn the hostess was expected to serve breakfast—hot cakes, eggs, side pork, coffee. Visiting families brought their own tableware and dishes.

A newcomer describing one of these western socials thought it "rather a peculiar gathering" because there was no music or dancing. "The time was principally spent in eating and drinking, and playing at silly, childish games mostly after the style of 'Kiss in the Ring.'" This observer was to learn in course of time that western party games included a surprising amount of kissing. "There are a great many Methodists and others," he added, "who look upon dancing as an unpardonable sin, and yet do not object to games of this kind. Upon this occasion, some game or other was proposed, but was ruled out and strongly objected to by one young lady, the daughter of a Methodist parson, because the game was too much like dancing. But she played in the other games, and seemed to enjoy them, kissing included. This I thought rather inconsistent." [11]

Some "play-party" games were actually dances without orchestras, the participants furnishing their own music by singing rhythmic verses as they moved through intricate dance forms. Spectators added their bit to the gaiety by clapping hands and stamping feet to the beat of "Skip to My Lou," "Weevily Wheat," "The Girl I Left Behind Me," or "Old Dan Tucker." These games were sometimes called "Presbyterian dances."

Another form of party amusement was described by a Kansas newspaper in 1878: "Hug socials are now the rage. It costs ten cents to hug any one between fifteen and twenty, five cents from twenty to thirty, one dollar to hug another man's wife, old maids two for a nickel, while female lecturers are free with a chromo thrown in. At these prices it is said that the old maids are most productive, because they can stand so much of it without getting tired."[12]

A newspaper editor of the same period wrote a vivid account of a candy pull: "After cooking sorghum a proper length of time you take it out and pull it, and the more you pull it the paler it will get, and then you go out and sit down on a pile of shingles and cool it. When it gets cool enough, you take hold of one end and your girl takes hold of the other end and you pull and then she pulls, and by and by it breaks in two and you turn a double back-action hand-spring towards the north star and she walks off on her ear in the opposite direction. If you want to change the programme you can take a chunk of the candy about as big as a small curly dog, and stretch it out exactly seventeen feet two inches and a half long, then take one end of it in your mouth and your duck takes the other in hers; then you commence chewing and prancing until you get yourself into a good state of perspiration, when you swallow eight feet seven inches and a quarter and clasp her in your arms, nose to nose."[13]

A milder variation of party-going was the frontier musicale, especially popular around Army posts where groups of musicians were more likely to be available than anywhere else on the frontier. Favorite numbers were such tunes as "Tenting Tonight," "Old Hundred," "Nearer My God to Thee," "Annie Laurie," and "When the Swallows Homeward Fly." The amateur theatrical was another specialty of military posts; the enlisted men could always be depended upon to form an audience.

The box supper was a later custom, widely prevalent in the early-settled Northwest, its primary purpose being to raise money for schools or churches. Girls and wives prepared the suppers and their escorts were expected to pay the final price, no matter how high the spirited bidding went. A Washington settler related the story of a bidding competition between one girl's sweetheart and a burly logger, the latter raising the price beyond reach of the young man. The logger's victory appeared to be a hollow one, for even though the code required that a girl must sit beside the buyer of her box supper, in this case she refused to talk to the woodsman or pay him any attention whatsoever. After eating the expensive box supper, the logger turned to the girl and in the racy language of the woods expressed his opinion of her as a female. The girl went home in tears, angry at her sweetheart for not punching the logger in the nose or otherwise defending her honor. Three months later she married the logger.[14]

One of the best-remembered incidents in Owen Wister's *The Virginian* is the ranch party, the high point of which is the practical joke played by the hero—the scene in which he mixes up the sleeping babies so their parents carry home the wrong offspring. Readers who enjoyed this most were undoubtedly westerners, many of whom had experienced the same confusion, for baby mixing at parties was an old western sport, noted in various contemporary accounts. Some thirty years before the time of the *Virginian,* a Californian recorded a factual baby mix-up in Sonoma Valley: "In the rear room of the hall where the ball was held, a dozen or so cots had been set up, upon which the mothers placed their babies and their wraps. While they were dancing, the babies had been shifted around, their clothes changed, and the ladies' wraps left in confusion. Some mothers found, on arriving home early in the morning, that they had boys instead of girls, who would not draw their nourishment from strange maternal fountains, and who were vociferous in their protestations and would not be comforted. General indignation prevailed."[15]

Westerners never permitted a wedding, a barn-raising, a national holiday, or any special event to pass without some lusty celebrating. Charivaris, or chivarees, accompanied almost every frontier wedding and were very noisy and violent affairs. A young bride, new to the West, told of being so frightened by the firing of guns she wanted to nail up the windows of her cabin. Members of a charivari party usually disguised themselves by wearing masks or blackening their faces, sometimes donning their clothing hind part before, and then marched in a body to the house of the newlyweds to the sound of rattling kettles and pans, banging drums, tootling horns, cracked fiddles, and continuous gunfire. The march was timed so that the party would arrive about bedtime. They would beat upon the front door with clubs, demanding admittance to hold a dancing party or to drink the bride's health, or in place of these a sum of money to treat themselves at the nearest saloon. Should the bridegroom ignore their demands, the din increased; dried peas or beans were fired against the windows; sometimes doors were broken in and the groom dragged out of bed into the night.

"We believe the practice of belling and fussing, generally, upon wedding occasions, prevails in all parts of the country," observed the editor of the White Cloud (Kansas) *Chief* in 1860, "but our Western people have a way of their own to do these things. We are informed that a wedding came off somewhere in the Missouri Bottom, a short time ago, and in the evening a crowd went to the place for a spree. They performed such tricks as shooting bullets through the windows, breaking down the door, dragging the couple out of bed, and tumbling them about on the floor, cutting open the feather beds, tearing up the floor, and indulging in other equally innocent tricks. It requires backbone to get married out this way." [16]

When Mary Heslip Knight and her husband arrived in Evanston City, Wyoming, to start their honeymoon, they learned that practically every pan, kettle, cowbell, and tin pail in town had been corralled in preparation for a charivari in their honor. Having been active in many violent charivaris himself, the bridegroom with great presence of mind secretly employed a friend to take a room in the hotel and pretend serious illness. As the din began beneath the windows of the little frame hotel, the hotelkeeper stepped outside and begged the crowd to desist. "A dying man lies in my hotel," he explained apologetically. The ruse was successful, and bride and groom spent a peaceful night.[17]

Social gatherings for work were called bees—quilting bees, barn-raising bees, logging bees. British-born Susanna Moodie was disillusioned by her experiences with bees. People on the western frontier, she said, "have a craze for giving and going to bees, and run to them with as much eagerness as a peasant runs to a race-course or a fair; plenty of strong drink and excitement making the chief attraction of the bee . . . noisy, riotous, drunken meetings, often terminating in violent quarrels, sometimes even in bloodshed." When her husband invited thirty-two men to a logging bee to clear part of their new homestead, she had to bake and cook for all of them over a three-day period. She fed them pea-soup, legs of pork, venison, raspberry pie, potatoes, and plenty of whisky to wash the food down. Although the men cleared sixteen acres, at the end of the three days she was convinced that more work would have been done at less expense and trouble if her husband had hired two or three industrious workers.

All accounts agree, however, that Christmas was one of the happiest times for women everywhere on the frontier. They took keen pleasure in decorating the trees with homemade candles, strings of popcorn, strips of paper painted various colors, silver foil salvaged from cigars, old Christmas cards, and ribbons. In the plains country, with nothing but scrub cedar and sage about, Christmas trees were ingeniously contrived from what was available. A Dakota woman told of hanging cedar scrubs in relays from ceiling to floor, the whole resting in a tub of sand. According to a Wyoming ranch woman, a tall bare cottonwood was always set up in the barn and then decorated with festoons of evergreens. On Christmas Eve, the cowboys would come in, washed up and painfully attired in tight new boots and celluloid collars, their wives in trailing velveteen and carrying crying babies. Christmas gifts of that day included mustache cups, scarlet plush sofa pillows, photograph albums, and polished steerhorn chairs and hatracks.

Christmas was also one of the year's big social events for Army wives, the custom being for the women to visit each other on Christmas morning, exchange greetings, and view each other's gifts. All the married women went in a body to the bachelors' quarters, taking along homemade candy, cake, or other little remembrances. Company officers and their wives were expected to visit also the enlisted men's dinner tables. Then as now the Army's Christmas dinner was a rich banquet, although the food was different in the Old West. A Christmas menu of 1871 at Fort Lyon, Colorado Territory, included buffalo, antelope, boiled ham, several kinds of vegetables, pies, cakes, pickles, dried "apple-duff," and coffee. In the center of each mess table was a huge, thickly iced plum cake, baked by one of the officers' wives. "When we entered the dining hall," wrote one of these wives, "we found the entire company standing in two lines, one down each side, every man in his best inspection uniform, and every button shining. With eyes to the front and hands down their sides they looked absurdly like wax figures waiting to be 'wound up' and I did want so much to tell the little son of General Phillips to pinch one and make him jump." [18]

Independence Day was the big event of summer in every early western settlement. Long orations, patriotic poetry readings, and spirited toasts at public dinners were the order of the day. Horse races and comic mule races were held in the town's main street. Several families often joined forces for outdoor picnics. With patriotism running high, flags were much in demand, although sometimes the Stars and Stripes had to be hurriedly fashioned from whatever materials were at hand. In California, July 1852, Dame Shirley had to make a flag from white cotton, red calico, and blue drilling taken from one of the mining camps' "cloth" hotels. To honor California, she added a large star of gold leaf, and the flag was then raised to the top of a lofty pine. She and the hotelkeeper's wife were the only women among the celebrating gold miners.

2

Although most western women were deeply religious and certainly did not consider churchgoing an amusement, they would have been the last to deny that "going to meeting" was also a social diversion, an opportunity to see and be seen, a pleasant change from the routine of daily life. Before churches could be built in the new settlements, the custom was to gather in an appointed cabin to hear preaching and sing the old familiar gospel hymns. "The ladies sit in the front room, the gentlemen outside on benches and in carriages, while the preacher stands in the doorway." [19]

Some of the rawer, male-dominated settlements did not always take readily to the missionary spirit, as Eliza Spalding discovered on her way west in 1836. While stopping over at Liberty Landing on the Missouri frontier, she wrote in her diary: "Attended a prayer meeting in the village which was got up a few months since by a number of pious females, who being deprived of the stated preaching of the gospel, felt the importance of social prayer. It was an interesting session, and we all seemed to enjoy it very much. The Sabbath here is regarded by the people generally as a day for amusements—the cause of religion has but few advocates." [20]

Camp meetings seemed to suit the western temperament better than prayer meetings dominated by "pious females."

Julia Lovejoy reported attending one in Kansas in 1857, "a glorious meeting . . . in true western style. The preaching, praying, singing, and shouting, was as if the citadel must surrender or be taken by storm. We alternately laughed and wept, and the grand old woods rung to celestial notes." [21]

These boisterous outdoor revivals were generally held in late summer, lasting for about a week. Most of those who attended lived in tents, some having come from as far as fifty miles away. A roofed altar for the preachers was constructed at one end of a pleasant grove, the congregation sitting on logs or hewn benches in the open air. The worshipers' day began at daybreak with the blast of a trumpet. Individual families then held prayer meetings in their tents, breakfasted, and prepared for eight o'clock services. The first hellfire-and-brimstone sermon was delivered about midmorning, the second at three in the afternoon, and the third around seven in the evening. Periods between sermons were given over to singing and exhortation, involving much leaping, clapping of hands, and shouting: "Glory, glory!" "Amen!" "Hallelujah!" and "Praise the Lord!"

As the day wore on, some women became hysterical with emotion, flinging their arms about, hopping, skipping, and fainting in fits of ecstasy. A traveler observing one of these meetings described a young girl leaping so that "the velocity of every plunge made her long loose hair float up as if a handkerchief were held by one of its corners and twitched violently. Another female was so much overcome . . . the vertebral column was completely pliant, her neck, and her extended arms bent in every direction successively." [22]

All this emotionalism sometimes sought outlets in activities other than those intended by the frontier preachers. One philosopher of the times noted that "religious love is the very neighbor to sexual love and they always get mixed up in the intimacies and social excitements of Revivals." A common saying was that at these camp meetings "more souls were begotten than saved." To prevent such excesses, rules were published, circulated, and enforced, reserving certain areas of the grounds for females and others for males. In some cases females were barred from the camp until "an hour after sunrise in the morning," and they could stay no later than "an hour before sunset at night." [23]

3

As the frontier matured, women formed cultural organizations also for mutual diversion and elevation. Some of these groups were rather formal, publishing rules for guidance of the members. For example, the Farmers' Wives' Society of Harrison County, Iowa, included the following articles in its rules for 1872:

Article 3. That this society may not become a burden and a care to any one person, every lady shall bring from her store of eatables whatever she may think most convenient; the lady of the house where said society meets providing the tea, butter, biscuits and condiments.

Article 4. That this society may not say bad things while it aims to do good, a fine shall be imposed upon any lady who speaks disparagingly of another.

Article 6. Lest we forget the object of our society and make it an advertisement of the latest styles in fashionable attire, every lady is required to wear a plain home dress.[24]

4

In 1840 the editor of the Boonville *Missouri Register* invited the attention of his female readers to a bookseller who had established shop in that rugged frontier village. "The ladies," he wrote, "can find there material to heighten their charms, enrich their minds, or please their fancies." [25] How

A White Squaw

To the white woman the most terrifying nightmare of all was
captivity by the Indians. For Josephine Meeker, captured in a Ute
uprising of 1878, the nightmare became reality. After her rescue she
told her story at an official investigation, recalling that, to the
Indians, "A white squaw was a pretty good thing to have."

The handcart pioneers crossed the country on foot, pulling their few precious possessions behind them.

Brown's "ranche-stop," a combination store, tavern, and primitive hotel, typical of the stopovers along stagecoach trails.

Many a Weary Mile

Whether by handcart, wagon train, or stagecoach, the journey west was always exhausting and often perilous. The scourge of disease took an even greater toll of lives than the dreaded Indian raids. Yet the evening campfire on the open plains was a setting for songs and dances, gaiety and romance.

Virginia Reed—At thirteen, she was a member of the tragic Donner party.

Susan Shelby Magoffin—Honeymooning on the Santa Fe Trail, she brought along a maid, a cook, and a coop of live chickens.

Elizabeth Custer and her famous lover-husband startled the Army with "wild games of romps."

Martha Summerhayes—As a young wife, she regretted Army protocol and admired Army mules.

The Army Girls

In mule-drawn Army "ambulances" they followed their husbands across the wilderness to set up housekeeping in isolated outposts. Despite dust storms, blizzards, and shortages of food and equipment, these young ladies from the civilized East brought to their temporary quarters a touch of home and an occasional feminine frill.

Frances Grummond—A gentle Easterner, she became a living epic of all the West could deal out to a woman.

At harvest time, cook wagons brought the mistress of the household, her kitchen, and dinner to the workers in the field.

A Home in the West

In a strange new land, where even a log cabin was a luxury, the settler-housewife learned to "make-do." The sod house, standard dwelling of the early western family, offered few opportunities for decoration or comfort. Furniture was rough, if available at all, food supplies were scarce, and primitive cooking facilities often gave the "little gray home in the West" its characteristic color by means of a blanket of soot.

On the pioneer plain, where wood was scarce, the typical home was the sod house.

A Bit of Ribbon

Try as she would, the woman of the West found it no light task to display her charms to the best advantage for her prairie beau. Her eastern hoopskirts, frills, and elaborate bonnets became on the plains a nearly insurmountable maintenance problem. But fashion was not to be denied. As a contemporary male observer put it, ". . . nearly every woman wore her bit of ribbon."

Mama in her new bustle inspects the wheat combine.

The reliable sunbonnet, standard defense against burning midday rays and all-enveloping dust on the prairie.

For such fashionable occasions as the Sunday school picnic, the sunbonnet yields to the latest styles in Paris millinery.

Square dancing was rare in frontier saloons; the sets ran too long between drinks. So round dancing it was.

In their summer finery, ladies of Kearney, Nebraska, attend a Chatauqua.

Dance hall girls pose on the roof of a Wichita saloon.

A Little Light Diversion

Like the clothes she wore, the entertainment and recreation enjoyed by the lady of the early West were largely homespun. Dances were eagerly awaited occasions, usually presided over by bands of amateur pioneer musicians, and often arrived at only after harrowing dashes over icy terrain. Box suppers, hug-socials, prayer meetings, and "bees" of every sort also brightened many a plainswoman's off hours.

Pink Tights and
Red Velvet Skirts

To a California rich in gold but short of
women came a glittering burst of theatrical
entertainment. The miners gave their hearts
and their nuggets to the stage darlings of
the hour: Caroline Chapman, of the Mississippi showboats; seductive and eccentric
Lola Montez; Lotta Crabtree, the gamin
with the air of innocence; Adah Menken,
who captivated Mark Twain.

Lotta Crabtree—"La Petite
Lotta, the celebrated Danseuse
and Vocalist."

Adah Isaacs Menken—"The
Frenzy of Frisco."

Lola Montez won notoriety for her sensational spider dance.

Theater lovers flocked to see Adah's sensational horseback ride in Mazeppa or The Wild Horse of Tartary.

Caroline Chapman—Illegitimate daughter of a legitimate actor, "Our Caroline" triumphed in She Stoops to Conquer.

An exception to the rule—A wife of Brigham Young, she was a low nineteenth on the totem pole of a plural marriage.

Julia Bulette, the reigning courtesan of Virginia City. "Her skin may be scarlet, but her heart is white."

Laura Fair—She left behind a trail of husbands.

The Great Female Shortage

The acute shortage of women made the West a profitable haven for ladies of easy virtue and a happy husband-hunting ground. Marriage ceremonies were casually performed and often, if a better prospect came into view, as casually forgotten. That rare and exalted creature, an attractive woman, could, and sometimes did, get away with murder. To right the ratio of male to female, grandiose schemes arose for the wholesale importation of young ladies, who might set out as schoolmarms, but usually wound up as wives.

Asa Mercer—Shipping ladies to the Wild West was his business.

Loretta Velasquez—She shed her soldier's uniform and set out to find a new mate.

The recovery of H. T. P. Comstock's elusive and expensive bride.

Esther McQuigg Morris, the first woman justice of the peace. Her tea party led to women's suffrage in 1869.

Louisa Ann Swain put on her apron, walked to the polls, and became, at seventy, the first woman in the world to vote in a public election.

The first female jurists made news across the country. Sketches and caricatures bore such captions as:

> Baby, baby, don't get in a fury;
> Your mama's gone to sit on the jury.

The imposing hall of justice in Laramie, Wyoming, where women first assembled for jury duty.

The Wyoming Tea Party and Women's Rights

The courage, determination, and stubborn strength of western women again triumphed in the battle for women's rights, launched in Wyoming Territory by Esther McQuigg Morris. While they were about it, the ladies of Wyoming won for themselves not only the right to vote, but that of serving jury duty and holding public office.

Clarina Irene Nichols—A fiery speaker, she advised women to refuse to marry unless they were given the vote.

A contemporary impression of local ladies casting their votes in Cheyenne.

Ladies in Rebellion

As she left behind the restrictions and conventions of the old way of life, the western woman carried the struggle for emancipation into areas previously sacred to the male. She competed in business and politics, in bronco busting and outlawry, and even dared to sample the masculine pleasures of smoking, drinking, and gambling.

The epitome of the free western female, Martha Conneray forsook feminine frills and inhibitions for sturdier garb and a legendary career as "Calamity Jane."

A bizarre example of feminine defiance, Carry Nation, hatchet in hand, launched a campaign of saloon smashing, hymn singing, and liquor spilling.

Calamity Jane

Tillie Baldwin—New stunts and new fashions for the Rodeo.

Mary E. Lease—A moving force in the People's Party, she urged the farmers to "raise less corn and more hell!"

Rose of Cimarron, gowned and gunned fit to kill.

Arizona Mary—Driving a sixteen-yoke ox team, she amassed a fortune.

The schoolmarm as she really was, surrounded by her charges.

The nineteenth-century stereotype of Teacher.

Between lessons, two young students share lunch and a secret.

The Frontier Schoolmarm

Encouraged by Catherine Beecher's exhortation to woman . . . "the best, as well as the cheapest guardian of childhood" . . . many a Prudence (or Grace or Charity) made her way west to take up the book, ruler, and switch of the schoolmarm. These prairie peda- gogues dispensed vital "book learning" to the children and did much to clean up the homes, hands, and language of the plainsmen.

many westbound females sampled the wares of the plucky bookseller in that busy little trading post on the Missouri is not known, but certainly most western women treasured their books highly, made sacrifices to obtain and preserve them, read them thoroughly, and rated them first among their solitary diversions.

Martha Summerhayes, for example, carried finely bound sets of her favorite authors—Schiller, Goethe, and Lessing—from New England to Cheyenne, then to San Francisco, down the Pacific and up the Colorado River to Fort Mohave, then back and forth several times across Arizona Territory. The books met with only one serious accident, when the box in which they were carried fell into a river during a crossing. As soon as she reached her destination, she unpacked them, but all fell out of their bindings, warped and almost unreadable. "I did the best I could," she wrote, "not to show too much concern, and gathered the pages carefully together, to dry them in the sun." [26]

Narcissa Whitman also had trouble with water damage during her trip to Oregon. "Our books, what few we have, have been wet several times," she noted in her diary. "The custom of the country," she added philosophically, "is to possess nothing, and then you will lose nothing while traveling." [27] Nevertheless, Mrs. Whitman held on to her books, and later sent back east for more.

A woman in Washington Territory recalled that her father's library when they first arrived in the West "consisted of the Bible and Webster's Dictionary—the only books we could not do without, and to make sure of them we had brought them all the way across the plains." [28]

Frances Grummond Carrington once observed that the surest way to make an Army tent seem homelike was to scatter a few books around it. And another Army woman, the wife of General Edwin S. Godfrey—who soldiered with Custer—was so smitten by Sir Walter Scott's *Guy Mannering* that she named her son in honor of the hero.

Encyclopedias often inspire awe and respect, yet one must admire the determination of Emily Meredith, who could not bear the thought of leaving her valued encyclopedia behind when she and her husband started west in an ox wagon in 1862. Finding it impossible to fit the huge leather-bound volumes into the wagon, she exchanged them for "a pasteboard bound edition in some sixty-eight volumes." The books survived the long journey to Bannock City, Idaho, were carefully preserved through the years, and eventually were donated to the Montana State College Library at Bozeman.[29]

Random examples of ladies' choices in reading can be found in almost any western diary or other contemporary account. Among the volumes Frances Grummond took from Tennessee to Fort Phil Kearney, Wyoming, in 1866 were two prayer books, a *Life of Benjamin Franklin*, and Jane Porter's *Thaddeus of Warsaw*. During the California gold rush, Dame Shirley read Shakespeare, Spenser, Coleridge, Burns, Shelley, and Isaac Walton's *Compleat Angler*. Mary Dodge Woodward, who lived in Dakota Territory during the 1880's, listed the following in her diaries: Jane Welsh Carlyle's *Letters*, Johan Holderlin's *Hyperion*, Charles Reade's *Hard Cash*, Ida Hahn's *Daughter of Faustina*, Elizabeth Gaskell's *The Grey Woman*, Charles Dickens' *Little Dorrit*, Victor Hugo's *Les Miserables*, and Estes and Lauriat's "Cobweb Series of Choice Fiction," of which Friedrich Hacklander's *Forbidden Fruit* was a favored title.[30]

Among a collection of books that an Illinois woman took to Oregon were "histories of Greece and Rome, Bibles, and a few miscellaneous ones." Mrs. Katherine Ide, who was born in Oregon in 1858, recalled reading "an unexpurgated copy of *Arabian Nights*" in Portland. She also read Goethe's poems.[31]

Byron and Scott were favorites in Texas, especially among

women who had come from the Deep South. A Norwegian woman in Texas wrote to a friend in her native country, heartily thanking her for sending six books, but adding frankly that she did not care for Ibsen's works.

Traveling book peddlers ventured into some areas of the West, Mary Woodward recording the visit of an agent who was canvassing Dakota Territory on foot in the 1880's, selling a *Life of Garfield* and an illustrated Bible. But most women obtained their books by mail, ordering from advertisements in newspapers or magazines such as *Atlantic Monthly* and *Harper's*.

Because they could be readily obtained by mail subscriptions, magazines and newspapers were widely read from the very beginnings of western settlement. Narcissa Whitman wrote from Oregon in 1838 that she was enjoying some issues of *Mothers' Magazine* sent by her sister Jane. The only newspapers she had seen since her arrival were copies of the *New York Observer*, about two years old, which had arrived after traveling by vessel around Cape Horn, then to the Sandwich Islands (Hawaii), and on to Oregon. A few years later, the demand for eastern newspapers in remote settlements was recognized by New York publishers, and weekly editions of the *Herald* and the *World* reached into all parts of the Far West.

Mail deliveries of printed matter were not by any means dependable in the wilder areas. "The weekly mail," one woman wrote, "was always an uncertainty. We were never sure that we should be able to understand the next chapters in serial stories, which were our delight. I remember being very engrossed in one of Charles Reade's novels, the heroine of which was cast on a desert island . . . the story was published in *Every Saturday*, and at first came weekly; but after we had become most deeply interested five weeks passed during which not a single number was received, and we were

left to imagine the sequel . . . Several periodicals of a more
solid nature always came regularly, which constrained us to
believe that we were furnishing light literature to the poor
inhabitants of some lonely stage station on the road." [32]

Periodicals most often mentioned by women in the West
included *Harper's Weekly, Harper's Monthly, Ladies Home
Journal, Scribner's Monthly, Atlantic Monthly,* and *Frank
Leslie's Weekly. Godey's Lady's Book* was, of course, very
popular with females of all ages. One of the incidents a Wyoming woman best remembered of her childhood during the
1870's was "turning the pages of *Godey's Lady's Book* and
gazing enraptured at the picture of a tall, stately lady in a
gorgeous blue silk dress, and tight-fitting basque buttoned
from neck to hem, flowing sleeves and frilled lace under-
sleeves, long, full, flounced skirt which swept the floor." [33]

Elizabeth Custer declared that *Harper's Bazaar* was as thoroughly read on the frontier as at any point on its wide wanderings, and Margaret Carrington found *M'me. Demorest's
Magazine* very useful for its clothing patterns; she cut many
yards of linsey-woolsey and calico by the Demorest designs.

In addition to several of the periodicals already mentioned,
Mary Woodward of Dakota Territory listed *American Agri-
culturist, Punch,* and *Police Gazette.* Magazine reading certainly was quite varied in the Woodward household; she was
especially fond of "The Easy Chair" in *Harper's.*

Other oft-mentioned reading matter included almanacs,
western guidebooks, religious tracts, and mail-order and seed
catalogs. In addition to various editions of "farmers' almanacs," almost every patent medicine on the market was repre-
sented—for example, Ayer's yellowback almanac advertising
medicinal sarsaparilla, or Hostetter's blueback almanac boost-
ing the manufacturer's "Celebrated Stomach Bitters." In later
periods of settlement by European emigrants, these almanacs
were published in several languages.

Paperback guidebooks were much in demand during wagon-train crossings. "We had guidebooks that were published by some pathfinder, or trapper, describing every camping place, the distance between the watering places, and all cutoffs and the names of creeks, etc. Each train had some of these books." [34]

Religious tracts brought by the missionaries were the common literature of early Oregon, although not always used for purposes intended by the authors. One collection of these pamphlets came to a practical end when pioneer Jesse Applegate caulked a boat with them, forcing the papers into cracks with a chisel and hammer and then pouring in hot pitch.

Even before they were recorded on maps, many settlements formed some sort of public book collection, a movement that was largely the work of women. Before women arrived such efforts did not always succeed; in a miners' camp at Volcano, California, during the early gold rush, the library failed "because the Association had no power to compel the restitution of books."

It should be acknowledged that there was a minority opinion among pioneer females against the reading of books. No one has recorded this side of the question better than Christiania Holmes Tillson, who toured the early West, listening with an ear for accents that was as true as Mark Twain's. While stopping in a frontier cabin she noted that the only reading matter in view was a greasy almanac hanging against the wall. A query brought a frank reply from the frontier hostess that she "didn't want books, did not think it was of any use to be allus reading; didn't think folks was any better off for reading, an' books cost a heap and took a power of time; 'twant so bad for men to read, for there was a heap of time when they couldn't work out, and could jest set by the fire; and if a man had books and keered to read he mought; but women had no business to hurtle away their time, case they could allus find something to du, and there had been a heap of trouble in old Kaintuck with some rich men's gals that had learned to write. They was sent to school, and were high larnt, and cud write letters almost as well as a man, and would write to the young fellows, and, bless your soul, got a match fixed up before their father or mother knowed a hait about it." [35]

If a woman was not inclined to escape humdrum routine through reading, she could climb upon a saddle—in this land of many horses—and fly away in reality. "To mount a horse such as can be found only in the west," said one, "and gallop over prairies, completely losing oneself in vast and illimitable space, as silent as lonely, is to leave every petty care, and feel the contented frame of mind which can only be produced in such surroundings. In those grand wastes one is truly alone with God." [36]

Or—in this land of much gambling—she could escape as so many males did through games of chance; although she would attract attention by doing so publicly. A correspondent for a Missouri newspaper noted a woman in a San Francisco gambling palace during the gold rush, "dressed in white pants, blue coat, and cloth cap, curls dangling over her cheeks, cigar in her mouth, and a glass of punch at her side. She handled a pile of doubloons with her blue kid gloved hands, and bet most boldly." [37]

Some women went hunting for wild game, even buffalo, but most of them indulged in this form of recreation vicariously, watching through field glasses from the safety of a carriage while their males performed the kill.

Another use for field glasses and telescopes in the flat country of the Great Plains was observing "the country round." From an upper window of her Dakota farmhouse, Mary Woodward amused herself for hours, watching activities in and around three towns and four country schoolhouses. This pastime also had its useful features; when her milk cows strayed she could locate them readily, and she also could determine the proper hour to start cooking supper by watching the men of the family quitting their threshing machines or completing the unloading of their wheat at a railroad stop miles away.

When trains first began to run on the new western railroads, settlers' wives quickly discovered a diversion that is only now beginning to disappear—watching the trains go by, or meeting the daily locals at the nearest station. A traveler through the West in 1871 told of seeing two frontier females standing on a station platform looking with friendly inquisitiveness into each car as it slowly moved past. As the last coach rolled by, one exclaimed sadly and wonderingly to the other: "Not a soul among 'em all what I knowed!" [38]

X

Pink Tights and Red Velvet Skirts

1

"THE mere appearance of a woman," declared historian Hubert Howe Bancroft, in describing the development of the far-western theater, "sufficed in early days to insure success."[1] And he went on to relate the story of an untrained Swiss girl who collected four thousand dollars for a few weeks' performances. In a land predominantly masculine, this adoration of female stage players is not to be wondered at.

The first actress to appear in Virginia City was Antoinette Adams, variously described as six feet tall, long-necked, Roman-nosed, cracked-voiced, and a faded blonde. Although her audience of miners was cruelly disappointed in what they saw and heard, they listened patiently through her first rendition. At the first pause in her performance, a burly miner stood up and ordered the audience to give three cheers for "Aunty." The cheers resounded, and Antoinette sang again. Once more the miners applauded her, then one man rose to suggest they give her enough money to retire from her profession. A shower of silver cascaded upon the stage, the audience rowdily saluting her retirement. After that, every time Antoinette opened her mouth to sing, the miners cheered her so lustily she could not be heard; they also hurled more silver at

168

her feet. At last the actress surrendered, ordered the curtains pulled. When she gathered the silver up, it filled two money sacks. But Antoinette could take a hint; she left town the next day.

The western masculine audience was a critical one, and some mining camps were not as tolerant as the gentlemen of Virginia City. Ordinarily they rewarded handsomely only those players who pleased them, expressing their displeasure of poor performers by such means as tossing the offenders up and down in blankets and sending them packing.

The few female spectators among western audiences were inclined to be more critical of actresses' costumes, or lack of costumes, than of dramatic abilities. A women's-rights lecturer attending a Denver theatrical performance in 1871 was shocked by actresses "in horrible undress, swinging and tumbling, and plunging heels over head out of their sphere . . . It was, to me, very dreadful—a revolting, almost ghastly exhibition of women's rights." She tried to excuse this near nudity by blaming it on high rates charged by western railroads for hauling baggage. Because of this prohibitive expense, she said, "actresses coming to Colorado have been compelled, at a painful sacrifice to their modesty to 'shed the light frivolity of dress' in great measure." [2]

Female performers knew, of course, what their rowdy audiences wanted and gave it to them. A man writing from Leavenworth, Kansas, in 1864, reported that a Mrs. Walters was the town's "beau ideal of an actress, a prima donna whose excellence consists in her half disguised (I was going to say) vulgarity, but modesty would be a prettier word. But she caters to her audience and receives her reward." [3]

Never before in history was it so easy for women to come to the fore on the public stage. The boards of a hundred frontier theaters were waiting for them. Both time and place "offered unparalleled opportunity for feminine initiative."

The flowering of the theater in California, particularly in and around San Francisco during the decade between the discovery of gold and the Civil War, has been compared to a similar phenomenon two hundred years earlier—the London stage of the seventeenth century. Theaters sprang up all through the mining regions; every town had at least one, varying from luxurious playhouses to canvas-sided flimsies. The land was gold-rich, bubbling with excitement and constant change, eager for entertainment. To see a favorite actress a miner would pay a hundred dollars for an opening-night seat and then toss more than that in nuggets or gold dust upon the stage. The demand for female performers was so great that young actresses frequently took the part of Romeo, and a girl of ten was said to have played Hamlet one night and Richard III the next.

One of the first actresses to take California by storm was vivacious Caroline Chapman. The Chapmans were a famed theatrical family who had originated the showboats of the Ohio and Mississippi Rivers. In 1852 they journeyed to California and according to newspaper accounts were an immediate success, audiences becoming "hysterical with pleasure." Caroline always played with her father, William Chapman, and they looked so much alike that theatergoers often assumed they were brother and sister; actually, Caroline was William's illegitimate daughter. At the end of their first performance in San Francisco, the audience saluted the Chapmans with so many buckskin sacks of gold dust that the stage appeared to be carpeted with them. Mobs began following the impetuous Caroline to and from the theater; they dubbed her "our Caroline," and showered her with coins until there was a shortage of minted money in the city.

When the Chapmans traveled to Sonora to open a new theater there with *She Stoops to Conquer,* a thousand miners met them and formed an escort of honor. One secret of the Chapmans' popularity was their willingness to perform anywhere under any conditions; at one mining camp during a tour they played with verve and spirit upon the sawed-off trunk of a huge tree.

2

No western stage performer ever equaled the glamorous Lola Montez in creating an aura of seductive mystery and exquisite scandal around her personality. Whether or not Lola was an actress is debatable—she was more in the class of modern burlesque queens—but the dubious legends of delicious sinfulness which she deliberately spread abroad and carefully nourished have spun down through the years until they are a part of the fabric of western history.

With her sensational spider dance, Lola burst upon San Francisco like a bombshell, making excellent copy for the newspapers with stories of her many marriages and her claim that she was the illegitimate daughter of Lord Byron. Offstage she dressed in the Byronic mode, wearing black jackets and wide rolling collars. Bronze-skinned, blue-eyed, she made a striking appearance strolling along the San Francisco streets, with two greyhounds on a leash and an enormous parrot upon her shoulder. She constantly smoked small cigars, forced her way into gambling saloons forbidden to women, and played tenpins with any male daring enough to take her on.

"A tigress," said one newspaper writer, "the very comet of her sex." Lola's celebrated spider dance shocked and titillated her audiences; the spiders were ingenious contraptions made of rubber, cork, and whalebone. She gave a spectacular benefit for an audience of San Francisco firemen, and they showered the stage with their fancy helmets and almost smothered her with enormous bouquets of flowers.

During this period of her glory, Lola took on a new husband, one Patrick Purdy Hull, because, she said, he could tell amusing stories better than anyone she had ever known. For some weeks she played to capacity houses, earning an enormous fortune; then suddenly she was undermined by a rival player, none other than the audacious Caroline Chapman. Annoyed by all the attention Lola was receiving, and noting a slackening in the size of her own audiences, Caroline decided to burlesque the spider dance. According to the press, Caroline's performances were as bold as Lola's and twice as ludicrous.

If there was anything Lola Montez could not bear, it was ridicule. She left San Francisco in a fit of petulance, determined to conquer other fields—the mining towns of California. The tour was not a success. She became temperamental, refused to play out scenes if the miners laughed during her dances. She quarreled with Patrick Hull, and a story went around that she had thrown him down the stairs of their hotel, pitching his baggage out the window after him.

Upset by the rapid decline of her meteoric popularity, Lola decided to retire for a while. She chose Grass Valley as an ideal spot for quiet living, took a small cottage surrounded by a white picket fence, and passed the time by tending a small flower garden. The miners of the area were so delighted by her presence they named the highest peak in that section of the Sierras Mount Lola in her honor.

Legends inevitably followed her even into this quiet retirement. One story still persists that when the local minister attacked her from his pulpit, she responded by donning her stage costume, knocking at his door, and performing the spider dance on the reverend's front porch. Afterward, it is said, she was so remorseful she sent him a large donation for his church. Another tale has it that after reading a published insinuation upon her character, she called upon the editor and gave him a thrashing with a riding whip.

Her major eccentricity during her stay in Grass Valley appears to have been the acquisition of a pair of bear cubs which she trained to do tricks; there were rumors that when Patrick Hull visited her to affect a reconciliation, she turned the bears loose, one of them chewed Patrick's arm, and he never came back. It is true that Lola did resume one of her former names, Countess of Landsfeld.

In recalling Lola's presence in Grass Valley, a local miner named Edwin Morse declared that she had the right to this title because she had been the mistress of the King of Bavaria. "When Lola Montez came to Grass Valley," added Morse, "a man named Johnnie Southwick was connected with the since-famous Empire mine. He had accumulated a snug little sum of money and became deeply infatuated with the dashing dancer. She was no fool and she knew a good thing when she saw it and that good thing was Johnnie Southwick, while his money lasted . . . Southwick purchased a little cottage on Mill Street and established her there . . . I had ample opportunity to observe and become acquainted with the dancer.

"She furnished the place in great style for that day, spending three or four thousand dollars of Southwick's money. Being a very lively person, she furnished the people of Grass Valley with plenty of entertainment with her various escapades and eccentricities.

"She kept a young bear chained to a stump in the front yard. She evidently did this for effect, and to make people think she had a fondness for ferocious pets. In reality, she was mortally afraid of the brute and used to stand at a good safe distance when she fed him, throwing his meat within reach, although the bear was only a cub and anything but fierce.

"Lola was said to exercise a great fascination over men, but for my part I failed to see her charm, notwithstanding the fact that I had quite often held conversations with her over her gate and had plenty of opportunity for observation.

"She had undoubtedly been a beautiful woman, but her

charms were then beginning to fade. She still retained a slender and graceful figure. She had heavy black hair and the most brilliant flashing eyes I ever beheld. When carefully dressed and gotten up, she was still very handsome, but ordinarily she was such a slattern that to me she was frankly disgusting. When attired in a low-necked gown, as was her usual custom, even her liberal use of powder failed to conceal the fact that she stood much in need of a good application of soap and water."

According to the observant Morse, Lola entertained frequently, but all of her guests were males. When the great violinist, Ole Bull, played in Grass Valley she gave an evening musicale in his honor. "I well remember Ole Bull's appearance as he came swinging down the street with great strides, Southwick trotting along at his side and trying to keep up with the tall, raw-boned Norwegian with the long, fair hair." [4]

In 1855, Lola at last tired of the quiet life of Grass Valley, packed her costumes, and sailed for Australia. After a series of triumphs there, she returned to San Francisco, gave some farewell performances of the spider dance, and then went to New York. She later went on a lecture tour relating the story of her life, wrote a book called *The Arts of Beauty; or Secrets of a Lady's Toilet, With Hints to Gentlemen on the Art of Fascination,* and then she gradually dropped from public notice.

In spite of her flashy front, her contrived improprieties, and her bursts of temperament, Lola Montez had no illusions of grandeur. "Notorious I have always been," she once said, "but never famous." In the Old West, however, Lola was something special; after a century, her glamor still glows brighter than ever, her fame deeply woven into the folklore of the California gold rush.

3

During the time Lola Montez was living in Grass Valley, only one woman in the town was friendly toward her—a boardinghouse keeper named Mary Ann Crabtree. The reasons for this friendship are not clear. Perhaps it was a common loneliness, a shared disillusionment with the male sex, or it may have been Mrs. Crabtree's six-year-old daughter Charlotte who brought this unlikely pair together.

Charlotte, or Lotta, was an appealing moppet, with her red hair in long curls, flashing black eyes, and a voice filled with melodious laughter, and she spent many hours playing around the Montez cottage. She was small for her age, quite shy, and there was an aura of innocence about her that was in direct contrast to the personality of the spider dancer. Lola was drawn to the little girl. She taught Lotta to ride horseback, to dance, and to sing a few simple ballads.

When Lola decided to tour Australia, she wanted to take Lotta along as an added feature of her act, but Mary Ann Crabtree refused permission. No amount of arguing on Lola's part could change Mrs. Crabtree's decision. As the theatrical world was soon to learn, Mary Ann Crabtree was a determined woman, a driver of hard bargains, bound on obtaining what she wanted for her talented daughter.

Mary Ann's inflexible personality may have been the result of suffering long years of poverty as the wife of a too-flexible male, John Crabtree, who had departed New York in 1852 to search for gold in California. The following year Mary Ann and little Lotta followed after him, taking the Panama Isthmus route. John Crabtree was one of the unblest, a gold digger who never made a strike, a prospector who kept going on the strength of dreams, hopes, and the receipts of his wife's boardinghouse in Grass Valley.

Chance brought Lotta Crabtree upon a public stage when

she was eight years old. A Grass Valley theater owner, Mart Taylor, needed a child actress to meet competition from a rival who was featuring his small daughter with great success. Taylor had seen Lotta's amateur efforts. Now, with Mary Ann's enthusiastic permission, he taught the little girl an Irish jig and reel; she already knew several other steps and the ballads learned from Lola Montez.

Proof of Mary Ann's keen interest in her daughter's early stage career is shown by the fact that she designed and made for her a handsome Irish costume of green—long-tailed coat, knee breeches, tall hat. Lotta's singing and dancing, combined with this costume, won loud acclaim from her audience of miners. An even greater success was the closing number, Lotta clad in angelic white, singing a tear-jerking ballad of innocence. As she sang the final note, gold and silver coins showered the boards at her feet; among them were several nuggets and a gold slug worth fifty dollars. This jingling rain of wealth frightened the child, but Mary Ann rushed out with a basket, carefully collecting every scrap of precious metal. Two precedents were set at this première performance; thenceforth Lotta Crabtree's signature trade-mark would be a lachrymose ballad delivered in a white costume, and Mary Ann would take care of the money.

Shortly afterward Mary Ann and Lotta, with Mart Taylor along as manager, set out on a tour of the mining camps. John Crabtree was left behind to continue his profitless digging for gold. Taylor played a guitar and Mary Ann a triangle, and Lotta added more dances and ballads to her repertory. Their luck was phenomenal. "The singing and dancing of little Lotta," said one newspaper, "was admirable and took our hearts by storm." In 1859, Mary Ann decided that Lotta was ready for San Francisco. Her timing was excellent, for variety was just coming into popular favor in the West's theatrical center. The headlines tell the story: "Miss Lotta, the

San Francisco Favorite," "La Petite Lotta, the Celebrated Danseuse and Vocalist," "Miss Lotta the Unapproachable."

Undoubtedly the secret of Lotta Crabtree's vast success was her innocence. Whatever she lacked in dramatic ability she made up in personality. Where other actresses traded on scandal and indecorum, little Lotta was above suspicion, a lamb among wolves. In that western gold coast of knavery and avarice she shone like a rare jewel, and her audiences showered her with their filthy lucre, Mary Ann gathering it up into her baskets, hoarding it carefully.

As she grew older and began smoking cigarillos, after the fashion of Lola Montez, Lotta Crabtree always smoked them with her special air of childish innocence. When she introduced gaminlike bits into her acting—showing her knees by pulling up her stockings, rolling off divans with a flurry of lifted petticoats, and wearing the briefest of skirts—it was all done with such guileless staging that even female spectators rarely objected.

For thirty-five years, Lotta was the princess, the perennial little-girl pet, of western theater—although she spent much of her time on tours elsewhere—and when she retired at the age of forty-four she still had her red curls and flashing black eyes. She never came out of retirement, living alone with Mary Ann, who had saved most of her daughter's enormous earnings. Probably no other stage performer of that time amassed such a fortune. By 1924, the year of Lotta's death, it had grown to four million dollars.

Naturally there were many claimants to the money, including one alleged illegitimate child—about as unlikely a possibility as could have been imagined, for all through the years of her youth Lotta Crabtree was prisoner to the insatiable, poverty-fearing Mary Ann. And after Mary Ann died, it was too late for romance. The four million dollars which had its origins in the California gold fields—tossed by hardened

hands of miners upon the rough boards of frontier theaters—
all went to charity.[5]

4

Still another favorite of male theatergoers in the West was
Adah Isaacs Menken, who made her stage debut in San Francisco a full decade after the first triumphs of Lola Montez
and Lotta Crabtree. The magnificent Adah was not a dancer
like Lola or a variety performer like Lotta; she preferred exciting melodrama. Although she operated in the "wicked" tra-
dition of Lola, and also sometimes dressed in Byronic costumes, Adah Menken was prompt to deny any professional
kinship with the spider dancer. "Lola Montez began with a
king and ran down the scale through a newspaper man to a
miner," she would declare vehemently. "I began with a prizefighter, and I will end with a prince!"

Adah knew the value of possessing a mysterious background, and she dropped hints that she had lived with Sam
Houston in Texas—though she was vague as to whether she
was his mistress or his adopted daughter. It was a fact that
she had been a ballet dancer in New Orleans and had performed in Cuba and Mexico, but there was no proof of the
rumors that Indians captured her in Texas and that Rangers
went to her rescue.

She conquered California, however. The press called her
"the Frenzy of Frisco," and she kept the journalists happy
with her cultivated eccentricities. Although the Civil War was
in full fury and California was pro-Union, she spread a large
Confederate flag across one wall of her hotel room. By day
she walked the streets clad only in a single yellow silk gar-
ment. Yellow, she said, was her mystical color, and when
Joaquin Miller called upon her he found her lying upon a yellow skin clothed in a yellow sheath. He was fascinated by the
costume. "I doubt if any other woman in the world," he wrote,

"could wear a dress like that in the winds of San Francisco and not look ridiculous." She went horseback riding with Miller into the California desert; she dismounted and dropped into the sand. "I was born in this yellow sand," she cried, "sometime and somewhere . . . in the deserts of Africa maybe." [6]

Adah's most sensational vehicle was *Mazeppa, or The Wild Horse of Tartary*, a banal dramatization of Byron's poem, presented in rapid-fire fashion like a three-ring circus. The high moment of the performance was her ride on horseback up a runway between cardboard representations of mountain crags. She was strapped to the horse's back, and the runway was narrow, yet critics disagreed as to whether there was any real danger involved. All agreed, however, that Adah's costume was extremely daring; her enemies charged indecency and nudity. Accounts differ as to what she wore while strapped to the horse; probably she varied her costume. Sometimes it was described as a short Greek chiton that showed off her plump legs to advantage; in Virginia City she stripped to a piece of gauze, a *maillot;* and one spectator reported she dressed only in tight-fitting cotton underwear. Records also disagree as to the sort of horse she used, the animal being variously described as a huge sorrel, a spirited black, and a gentle mare which toddled up the ramp to a trainer waiting with lumps of sugar.

Adah Menken's visit to Virginia City during its booming heyday of 1863 was like a royal jubilee. For weeks colorful posters displaying her half-naked form upon the back of a black stallion had been hanging in all the bars of the town, and every miner in camp wanted to see this beautiful body in the flesh. As soon as she arrived at the International Hotel, local firemen gathered beneath her window to serenade her.

All did not bode well for Adah, however. Before her arrival three reporters on the Virginia City *Territorial Enterprise* had already decided to write derisive notices of her first performance for their paper. They had seen the posters and had made up their minds that she was nothing but a circus performer. One of these reporters was Mark Twain.

That first night the theater was packed with enthusiastic males, all waiting for the long-heralded undressed ride up the mountain peak. And before the performance was well along, Adah had conquered the three literary cynics of the *Territorial Enterprise*. Mark Twain was especially enthralled by her voice; his glowing review of Menken in *Mazeppa* was reprinted by newspapers all over the country. He later called upon Adah at her hotel, found her seated at a table sipping champagne and feeding her pet lap dog sugar cubes dipped in brandy. He was so infatuated that he showed her some of his writings, asking for criticism, and composed a conundrum about her lovely hands.

Apparently the only male in Nevada not captivated was a hypercritical writer from the Carson City *Independent,* who must have been an outlandish cad indeed. "We hope there were no butchers in the audience, for they must have been lost to the play, and thought of nothing but veal. Such calves! they were never reared on milk. The acting consisted of sneezing, smoking, and coughing on the part of the supes, and some elegant posturing on the part of the Menken." [7]

Adah remained in Virginia City for quite a while, enjoying her glory. The miners presented her with a bar of bullion worth two thousand dollars; they named a street and a mine in her honor, and gave her fifty shares of the mine's stock—which she later sold for a reputed thousand dollars a share. One night in the Sazerac saloon she announced that she could box as well as any man (one of her husbands had been a prizefighter) and volunteered to put on the gloves and spar with anyone willing to volunteer. A rash miner stepped forward, and the story goes that she knocked him out in the second round. Another volunteer lasted a bit longer, but he admitted that "Adah's left was a thing with which to conjure."[8] This was theater in the Far West, glittering and extravagant, where femaleness—not the play—was the thing.

5

In the more sparsely settled Plains and Rockies, theater was cruder, the actresses not quite so flamboyant, yet stage entertainment was just as eagerly sought after as along the more sophisticated gold coast. Many troupes of actors made the journey to California by covered wagon, and some of them earned their passage by giving performances en route. Wyoming's first drama was staged by a Chicago troupe bound for California in 1864. While their wagon train was camped in Snyder Basin, the actors entertained a few ranchers and fellow members of their train, using the floor of an old blacksmith shop for a stage and a wagon canvas for curtains.

The audience, numbering about two hundred persons, joined forces with the players, cut down several large cottonwoods, and dragged the logs into a wagon corral for pit seats. The play was melodrama; a young girl forced into a repugnant marriage by her mercenary parents was saved in the nick of time by her young sweetheart, who exposed the villainous past of her elderly suitor. An orchestra composed of violin, flute and guitar furnished music; popular songs, instrumental numbers, acrobatic performers, ventriloquists, and jig dancing followed presentation of the drama.[9]

Three years later, the Julesburg Theatrical Troupe arrived in Cheyenne for a long run. The performers were two months ahead of the Union Pacific tracklaying crew and had to build their own theater, a small clapboard structure with "parquet, dress circle, private boxes, and all modern improvements." This was accomplished in less than a week.

In western communities too small to support theaters, patent-medicine shows served as substitutes for legitimate drama. The personnel of these shows consisted of only three or four persons—the alleged doctor or medicine man, a buxom, well-proportioned female to excite the predominantly male audiences, and one or two assistants to double as performers and medicine salesmen. During good weather, they operated from a platform on a vacant lot; in bad weather they hired a hall.

The show, free to all, opened with music—guitar, banjo, and very loud drum. As soon as an audience assembled, the performers went through a few variety acts, then passed out songbooks advertising certain wonderful remedies soon to be offered for sale. In exchange for these "valuable, absolutely free" songbooks, the audience was expected to join in singing several well-known ballads of the day. At the proper psychological moment, the medicine man began his pitch, first attacking doctors, claiming they not only charged too much for their services but kept secret the medicines they used. Then he would launch into a panegyric description of his own patented medicine, emphasizing the word "patented" as an indication of government sanction and approval of his product.

Almost always the medicine was an "Indian remedy," a cure-all concoction of herbs originated by some fictitious Indian medicine man who possessed mystic and divine powers. To the rhythmic beat of the drum and the merry thrumming of banjo and guitar, the nostrum was passed through the audience. After the first flurry of sales, more entertainment followed, then more sales, and so on until the audience began to thin out. No doubt many buyers were aware that alcohol was the main ingredient of these patent medicines. They bought cheerfully, laughed uproariously at the minstrel skits, and loudly applauded the female performer's singing and dancing.

Frontier doctors bitterly opposed patent-medicine shows; a newspaper of 1854 ran an indignant letter from a local physician condemning medicine shows and "Indian doctors in whom credulous females, children and ignorant, superstitious men, have great confidence." [10] Opposition had little effect, however; medicine shows provided something that small western communities wanted, and they thrived until the early years of the twentieth century.

Immediately after the Civil War, tent shows began touring the western states, offering drama and variety in all degrees of quality. Lyceums and chautauquas came along later, presenting lecturers, poets, musicians, and occasional plays. A woman visiting in Caldwell, Kansas, during the 1870's witnessed a precursor of modern carnival, a tent show that included everything from side-show freaks to an evangelist. "Small tents set around on vacant lots dispensed whiskey, tobacco, physic, raisins, and other groceries, while in one a thin-faced traveling evangelist, with a natty dark suit, a white tie, and a hat dexterously pulled over his eyes, was exhorting his fellow-man. Before him was a mob of struggling, tugging, hauling, roaring, hoodlums, hallooing: 'Oh, mamma, come down, come down, git back to your mamma.' While the arms of this inspired genius sawed the air in gesticulations, his face growing red with the violence of his exertions, no one, not even himself, could hear a word he said. As each of the wild exhilarated listeners succeeded in gaining a point of vantage, they would bawl out some incoherent western slang, while one of their number, an expert, would swing his lariat-noose a few times high in the air, as a threat that he would be 'roped' if he didn't desist. The grizzled chin-whisker of this unique product would fairly quiver with stern indignation, as he tried to maintain his dignity against both this disrespectful diversion, and the illuminated canvas museum next door that had other natural curiosities . . . an electric girl, armless man, fat boy, skeleton dude, providing strong competition, and a fakir with yellow tickets in hand was filling the air with 'Now, ladies and gentlemen, the great show of the earth is open. You will never see again what I have to show you, ladies and gentlemen. One of the wonders of the world . . .' " 11

Serious drama did not always win the approval of western audiences, and renowned actresses certainly had their troubles with local critics. One of the classic reviews of a Sarah Bernhardt performance was the work of Ed Howe of the Atchison (Kansas) *Globe*. Howe is best known for his *Story of a Country Town*, but he also enjoyed harassing visiting actresses in his newspaper columns.

In 1881 he attended a performance of the great Bernhardt in *Camille*, given across the border in St. Joseph, Missouri. "At exactly 8:31 last night, Sarah Bernhardt made her appearance on the stage of Tootle's Opera House, walking down the centre as though she had but one joint in her body, and no knees. Her first action was to shake hands with the stage company with arms as long and wiry as the tendrils of a devil fish, which wound around them occasionally with the soft grace of a serpent. Perhaps the first thing remarked of her by the average auditor is that she is almost red-headed, and that she wears her hair in light Dutch braids. The second, that she is distressingly ugly, and that her smile is painful, because it displays a big mouth and a prominent row of butter teeth . . . Her dress was of white and costly stuff, and cut so low in front that we expected every moment that she would step one of her legs through it. She talks fast, and takes tremendous strides across the stage. Her arms were encased in white kid to within an inch of her shoulders, and whenever she pointed the villain or other disagreeable person to the door and said 'Go!' we saw that the color of the hair under her arms was sandy. This was our first impression of Bernhardt, and the second was that a lady so ugly and ill-shapen should not, in justice to her sex, challenge the criticism and opera glasses of the public.

"We waited patiently for the embrace for which she is said to be the champion of two countries. It came in the third act, and Armand was the recipient. He parted with her, and started to go out, but she followed, and finally embraced him by shambling up, breaking in two at the middle, and throwing her tendrils around him. It was neither graceful nor natural, and only original in its awkwardness. In these scenes the middle part of her body strikes the recipient first—her arms swing wildly a moment, and then twine two or three times around the person she loves. This is the Bernhardt embrace as we saw it through an opera glass.

"The Bernhardt kiss is little better. Perhaps *Camille* does not afford opportunity for this sort of acting, but there are millions of women who can kiss a man more naturally and acceptably than Sarah Bernhardt. She has no new ideas on the subject, unless kissing on the ear is new.

"The only thing Bernhardt does extraordinarily well is to put her arms around a man, and look into his eyes. If her face could be hidden at these moments, she would be sublime."

After the performance, Ed Howe attended a reception at the local hotel. "Bernhardt," he reported, "consented to come down and watch the mob if nobody spoke to her. She stood around for an hour, and all St. Joe walked in front of her, stared her in the face, jostled her, eyed her dresses through glasses, and had a good time. At one o'clock she retired, and at nine this morning her maid shook the sheets to find her, as the time had arrived to depart for Leavenworth." [12]

During a highly publicized tour of the west in 1877, Mrs. Frank Leslie was entranced by the rip-roaring lustiness of Cheyenne's theaters. Accompanied by a bodyguard of males from her traveling party, she attended a performance in a

theater built to connect with a gambling room and bar. She
described the place as "a long, low brick building, which
hangs out numerous flaming red signs under the moonlight."

She climbed a stairway to a private box that was gay with
tawdry paintings and lace hangings. "The auditorium departs
from the conventional horseshoe pattern, and is shaped
rather like a funnel, expanding at the mouth to the width of
the stage. It is so narrow that we, leaning out of one box,
could almost shake hands with our opposite neighbors. The
trapezes through which the wonderful Mlle. Somebody is flying and frisking like a bird, are all swung from the stage to
the back of the house, so that her silken tights and spangles
whisk past within a hand's breadth of the admiring audience,
who can exchange civilities, or even confidences with her in
her aerial flight.

"Below, the floor is dotted with round tables and darkened
with a sea of hats; a dense fog of cigar smoke floats above
them, and the clink of glasses rings a cheerful accompaniment
to the orchestra, as the admiring patrons of the variety business quaff brandy and 'slings,' and cheer on the performers with liberal enthusiasm. The house, for all its cheap finery
of decoration, its barbaric red and yellow splashes of paint,
and *bizarre* Venuses and Psyches posing on the walls, is won-
derfully well-ordered and marvelously clean; the audience,
wholly masculine, is unconventional (let us put it courte-
ously), but not riotous. As for the performance, it is by no
means bad, and the trapeze feats are indeed exceptionally
startling and well executed. The hours of the entertainment
are from 8 P.M. to 2 A.M., while the doors of the connecting
gambling saloon are never closed." [13]

For males, one of the added attractions of attending cow-
town theaters such as this was a visit after the performance to
the "green room," a secluded place where for a price cowboys

could drink and indulge in "familiar pleasantries with the stage girls." A Kansas newspaperman writing in 1873 reported that in Ellsworth the acme of a cowboy's ambition was to obtain access to the "green room" and crack a bottle of wine with the girls. "These visits frequently cost a dozen head of steers, but Texas is able to stand the damage and don't care for the expense." [14]

6

Out of this love for theater and spectacles, westerners created a native form of pageantry, the rodeo. From simple beginnings in the roundup camps of cowboys, rodeo developed into vigorous organized competitions among males, but, as in every other activity in the West, females quickly invaded their ranks as participants.

According to a woman who lived in Santa Clara Valley during gold-rush days, in the cool of late afternoons "youths and maidens could be seen collecting in a corral near by for the purpose of enjoying the sport of riding calves. Upon mounting, the calves would jump and plunge, frequently throwing the riders; but being young and active, they were on their feet again, and upon the calves' backs in the twinkling of an eye." [15]

From earliest settlement, California ranch girls were noted horsewomen, and during the 1850's one Mary Ann Whittaker made a career of her skill, giving public exhibitions under the title of "First Female Equestrian Artist in America." Her specialty was performing pantomimic sketches on horseback, and she billed one of her acts as "Xanthe Driven Mad by Her Own Infuriated Horse."

After attending a circus in Denver in 1871, Sarah Lippincott told of her delight in watching the wonderful riding skill and daring of another young California girl, Polly Lee. "She managed with the utmost ease and grace, four horses, having four younger brothers and sisters swarming all over her. She supports, in more ways than one, the whole family." [16]

From equestrianship to rodeo was but a single step, and the hard-muscled males of the range had to make room for divided skirts and spangled shirts. In fact, the first female entrant in organized rodeo distinguished herself by shaming the male riders into performing in the mud. This incident occurred during one of the first Frontier Days celebrations in Cheyenne, which was almost washed out by a torrential rain. The cowboys decided it was too dangerous to ride in all that mud and asked for postponement until another day. But there was this slip of a girl, Bertha Kaepernick, entered in the bucking contest, and she objected to waiting around for a dry track. She volunteered to ride a wild horse in front of the grandstand to prove it could be done.

According to an enthusiastic spectator, the horse she rode was "one of the worst buckers I have ever seen—and she stayed on him all the time. Part of the time he was up in the air on his hind feet; once he fell backward, and the girl deftly slid to one side only to mount him again as he got up. She rode him in the mud to a finish, and the crowd went wild with enthusiasm. Result—the cowboys thought if a girl can ride in the mud, we can too, and the show was pulled off. The real active idea of Woman Suffrage was thus demonstrated in Wyoming at a Frontier Days show—the idea that has gone around the world. Hurrah for the Wyoming gals! They lead in everything!" [17]

After Bertha Kaepernick's success, other equestriennes entered rodeo contests in increasing numbers, among them such names from rodeo's hall of fame as Prairie Rose Henderson, Prairie Lillie Allen, Lucille Mulhall, Bertha Blancett, Tillie Baldwin. In the early years of motion pictures, rosters of female rodeo champions and rosters of western movie actresses were virtually the same; in those times a rodeo championship was the easiest road to a career in the silent films. Lucille Mulhall could rope eight horses with one throw of a lariat, and she once astounded Theodore Roosevelt, who was visiting her father's ranch, by roping a coyote from horseback. Lucille made a million dollars from silent westerns, then lost it all and died a pauper. Tillie Baldwin was the first female to bulldog steers. Then she introduced the "Roman Stand," which became a specialty of Bertha Blancett, "champion lady bronco buster of the world."

As was to be expected, all these females had a profound effect upon rodeo costuming. Blue jeans and buckskins were too drab for them; they began wearing red velvet skirts with brilliantly decorated hems, then exchanged the fancy skirts for bright-colored trousers with flaring hips. From there they went to silk shirts of all hues and fancy neckpieces. With all this colorful competition, the males eventually capitulated, and that is why rodeo cowboys dress the way they do today.

XI

A Home in the West

1

FOR most women the only real reason for going west was to found a new home, and the dream of many an emigrating female was a snug log cabin nestling in some pleasant valley. Log cabins were traditional abodes of pioneers from the time of the first eastern settlements, and their construction had become a national craft. A skilled artisan could put one together with only an ax and an augur, using no nails or other pieces of metal. He sealed his logs together with wooden pins, chinked the cracks with mud, swung the doors on leather hinges, and fastened them with wooden latches.

A log cabin, for a woman, was a symbol of security; for a man it meant self-reliance; but in many parts of the Old West a log cabin was not easy to come by. Even in wooded areas, the immediate pressure for earning a livelihood led many a settler's family to spend the first year or so in a temporary dugout. If an earthen bank was handy, the newcomers would dig into it, wall up a stone fireplace at the back, extend poles out for a roof, pile bark and strips across the poles, cover the whole with grass, and then shovel on dirt. To prevent muddy water seeping through during rains, wagon canvas was sometimes laid over the top.

In California during the gold rush, the petticoated pioneers' first abode almost invariably was a tent. The reason for this was not lack of trees, but lack of manpower; the males were all too busy searching for gold to take time to build solid habitations. Sarah Royce told of trying in vain to persuade men to hew timbers so that she could move out of her over-crowded tent; the only solution she could find was to erect a second tent and add some packing boxes to strengthen the sides. Eventually she learned to feel as secure in a tent with the curtain tied in front as she had felt behind locked and bolted doors back home.[1]

Another eastern woman arriving in Nevada to join her husband found her new home was to be two tents, each only eight feet square. They were divided by a calico curtain, one tent to be used for a sleeping room, the other for a sitting room. Windowless and doorless except for one entrance, the interior seemed to her like a prison, and when the temperature dropped below zero the stove provided little warmth against the cold penetrating the canvas.

In areas where logs were scarce, settlers made the supply go further by splitting them into shakes, sometimes smoothing them out with drawing knives. Before the Civil War, enterprising suppliers were selling shakes to settlers on the treeless Great Plains. The rough boards brought two dollars a hundred in Kansas during the 1850's, Hannah Ropes recording that her husband was able to build their home for an outlay of sixty dollars for shakes. Her cabin, fifteen feet square and eleven feet high, was constructed by driving joists into the ground four feet apart, and nailing oak shakes outside, "after the manner of clapboards at home. These shakes are split out with an axe, after the blocks are sawed the proper length." She admitted the shakes did not fit well together and that at night "the stars can take a peep at us and we at them as well." [2]

Wooden floors were a luxury because of scarcity of smooth boards. If the ground was soggy it was covered with sand or gravel, perhaps temporarily carpeted with grain sacks. A housewife in Washington Territory said that she and her neighbors found it impossible to wear shoes on their graveled floors. They grew accustomed to wearing moccasins and sweeping the floors with rakes. They would ask each other, "Have you done your house raking today?" When at last they were able to obtain wooden flooring, "the women put on shoes again. They stepped high and had to become accustomed to walking in them." [3]

Some other temporary houses in the early west, as described by women who lived in them, included teepees taken over from the Indians, canvas stretched across wood frames, zinc sheets, and some rare but luxurious rolling quarters on railroad wheels presided over by wives of railroad construction engineers of the 1870's. A woman who occupied a zinc-sheet house in Marysville, California, declared that in summer "the sides of the house were so hot that she had only to place her dough, when she was going to bake bread, in close proximity to the wall, where the heat was sufficient to cook it." [4] Canvas and unbleached cotton houses also were quite common in California. Canvas formed the outer walls, cotton sheeting the inner walls. Women forced to live in these structures often pasted paper over the interior cloth to strengthen and decorate it. Sounds carried easily, of course, and fires were frequent.

Settlers moving into the arid Southwest adopted the native adobe, one of man's oldest forms of habitation. They learned to make bricks of clay mud mixed with grass or pine straw, drying them in the sun, and in that hot climate they had the most comfortable of all western abodes.

The classic western home was the sod house—as symbolic

of the pioneer plains country as the log cabin was of the for-
ested frontier. During the period of plains homesteading after
the Civil War, sod was the only building material available,
unless the settler happened to be one of the few fortunate
enough to secure a creek claim with timber suitable for logs.

In new settlements, sod-house building "bees" were shared
in by entire families, the men constructing the house and the
women preparing dinner and supper. When the prairie was
soaked by rain or melting snow, it was at its best for breaking
sod for building purposes. Buffalo grass was preferred because
of its toughness. The homesteaders cut the sod with plows
and spades into sections about twelve inches wide by eighteen
inches long and two or three inches thick. They set door and
window frames in place first, building the walls around them;
it was quite an art to bind the corners of a house so it would
not leak.

Next they erected forked tree trunks at the ends, laid a
ridgepole across so that it rested between the forks, and then
fastened rails from the ridgepole to the walls. Collecting whatever was at hand, corn or sunflower stalks, willow boughs or
straw, they strewed this supporting material over their crude
rafters, then laid sod strips upon all this to form a tight roof.
As time permitted, settlers finished up the interior of their
rough habitation with plaster made of sand and clay, which
when dry could be coated with whitewash. These houses were
cool in summer and, as one plains dweller attested, "are
mighty comfortable places to go into in cold weather, and it
don't take much fire to keep them warm." [5]

Regardless of what materials her home was built of, the
pioneer housewife had one recurring complaint—the houses
were too small. A typical letter is this one from a New England woman writing from Kansas in 1855: "We have but one
room, in which we all eat, drink and sleep, and that is not as

large as your kitchen, and has got four chests, two trunks, a cook stove, an apology for a table, half a dozen bags, three or four stools, &c." [6]

Another woman, fretting over her problems of space, said that one of her two rooms was occupied almost entirely by the family bed, leaving only just enough room in front of the fireplace to seat oneself, requiring constant alertness to avoid setting one's clothing on fire.

"Some of the habits of western life," wrote another, "originating doubtless in necessity, are truly shocking to our Yankee notions of propriety; especially, when so many of different sexes lodge in one room, in uncurtained beds. If you wish to change your linen, why haste away to the grove, to perform your toilet." [7]

Homesickness, temporary disillusionment, and an envious longing for comforts known back in the East, are also revealed in letters of women forced to live in rough quarters. "Oh, you who lounge on your divans & sofas," one wrote from Yuba River, California, in 1850, "and sleep on your fine, luxurious beds and partake of your rich viands at every meal know nothing of the life of a California emigrant. Here we are sitting, on a pine block, a log or a bunk; sleeping in beds with either a quilt or a blanket as substitute for sheets (I can tell you it is very aristocratic to have a bed at all), & calico pillow cases on our pillows. Our fare is very plain, consisting of meat & bread, & bread & meat, with some stewed fruit, either apples or peaches, now and then (as a great delicacy) some rancid butter that has been put up in the Land of Goshen and sent around a six months cruise by Cape Horn, for which we at times have given the moderate sum of $2 per pound . . . I have not seen an egg or a drop of milk since I have been in this country." [8]

2

Keeping food on the table of a frontier home was never easy and at certain times of the year presented problems to baffle the most resourceful. Money was scarce, grocery stores were few and poorly stocked, and present-day methods of preservation unknown. Meat was no problem in season, wild game being present in great variety in most parts of the West. Buffalo and deer kept more than a generation of westerners alive, with dried beans and corn furnishing the necessary starches. Meat was preserved by cutting it into strips and drying in the sun, or by salting it heavily and hanging in a smokehouse or by the fireplace.

Scurvy was an ever present danger, and though vitamins were then unheard of, wise pioneer women knew that they must provide their families with vegetables and fruit throughout the year. "As we had no jars in which to preserve wild fruit for winter," a Wyoming ranch woman recalled, "we cooked it to the consistency of thin paste, put it through a sieve and dried the mixture on large platters before the open fire until it was like leather. These flat cakes were then hung from the roof beams to be taken down when needed, boiled with water and sweetened sometimes with brown sugar." [9]

Because of their antiscurvy properties, potatoes in winter were as valuable as gold. John Bozeman, who opened the trail named for him into Montana, was a hero to the women of Fort Phil Kearney, because he sent sacks of potatoes from his ranch down to the fort. A few of these potatoes, "as precious as grain in the sacks of Israel's sons in Egypt," were doled out to officers' wives, the remainder going to the fort hospital for men afflicted or threatened with scurvy.

Foresighted housewives kept their cellars stocked as for a long siege. A contemporary description of a frontier family's food cellar told of how in the autumn months "huge barrels of buttermilk were stored for drinking and making biscuits during the winter when the cows 'went dry.' Wine, malt, spirits, sauerkraut, jerked deer and buffalo tongue, bear bacon, and a thousand other things were also stored there." [10]

New settlers had to adapt to peculiar cooking problems. They discovered that eggs were slow to boil in the Rockies, not because of a faulty fire or kettle but because of the high elevation. They learned to use Dutch ovens and johnnycake boards. "Take a board eighteen inches long and eight inches wide," advised one pioneer housewife, "round the corners off and make the edges thinner than the middle, spread it with well-made corn dough, set it on edge before a hot fire in a fireplace, and it will bake nice and brown, then turn and bake the other side the same way, then you have corn bread that no one will refuse." [11]

From the Indians they also learned of strange edible plants, such as the camas root in the Northwest. "It resembles an onion in shape and color," Narcissa Whitman wrote in her diary. "When cooked it is very sweet and tastes like a fig." [12] Another pioneer wrote that the only bread her family had in the early days was made from camas roots. The Indians cooked them by digging a hole in the ground, dropping in a heap of stones, heating them to a red heat, and covering them with green grass, upon which they put the camas, covering the whole with earth. When taken out the root was black and unappetizing in appearance, but during winters it was the chief food of many northwestern tribes.

In some cases, women could not bring themselves to adopt certain Indian delicacies. A California woman visiting a Digger tribe was fascinated to learn they made bread from powdered acorns. "They generously insisted upon our eating a piece," she wrote, then added that the keenness of her appetite was diminished when she learned the Diggers had included crushed earthworms for shortening. [13]

Coffee and sugar were two staples often in short supply, but resourceful women managed to find substitutes. Wild honey, molasses, and watermelon centers crushed and strained and added to juice from boiled corn cobs were frontier "sweeteners." Letters of the day mentioned various "coffee" recipes—parched wheat, barley and dried peas being common ones. "Take a gallon of bran, two tablespoonsful of molasses, scald and parch in the oven until it is somewhat brown and charred. Bran treated this way and cooked the same as coffee provides a very tasty drink." [14] Another frontier housewife recommended dandelion roots, advising that roots gathered in autumn were more flavorful than those gathered in the springtime. Leaving the skin on because it contained the "coffee" flavor, she cut the roots into small pieces, roasted them on an iron baking pan in her oven until they were brown and crisp, then ground them into a powder. She claimed this coffee substitute was superior to much of the green berry coffee on sale in stores.

For breadmaking, every housewife kept yeast handy in her pantry. If the yeast turned bitter, she freshened it with charred bread, or by straining through bran. She learned to store sour dough in an earthen jar; it would turn green in tin containers. If she was a newcomer and there was no dough starter in the neighborhood, she made salt-rising bread, or was reduced to using the unpopular saleratus, or soda and baking powder. She also made her own vinegar, starting it by mixing a quart of molasses and a pint of yeast. After the vinegar matured, she would likely flavor it with tincture of roses, prepared by pouring whisky over rose petals and keeping the mixture corked for two or three months.

Obtaining water for cooking was a real problem in some western areas. Alkali water had to be boiled before it was potable, and even then it was so distasteful that it was often flavored with citrate, or sugar of lemons. After railroads penetrated the Southwest, water was hauled in and peddled on the streets in wagons, sometimes at exorbitant prices. As one woman put it, "the only alternative was a choice between the strong alkaline water of the Rio Grande or the purchase of melted manufactured ice at its great cost." [15]

3

To furnish a western home required a combination of skills, hard work, and sufficient ingenuity to utilize whatever materials were at hand. "There was not sufficient furniture to be had," wrote an Oregon wife. "My husband made a table of split boards, and I went to work making stools, which I cushioned with moss and covered with oil calico. I made a rocking chair out of a sugar barrel, cushioned and covered it the same way. Cupboards and other conveniences I also manufactured. I was very proud of my new home." [16]

A woman just arrived into the midst of the California gold rush quickly furnished her canvas abode by covering the floor with matting, converting a wooden box into a trundle bed for her children, upending trunks for closets, and covering some kegs for use as ottoman seats. She finished up by arranging several packing boxes as storage walls to divide her little habitation into kitchen, bedroom and parlor.

Most families brought along mattresses in their covered wagons, using them en route; sometimes they added a few empty bed ticks and a bale of feathers to their baggage. But as time passed, old mattresses had to be replaced, new ones added to the family supply. Two readily available materials for stuffing beds were prairie grass and buffalo hair, or manes. Buffalo hair made a comfortable mattress, but grass was decidedly inferior. "A bed of 'prairie feathers' is not very comfortable at any time; and warmth is not one of its inherent qualities." [17]

Husk beds were highly recommended as replacements for

mattresses by a frontier newspaper editor of 1858: "No one who has not tried them knows the value of husk beds. Certainly mattresses would not be used if husk beds were tried. They are not only more pliable than mattresses, but are more durable. To have husks nice, they may be split after the manner of splitting straw for braiding. The finer they are split the softer will be the bed, although they will not be likely to last as long as when they are put in whole. Three barrels full, well stowed in, will fill a good sized tick. The bed will always be light, the husks do not become matted down like feathers, and they are certainly more healthful to sleep on. It is calculated that a husk bed will last from twenty-five to thirty years. Every farmer's daughter can supply herself with beds (against the time of need) at a trifling expense which is quite an inducement now-a-days." [18]

The center of a frontier home was the fireplace, used for heating, cooking, and furnishing light. A well-equipped fireplace had a turnspit for cooking meat, one or two heavy black iron kettles, an iron skillet, and a Dutch oven for baking bread. Near the hearth usually stood a broom, made with a straight pole to which stiff brush was bound tight with soaked strips of rawhide which when dried held the brush tight. Fires were always banked to save matches. In western frontier days boxed phosphorous matches were scarce, undependable, and expensive; the cheaper "China matches" came in blocks, a square inch of wood split into many pieces, dipped and treated, and the user tore them off in the manner of modern paper matches.

Glass for windows was another scarce item in early western homes. During the homesteading era, lack of window glass could be a serious matter because the law required that each family, to prove up on its claim, must have at least one window glass in the house. An Oregon woman told of how several families went together in the purchase of a single glass win-

dow: "As a man got ready to prove up on his claim he borrowed the window, put it up, and invited the inspectors. After
their visit, he took the window down, put it under the bed
ready for the next homesteader, and nailed up a sheep hide
to keep the wind out." [19]

Before kerosene was available, every family kept molds for
making candles. The women of the house were responsible
for melting deer tallow in pans over the fireplace, arranging
wicks on the molds, filling them with hot tallow, and then setting them outside to cool. Glass bottles, or nails driven into
blocks of wood, served as candlesticks. If the tallow supply
ran out, pitch pine thrown into the fireplace made a light
bright enough to read by. Women also learned to make temporary lights by twisting rags together into a ropelike wick
and placing them in pie plates filled with bear grease. Another
method was to dip the rag wick into pork lard and stick it in
a bottle.

One of the keenest joys of western women moving into a
previously occupied house was "reading the walls," as it
was the custom for everyone to use newspapers and magazines for wallpaper. No other wallpaper was available, and
in cold climates several thicknesses were pasted one above
the other. Army wives even papered the insides of their tents,
favoring illustrated journals because, as one said, "it was di-
verting to inspect those pictures which reflected many scenes
of our former lives." [20] A woman newly arrived in Oklahoma
Territory was startled on visiting a settler's wife to find the
cabin "papered with pictorial newspapers, showbills and other
professional incidentals. It was a printed landscape that
would have caused a most casual observer to give it a second
glance. All sorts of pictures budded and blossomed and
blushed from the walls." [21]

A Wyoming ranch wife left her kitchen one day in the care
of a crew of cowboys who were to prepare supper for the

ranch hands while she was away. In an effort to impress the lady with their neatness and love of homey surroundings, the cowboy cooks repapered the walls. "Upon returning," she said, "I found the walls covered with pink *Police Gazettes*, a sports publication permitted in the bunkhouse but not in the house. The apologetic cooks spent the evening tearing them down and in the morning covered the soiled places with whitewash." [22]

One of the most time-consuming of a woman's household duties was making clothing for herself and other members of the family. Many women brought wool cards and spinning wheels from the East and spun yarn from wool to make stockings and winter underclothing. In the early years wool itself was scarce; Jesse Applegate told of his aunt carding the fleece of wolves into rolls and spinning them into yarn. First arrivals had to cut up their tents and wagon covers to make coats, lining them with remnants of old woolen garments. They made buttons of pewter cast in molds cut in blocks of soapstone. "Old spoons, plates and other pieces of worn-out table wear that had seen service around many a campfire on the plains and in the mountains were used for this purpose." [23] Oregon Trail pioneers found serviceable cloth, an unbleached muslin called "factory cloth," in the Hudson Bay trading posts of the Northwest. Women dyed it brown, using the bark of alder trees for dye, and it made quite serviceable dresses and trousers. From braided oat straw, these same early pioneers also devised comfortable and attractive hats.

An Army wife in Wyoming Territory of the 1860's reported that calico, flannel, and linsey-woolsey, with gray Army blankets for use as material for children's outer coats, were available from the sutler's store. "Our buffalo boots were of a pattern emanating from or necessitated by our frontier locality, a counterpart of the leggings worn by the men, except that theirs did not have the shoe attachment. They were made by the company shoemakers of harness leather, to which was attached buffalo skin, with the hair inside, reaching almost to the knee and fastened on the outside with leather straps and brass buttons. The brass buttons were not for ornament, but a necessity in lieu of any other available kind." [24]

4

For a frontier housewife, washday meant exactly what the word implied—an entire day devoted to doing the family laundry. If she had no soap, and quite often she did not, she started the day by soaking a batch of hardwood ashes, preferably oak, in a kettle of water. When the water boiled and became lye, she dipped it into another kettle, stirring until a white, flaky scum appeared. This indicated that the water was "broken," and after clearing away the scum she poured it into washtubs, leaving it to stand until a sediment formed. The water was now clean and soft, but all this work used up the first half of her washing day.

To save time, women usually made up a quantity of soap every two or three months, mixing lye water with grease or with pork rinds, boiling the mixture, and then storing it in a dry place for a few weeks. If used before it was properly set, lye soap would melt away too rapidly in laundry water. A pioneer Kansas woman had an unusual experience with a party of Kaw Indians, who invaded her yard one day while she was making lye soap in a big iron kettle. Three of the Indians approached the kettle, and made signs indicating that they wanted to eat from it. The woman kept shaking her head no, but could not make the Kaws understand her. They thought she was unwilling to share with them. Finally, one Indian seized the stirring spoon from her and took a big bite of the thickening batch of soap. Tears came to his eyes but he never changed the expression on his face. He passed the spoon to the Indian next to him, who ate with tears in his eyes and then in turn passed it on to the third, who did likewise, after which they turned away and rejoined their party.[25]

Another household chore usually left to the woman of the house was that of planting and tending a vegetable garden. Crops that grew above the ground, peas, beans, and squash, were planted when a new moon was developing; root crops such as carrots and turnips were planted when the moon was on the wane, the theory being that as the moon ascended plants ascended, as the moon went down root crops would grow down.

The first arrivals brought their own seed, guarding them as carefully as gold. A woman just arrived in Washington Territory had brought along a precious cupful of seed corn, but as she walked along the newly opened furrow in her garden, dropping the seed, her old rooster sneaked along behind her gobbling up each grain. When she turned and saw what had happened, without a moment's hesitation she seized and killed the rooster, recovered the seed corn from its craw, and re-planted her garden.[26]

Women had a tendency to add a few flowers each year among the vegetables, but in such rigorous climates as the northern plains the delicate plants usually froze to death or were beaten to pieces by the wind. The wife of a pioneer who had lived in this area for three years told of the delight with which she discovered a dandelion growing near her doorstep; the seed had been brought in with some timothy hay, and the yellow blossom was a pleasant reminder of old home associations. "I felt less lonely," she said, "all that day." She cultivated the dandelion as carefully as a hothouse plant, and took care to see that the seed did not run out.

Pregnancy, childbirth, and child-rearing being universal experiences of women, they were subjects seldom more than barely mentioned in contemporary letters and diaries. "I do think a pregnant woman has a hard time of it," Susan Magoffin confided to her journal not long after moving into her first home, in Santa Fe. "Some sickness all the time, heart-burn, headache, cramp, etc., after all this thing of marrying is not what it is cracked up to be."[27]

A woman traveler touring the early western frontier was dismayed to discover that "western women felt that water was a deadly application for babies. They kept their babies' heads covered with a thick calico cap until they were several months old, in which time a black surface would form and cover the scalp. They would then commence a season of cleaning by saturating the head with either hog or bear's grease, and then as it would come loose, pick off the black coating."[28]

Care of older children was also rather loosely exercised in the California mining towns, according to Elizabeth Farnham, who was there during the gold rush. "The children participate in all the vices of their elders. I saw boys, from six upwards, swaggering through the streets, begirt with scarlet sash in exuberant collar and bosom, segar in mouth, uttering huge oaths, and occasionally treating men and boys at the bars."[29]

One of the hazards of pregnancy was the scarcity of doctors, and if childbirth occurred on a lonely homestead or en route overland, midwifery was performed by whatever person was closest at hand. For example, a young cavalry lieutenant bound for Fort Leavenworth in an army ambulance was called upon to officiate at the birth of a child when a woman passenger suddenly was seized with birth pangs. He had had no experience, but he spread gunny sacks on the ground and performed the birth by following instructions from the woman, using only water, a few handkerchiefs, and a penknife. The baby lived.

By force of necessity, western women learned the elements of nineteenth-century medicine, combining folklore with pills, purges, and poultices, so that if a physician was not available at least something was done to alleviate pain and discomfort among the members of her family. "In those days," said Jesse Applegate, "nothing was accepted as medicine unless it were offensive to the taste, and disagreeable to the stomach, and the more offensive and nauseating, the greater its medicinal virtues were supposed to be . . . The opinion also seems to have been general that the surest way to cure a man of disease was to reduce him almost to the point of death; that the less life there was left in a man, the less disease there would be. Where the disease was said to be in the blood, the blood was to be drawn off, leaving enough blood in the body to keep the spark of life burning until new blood could be supplied. In those days I think it would have been difficult to find a man or woman without scars from the lance."[30]

Home medicine chests contained a wide variety of staple remedies, ranging from whisky through powdered alum, sulphur, and turpentine. "Each family should have a box of physicking pills, a quart of castor oil, a quart of the best rum, and a large vial of peppermint essence."[31]

A common home remedy for fevers and "summer complaints" was to bind the sufferer's head in a cold cloth, the feet in cabbage leaves, and then administer a diet of sage tea, rhubarb, and soda. When children were ailing, mothers applied mustard plasters to their chests and onion poultices to the soles of their feet, and then forced castor oil and sage tea down their unwilling throats.

Spirits of turpentine was a favorite wound disinfectant, a more drastic treatment being the application of a live coal over the cut. Bleeding was checked by applying cobwebs, and if no cobwebs were at hand, a mixture of flour and salt was bound on with a cloth. For insect bites, a pack of wet earth or soda was applied. A popular earache cure was onion and tobacco, leaves of tobacco being inserted between onion slices and cooked over a fire; the juice was squeezed hot into the aching ear. Pioneers, incidentally, attributed considerable curative powers to onions and gunpowder. They dosed colds and coughs with onion syrup, treated sore eyes with gunpowder in a solution of water, and applied a salve of gunpowder and hog's lard to frostbites.

But the most valued remedy of all was strong whisky, which they used for snakebites, sore throat, burns, and rheumatism. They drank whisky toddies or gargled whisky and salt to cure bad colds. They treated burns with a mixture of whisky and peppermint oil and used it straight in cuts and wounds. Women used whisky for "female complaints," keeping the bottle well concealed on a private pantry shelf and taking their doses in secrecy.

About the only westerners enjoying ready access to professional medicine were military families, who could call upon the services of the post surgeons. After reading contemporary accounts of some of these treatments, however, one may wonder if Army wives and their children were any better off than the self-sufficient settlers. The wife of Lieutenant Orsemus Boyd related that when her young son fell ill of malaria at a Texas post, the surgeon kept the patient's temperature below 102 degrees by plunging him into a tub of the coldest water procurable, holding the child there until his body turned blue and his teeth began to chatter. "Heroic treatment that could not fail to wring a mother's heart!" commented Mrs. Boyd.[32]

5

Judging from their own comments, the major irritations to women in their new western homes were the weather, especially winds; unfamiliar reptiles, rodents and insects; prowling Indians; and poor mail service.

The first settlers had no official mail service. If they did not live near a Pacific coast port they had to put their letters and faith in the hands of some trapper or trader bound east for Independence or St. Louis, Missouri, where the communications might or might not be delivered to a post office. As there were no stamps, the receiver back east had to pay the postage, about twenty-five cents. Settlers living near a Pacific port could avail themselves of ship's mail, but the long route around Cape Horn was even slower than land passage. In a letter from Oregon Territory in 1838, Narcissa Whitman reminded her sister that "three years must elapse from the time of your writing, to receiving an answer, if sent by way of the Islands."* She requested that letters from home be sent to Boston to await a ship sailing for the Sandwich Islands. "We can always get them from there once or twice a year."[33] Mail service improved, of course, as the West filled with new settlers, but even as late as 1887 a Dakota woman was writing yearningly: "If we only lived where we could get our mail twice a week!"[34]

Of all the natural pests, none was feared as much as the rattlesnake, although insects caused much more actual discomfort. After becoming accustomed to seeing a rattlesnake thrust its head periodically through a hole in her adobe floor, a southwestern woman admitted she preferred the reptile to the armies of wasps, gnats, flies, fleas, and mosquitoes which plagued her constantly. In colder climates, when the first home fires were lighted in the autumn, rattlesnakes sometimes made sudden and unexpected appearances. Katherine Gibson was thus warming herself at Fort Rice one cold fall morning when a huge rattlesnake came undulating across the floor toward her and the fire, with a retinue of offspring following behind. She leaped out the nearest window and ran for help.

Flies of all sizes were a great nuisance everywhere. As soon as a house was built far out on an isolated plain, a cloud of flies enveloped it; where they came from was always a mystery, but no one had screens, and the flies swarmed freely over dining tables and awakened sleepers before daybreak. Even worse than the flies were biting gnats, so small they could

---

* Sandwich Islands, or present-day Hawaii.

penetrate mosquito netting. Not being trained naturalists, most women labeled their household pests merely as "bugs"; a woman living in a log cabin in Indian Territory complained that sleep was impossible because of "the army of bugs that hide underneath the bark during the day and march upon us at night."[35]

Centipedes and scorpions were a terror to women in the Southwest. It was unsafe to place a bed closer than two feet from a wall, or one might awaken amongst a company of those pests. Tent dwellers endured tortures from colonies of wasps which habitually took possession of the canvas over the ridgepole, darting down and buzzing the occupants below, disputing possession with painful stings.

Although grasshoppers seldom attacked human beings, settlers learned to fear them for the plague they were. During the 1870's, armies of grasshoppers attacked homesteads from Missouri to Oregon, moving in flying armies more than a hundred miles long, descending without warning upon fields and beating like hail against farmhouses. Within a few minutes they could destroy a housewife's laundry hanging on a line. "They came down like great clouds and settled all over the farm and garden and on the peach trees which were not far from the house. They ate all the leaves off and devoured the bark of the small limbs, there being hundreds on quite a small twig. They destroyed our sweet corn in a few hours the first day, and still they came—the earth was literally covered with them. I saw heaps of grasshoppers as large as a washtub. They commenced on a forty-acre field of corn about ten o'clock, and before night there was not an ear of corn or green leaf to be seen. I assure you it was sad, but it was so all over the country."[36]

One other native pest, thoroughly disliked by women with young children, was the cactus plant. "In all my rough trav-

els," declared one victim, "I never met with anything else
which gave me so much trouble as the cactus plant. Wherever
we went and whatever else we missed, that plant was always
present in some shape or form. If very young children were
allowed to wander in the least, one could depend upon finding them in the vicinity of the dangerous cacti. Days passed
before all could be picked out of the skin."[37]

Indians could be good friends, they could be dangerous
enemies, or they could be as troublesome as pests to a western
housewife. Most Indians were naturally curious, and would
often walk into a new home unannounced for a look around,
disconcerting the women, particularly if their husbands were
away. Indians distrusted doors, could not understand why
the white settlers would walk up to another's door and hit it
several times in order to have the owner open it for him. One
old warrior in Washington Territory, calling upon a new settler, found the door locked; the settler's wife was alone with
her children and refused to open it. The Indian expressed his
opinion of doors by beating that one down with his war club,
and stood on the threshold boasting, "If the white man thinks
an Indian will stop and peck at his door like a jaybird, he is
very much mistaken." As he finished his speech, the mother
reached for a gun and shot him full of buckshot. Later she
dressed his wounds, and the warrior eventually became a good
friend of the family.

Another warrior of a northwestern tribe also met his match
in a pioneer woman. He and a small band visited a tent camp,
and seeing bright-colored quilts and shiny utensils all about
and no one near but a few "white squaws," he decided to help
himself. One of the "white squaws," however, began defending her possessions with a heavy tent pole. "She laid it about,
right and left, over heads, shoulders, and backs until she put
them to flight."[38] Next day the warrior returned, apologized

for his conduct, and offered the woman's husband five hundred dollars for her. He was quite disappointed to learn she was not for sale.

Indians could be tamed, or at least confined upon reservations, but there was little that could be done to domesticate the rambunctious western weather. In the plains country, wind was every woman's enemy, shredding her weekly washing, ripping sheets and shirts from lines, and sweeping them into "regions unknown." It blew dust into houses through closed doors and windows, settling even into windowless closets, and blackened the faces of the inhabitants. It turned prairie fires into fearsome death-dealing walls of flame.

"Most disagreeable outdoor arrangements," was the way a Kansas woman described the winds of early spring. "It is quite useless for a person of little gravity or strength, to attempt much progress in locomotion, when from out of the halls of Aeolus the winds have rushed untrammeled, and unrestrained."[39]

But plains dwellers learned to laugh at their winds, newspaper editors vying with each other in colorful reporting of local storms. "On Wednesday a gust of wind removed seven dollars out of the stocking of Alice Chambers as she was walking up Front Street," reported the *Dodge City Times* in 1877. "After a six-hour search participated in by all the tramps in town, one dollar was recovered."[40]

Few people, however, were amused by winds bringing blizzards which sometimes lasted for days, drifting snow to rooftops and halting trains. Even in sturdily built houses it was impossible to keep warm with wind-driven snow beating unceasingly upon windows and whistling eerily through every crevice. In the middle of the night, storms would cease abruptly for a time, the cold silence as frightening as the howling snow-laden wind. Women felt as if they were buried in icebound tombs and wandered from one ice-sealed window to another, thawing frost from the glass with warm flatirons to let in the daylight.

Mary Woodward, who lived through several Dakota winters, declared that a blizzard was not a blizzard outside of Dakota. She was amused by reading a newspaper description of one in the East, the snowflakes "eddying by," according to the account. "Flakes don't eddy here," she wrote. "They whistle and go straight by as though shot from a cannon." When her husband built a high board fence around house and barns to keep the horses in and the blizzards out, she named the place "Andersonville," after the notorious Civil War prison stockade.

During one severe storm, Mrs. Woodward noted John G. Whittier's portrait in a copy of *Harper's Weekly* that she was reading. "If he were here," she commented, "he might write another *Snow Bound*, but it would have to be on a different plan. I doubt if there is a poet living who possesses enough vim to write a poem about a Dakota blizzard. I guess a blizzard would knock all the poetry out of a man."[41]

XII

The Great Female Shortage

1

WHEN the first white males ventured into the West, they left their women behind in the East or in border settlements. For female companionship they turned naturally to women of Indian tribes, buying or bartering for "wives" whose status sometimes became permanent, more often was quite temporary. "The man is thought a decent wooer who comes with money in his pocket to an Indian lodge," said a contemporary traveler, who observed that squaws were sold as one would sell "a buffalo hide or catamount skin."[1]

For twenty dollars a frontiersman could buy an Indian girl and claim, through her, adoption in the tribe. Sometimes the price was cheaper, one of George Custer's officers being offered a bride by a chief who asked only a cup of sugar in exchange. And sometimes it seemed too high, as fur trader Alexander Henry noted in his Fort George diary after his associate, Donald McDougall, purchased one of Chief Concomly's daughters. "He gave 5 new guns and 5 blankets, making a total of 15 guns and 15 blankets, besides a great deal of other property, as the total cost of this precious lady. This Concomly is a mercenary brute destitute of decency."

This same diarist declared that "for a few inches of twist

tobacco a Gros Ventre will barter the person of a wife or daughter with as much sangfroid as he would bargain for a horse . . . all those tribes (Blackfoot, Blood, or Piegan) are a nuisance when they come to the forts with their women. They intrude upon every room and cabin in the place, followed by their women, and even though the trader may have a family of his own they insist upon his doing them the charity of accepting of the company of at least one woman for the night. It is sometimes with the greatest difficulty that we can get the fort clear of them in the evening and shut the gates; they hide in every corner, and all for the sake of gain, not from any regard for us, though some of the men tell us it is with a view of having a white child—which frequently is the case."[2]

The white man's motives for uniting with Indian women included security as well as convenience. While traveling in the West in the 1830's, Gottfried Duden noted that Indian women often acted to protect white men, warning them of tribal treachery. "It is commonly stated here," said Duden, "that Indian women are easily seduced by Europeans. A white man who lives among the Indians for any length of time often takes an Indian girl as a temporary wife, and as a precaution for his safety . . . incidentally the Indian girls are not by any means all ugly to look at."[3] Some thirty years after Duden's observations, a Kansas newspaper reported that " 'Old Man Hathaway,' who lives on Drywood, near the state line, has, in order to save himself from being driven off by the Indians, been down to the Cherokee Nation and married a Cherokee woman. Unmarried men living on the Neutral Land, and who wish to remain there, can do so, by following Mr. Hathaway's example."[4]

Many of the great names of western exploration and settlement were "squaw men"—Jim Bridger, Kit Carson, John McLoughlin, William Bent, Joe Meek, Peter Skene Ogden,

Jim Beckwourth, Milton Sublette—and not all limited themselves to one wife. Jim Beckwourth admitted to owning eight wives, all of the Crow tribe, yet he came down to Denver in 1860 and proposed to and married Elizabeth Lettbetter, daughter of the town's first laundress. Some early fur trappers swapped, borrowed, or stole each other's squaws. Joe Meek and Milton Sublette, although partners, were rivals for the hand of a beautiful Shoshone girl named Mountain Lamb. Sublette won out because he owned more horses, but when he had to go east for surgical treatment of an ailing leg, Joe Meek "so insinuated himself into the good graces" of Mountain Lamb that she consented to join her fortunes with his.

"She was the most beautiful Indian woman I ever saw," said Meek, "and when she was mounted on her dapple gray horse, which cost me three hundred dollars, she made a fine show. She wore a skirt of beautiful blue broadcloth, and a bodice and leggins of scarlet cloth, of the very finest make. Her hair was braided and fell over her shoulders, a scarlet silk handkerchief, tied on hood fashion, covered her head; and the finest embroidered moccasins her feet. She rode like all the Indian women, astride, and carried on one side of the saddle the tomahawk for war, and on the other the pipe of peace."[5]

In fairness to the mountain men and fur traders, it must be said that most of them limited themselves to one mate at a time. The numerous Scotchmen representing the North West and Hudson's Bay fur companies often settled down for years with one tribeswoman and raised respectable families. For example, Angus McDonald, stationed at Fort Colville, had ten children by the same woman and considered himself as solidly married as any *pater familias* of his native Scotland.

In 1850, a traveler en route to California stopped at Jim Bridger's fort, recording that Bridger "had a squaw and two children, a boy and girl, half casts, of whom he seemed to be very fond. Old Jim, as the lord of the castle was called, was anxious for us to hear them read, which we did. Madam Bridger, the squaw, cooked us a good supper, making some light biscuit . . . the best I had ever eaten."[6]

One of the curious aspects of these relations between white men and Indian women was that there was no social reproach whatever to such unions until white women began arriving in the West in increasing numbers. Almost as soon as the first wagonloads of females arrived from the States—hardly before they could unpack their household goods—it was considered a disgrace for a white man to live with a squaw. For example, a reformed drunkard named Hauxhurst was living contentedly with an Indian girl in Oregon until the female missionaries arrived. Almost immediately, Hauxhurst's conscience began troubling him, and one morning he handed the girl some blankets and other farewell presents and sent her back to her people.

According to one of Hauxhurst's neighbors, who recorded the incident in a diary of 1845, the girl returned that night to the man's door, "beseeching him to let her in, averring her love to him and promising to be good to him if he would let her live with him; he let her in; and knowing it was wicked for them to live together as they had done, he, in a short time soon experienced religion, and is now a respectable man in the community, only he has a squaw for a wife. This, it is presumed, is the source for great mortification to himself and affliction to his friends."[7]

The first white men coming into the wilderness, straight out of a nineteenth-century civilization which professed to abhor the human form, had to make abrupt adjustments to a people who regarded clothing merely as protection from sun and weather rather than as concealment for the natural state of nakedness. Costumes varied, of course, from tribe to tribe, but in general the first difference noted was the dress, or lack of it, of Indian females. Eighteen-year-old Lewis Garrard considered the costumes of southwestern Indian women "a pleasing and desirable change from the sight of the pinched waists and constrained motions of the women of the States, to see these daughters of the prairie dressed loosely—free to act, unconfined by the ligatures of fashion . . ."[8]

Colonel W. H. Emory was fascinated by an Apache beauty of the same area: "She had on a gauzelike dress, trimmed with the richest and most costly Brussels lace, pillaged no doubt from some fandango-going belle of Sonora; she straddled a fine grey horse, and whenever her blanket dropped from her shoulders, her tawny form could be seen through the transparent gauze. After she had sold her mule, she was anxious to sell her horse, and careered about to show his qualities. At one time she charged at full speed up a steep hill. In this, the fastenings of her dress broke, and her bare back was exposed to the crowd, who ungallantly raised a shout of laughter. Nothing daunted, she wheeled short round with surprising dexterity, and seeing the mischief done, coolly slipped the dress from her arms and tucked it between her seat and the saddle. In this state of nudity she rode through camp, from fire to fire, until, at last, attaining the object of her ambition, a soldier's red flannel shirt, she made her adieu in that new costume."[9]

Ernest de Massey, a Frenchman in the gold rush, was less appreciative of the types he saw on the West Coast. "When I first saw these Indian women walking around in the open, and talking and laughing in the most natural manner before strange men when wearing scarcely more than the proverbial fig-leaf, my only feelings were those of indifference for they were neither beautiful nor appealing. Every time I touched their rough, cold, oily skin I had a feeling of repulsion just as if I had put my hand on a toad, tortoise, or huge lizard."[10]

As for Alexander Henry, he was equally repelled and tantalized by the abundance of feminine nudity around Fort

George: "This afternoon I had an opportunity of observing the total want of modesty, or even decency, in the women on this coast. I was walking on the wharf, where several women were washing themselves, as is their daily custom, in the small ponds left on the beach at low water. They were perfectly naked, and my presence did not affect their operations in the least. The disgusting creatures were perfectly composed, and seemed not to notice me. Although they stood naked in different postures, yet so close did they keep their thighs together that nothing could be seen. The operation over, they used their cedar coverings as towels, and, after drying themselves, tied them around their waists and walked away."[11]

Callous disregard for, and sometimes outright cruelty toward, Indian women increased in proportion with the deepening social disgrace accorded "squaw men" which had begun with the arrival of the first white woman. A California Indian agent received a report in 1855 from Klamath County referring to mistreatment of female natives by miners. "They have singled out all the squaws, compelling them to sleep with some man every night. This causes great excitement. The Bucks complain daily of it."[12]

The low status of Indian females during this period is indicated by an account of a party traveling by horseback to Oregon. The travelers came upon a naked Indian girl, suffering from hunger and almost eaten up by flies. She had evidently become lost from her tribe. A council was held among the men as to what to do with her; some wanted to take her along, others thought it would be best to kill her and put her out of her misery. A vote was taken and it was decided to leave the girl where they had found her. The women of the party protested, but they were overruled. After the party had gone on a short distance, one of the men went back and "put a bullet through her head and put her out of her misery."[13]

One other reason for the change in attitude toward Indian

women was the high rate of venereal disease among many tribes, a disease introduced, of course, by white men. Alexander Henry's diary has several illuminating comments on the subject. "At 11 P.M. I went to bed; Mr. McTavish was inclined to sit up. Mr. J. Cartier discharged his lady, she being so far gone with the venereal disease that he already has two pimples, and on examination the doctor gives it as his opinion that he is in a very bad way. Mr. Bethune keeps his, though he is very dubious about her." On another day, Henry recorded the death of a girl from the disease. Her owner, a former Canadian *voyageur*, sent for her family to come and bury the body, "lest the hogs should devour it. They did so, but in a barbarous manner, by dragging it perfectly naked down to the water, tying a cord around the neck, and towing it along the beach for some distance; they then squeezed the body into a hole, pushed it down with a paddle, and covered it over with stones and dirt. The poor girl had died in a horrible condition, in the last stage of venereal disease, discolored and swollen, and not the least care was ever taken to conceal the parts from bystanders."[14]

2

Any commodity that is both uncommon and universally desired becomes overvalued in the market place, and that was the situation applying to white women in the Far West during its earlier years. "Women were queens," was the comment of one observer during the spring of 1849 when there were but fifteen women in all San Francisco. And by October the number had increased to only fifty. The following year, when an official census was taken, females composed less than 8 per cent of the total inhabitants of California, a statistic which told only part of the story, for in many mining regions there were no women at all. It was no wonder that male passersby turned to salute every female stranger encountered on streets and roads.

This acute scarcity resulted in a goodly amount of full-blown, heart-bleeding prose on the part of some of the literate males. Walter Colton, alcalde of Monterey at the time of the gold strike, set down his feelings in this manner: "There is no land less relieved by the smiles and soothing caress of woman. If Eden with its ambrosial fruits and guiltless joys was still sad till the voice of woman mingled with its melodies, California, with all her treasured hills and streams, must be cheerless till she feels the presence of the same enchantress." [15]

Caspar Hopkins, a less mellifluous writer, struck a more cynical note: "As yet the female part of our population is only about two per cent of the whole, and of these, including all nations, the proportion who are what women ought to be is not more than twenty per cent. To say nothing of the large number of French women who are imported, like other French frail manufactures, only to take their places among the bottles and decanters, a great many American women who have started to join their husbands here, have found the journey too much for their principles. The attentions of extempore gallants have rendered the husbands they set out to meet the last persons they wished to see on their arrivals. Happily, however, these instances are in the minority; though were it otherwise, the universal depravity of the male population would be sufficient explanation for it."[16]

In the back country, the female-starved miners came to consider it a privilege just to look at a member of the opposite sex. A typical story concerns a young man who learned one evening that a woman had arrived at another mining camp some forty miles distant. The young man went to his uncle and asked: "Uncle, will you lend me your mule tomorrow?"

"What do you want with my mule?"

"I've heard there's a woman over at the next camp, and I want to go and see her."

The uncle lent his nephew the mule, and he was off at daybreak, and never stopped until he had covered the forty miles and had a good look at the lady.[17]

As late as 1860, in the Colorado mining country, a similar condition prevailed. "We were all in the habit of running to our cabin doors in Denver, on the arrival of a lady, to gaze at her as earnestly as at any other rare natural curiosity."[18]

Not since the days of knighthood had women been accorded such courtesy, respect, and unobtrusive chivalry. The miners even went so far as to flatter the vanity of fair visitors by "salting" their diggings, and as Dame Shirley observed, "the dear creatures go home with their treasures, firmly believing that mining is the prettiest pastime in the world."[19]

And one winter when Downieville was snowed in with deep drifts and food became short, the entire male population was ordered to leave town in order that the few women in camp would have sufficient provisions.

"I never knew a miner to insult a woman," wrote an observer of the times, "but, on the other hand, I know a woman could visit among a camp of miners and be treated with higher consideration than many honorable wives, mothers, and sisters are treated by men in passing along the streets of our cities in the evening, or even in the day time. Every miner seemed to consider himself her sworn guardian, policeman and protector, and the slightest dishonorable word, action or look of any miner or other person, would have been met with a rebuke he would remember as long as he lived, if, perchance, he survived the chastisement."[20]

A woman traveling in upper California during this period was astonished at the honors shown her by the miners. "I am afraid I should have had a very mistaken impression of my importance if I had lived long among them. At every stopping-place they made little fires in their frying pans, and set them around me, to keep off the mosquitoes, while I took my meal. As the columns of smoke rose about me I felt like a heathen goddess, to whom incense was being offered." [21]

Weddings were both rare and costly. Two thousand dollars was expended on a wedding celebration in Marysville, though the bride may have shared part of the expense, she being described as "a fair widow of thirty who had been left a fortune by a former husband." A miner in Shasta decided to defray part of his expenses by selling admissions to his wedding at five dollars per ticket; so many guests came and paid that he took in enough extra to furnish a house.[22]

The female shortage was felt most acutely at dances or other social gatherings where the gaiety depended upon an even number of partners of opposite sexes. In the cattle country of western Washington, one rancher recalled attending a dance where there were sixty cowboys and three women. They had to resort to the old trick of tying handkerchiefs to the arms of a number of cowboys to designate them as females. Because of the woman shortage in that area, "a man bringing one girl to a dance got a free ticket, and if he brought two girls he got 25 cents to boot."[23]

A Montana cowboy of the 1880's complained that girls were so scarce up there that engagements for dances had to be made eight months ahead. He told of trying to arrange a dance with several other cowboys, but found it impossible to round up nearly enough women. "One of the boys went into the back room of the honky-tonky where they were staging the dance and came out with a pair of woman's white ruffled drawers pulled on over his pants. He was the attraction of the evening."[24]

Eleanor Alice Richards, daughter of a Wyoming governor, recalled that during one winter when she was a girl of eleven living in the Bighorn Basin, there were a hundred men in the

Basin and seven women, if she included herself. She attended the all-night dances with her parents. "The men were very respectful and well behaved. I remember at one dance that a couple of the boys who became intoxicated were taken out, placed on their horses and shown the way home. There were so many men and so few women, they knew they must behave if they wished to have a good time."[25]

Westerners who could afford servants found it impossible to keep female help longer than a month or so. "The parlor-maid or the kitchen maid," commented Janos Xandus in a letter from California in 1857, "who weeks ago had cooked, charred, and washed the laundry, has become the wife of a banker or a rich merchant, because she has a nice face."[26] And it was not always necessary to have "a nice face." An Army wife told of deliberately selecting a homely nurse so she would not marry one of the soldiers in the fort and leave her service. "The girl was almost a grenadier in looks and manners, and although not absolutely hideous, was so far from pleasing that we were confident of retaining her services . . . She had not been in the fort three days before the man who laid our carpets proposed to her."[27]

After Fort Lincoln was fitted up as a sort of frontier luxury station in 1876, and maids were imported to keep the officers' quarters clean, the Army command itself was forced to take cognizance of the servant problem. When experience showed that all the imported maids married soldiers within two to six weeks after arrival, the military instructed employment offices in Chicago and eastern cities to supply only the homeliest females obtainable. The agencies complied, shipping out a troop of knock-kneed, cross-eyed, buck-toothed females to Fort Lincoln. At the end of two months, however, every one of them had landed a man.[28]

Thousands of women of all classes went west in those days with that single purpose in mind—to get married as quickly

as possible. Loreta Velazquez, the incredible male imperson-
ator who took her dead husband's place as a soldier in the
Civil War, discarded her disguise as soon as the fighting
stopped and headed west to find a new mate. Dressed in a
most feminine manner, she reached Omaha almost penniless,
but she charmed old General W. S. Harney into supplying
her with a buffalo robe, a pair of blankets, and a revolver—
which she needed to continue her journey into the Nevada
mining regions. Two days after Loreta arrived in Austin,
Nevada, she received her first proposal of marriage, but the
gentleman was sixty years old and she waited a few days for
a younger suitor. She married, settled down, and lived a full
and happy life.

Wedding ceremonies in the West were as short and swift
as the engagement periods. For example, a marrying squire
of Kansas is said to have used this one:

Squire: Have him?
Bride: Yes.
Squire: Have her?
Bridegroom: Kinder.
Squire: Done. One dollar.

A young single woman just arrived in the West attended a
funeral on horseback. As she turned to leave, the bereaved
widower rode up beside her horse and "expressed a wish that
she might be induced to consent to fill the place of the dear
departed one whose mortal remains had just been laid in the
grave." [29] The young woman rejected the suitor for lack of
emotional delicacy.

Sometimes husbands were acquired through unusual circumstances, as in the case of a woman arrested for vagrancy
in Meade, Kansas. On that same day a man was arrested for
disorderly conduct. Both were sentenced to jail, creating a
dilemma for the court, because the jail had only one cell. The
defendants, however, solved the quandary by offering to get

married. A collection was taken up, a marriage license was procured, the justice performed the ceremony without charge, and the honeymoon was celebrated in the calaboose.

3

Too much adoration poured upon a minority of females was bound to have pernicious psychological effects upon even the more worthy of the creatures. Naturally, many of them took advantage of their scarcity, and for a time made life almost intolerable for the competitive males. Historian Hubert Howe Bancroft observed that the excessive attention paid them "made modest women uncomfortable, while others encouraged it by extravagant conduct. Loose characters flaunted costly attire in elegant equipages, or appeared walking or riding in male attire."[30]

Special privileges accorded females annoyed some men; a few were highly critical because western juries would not convict a woman for any crime, not even murder. "A white woman is treated everywhere on the Pacific slope, not as man's equal and companion, but as a strange and costly creature, which by virtue of its rarity is freed from the restraints and penalties of ordinary law. In San Francisco there is a brisk demand for wives, a call beyond the market to supply. A glut of men is everywhere felt, and the domestic relation is everywhere disturbed."

The diaries of male gold seekers are filled with continuous entries decrying the shortage: "Would give my little finger to go to the theater or museum with some certain Baltimore girls, tonight—hush memory—or I'll go mad." This same young man complained that before he could induce a homely woman to wash his linen he had to pay court to her as well as the six dollars a dozen she charged for his laundered shirts.[31]

Polyandry without benefit of formal marriage—quite common among Chinese emigrants—was probably more generally practiced among the whites than the records indicate. Ernest de Massey told of visiting a ranch in southern California where two men were living with one woman in a congenial *ménage à trois.* "Perhaps in California," he commented primly, "there is a sacrament that blesses such a union, but it does not meet with local approval."[32]

The ease with which some women shifted from one husband to another is exemplified in the rocky marital adventures of Henry T. P. Comstock, discoverer of the rich Nevada lode which bore his name. Comstock fell in love at first sight with the wife of a Mormon who arrived one day in Nevada City riding upon a dilapidated wagon. The woman was plainly dressed in drab calico and poke bonnet, but the grizzled old miner could not resist her charms. He persuaded her to leave her husband and run away with him to Washoe Valley, where a preacher friend married them. Proceeding to Carson City for a honeymoon, Comstock and his bride had scarcely settled into a hotel when the original Mormon husband arrived in a state of high indignation.

Comstock blithely produced a marriage license and dared the Mormon to do the same. When the Mormon admitted he had no license, the old miner graciously agreed to give him a horse, a revolver, and sixty dollars to settle the matter with no hard feelings. Probably because there was nothing else he could do, the Mormon agreed to the bargain and went on his way.

A few days later, Comstock left his bride comfortably ensconced in the hotel and started out to San Francisco to attend to some business matters. He had gone no farther than Sacramento when he received a message from a friend informing him that his new bride had absconded with "a seductive youth of Carson City" and the pair were on their way to Placerville. Rushing to Placerville, Comstock intercepted the runaways, had a long private talk with his sixty-dollar wife, and apparently convinced her she had made a rash mistake. But when he left her for a few minutes and then returned to her room, she was gone again. She had climbed out the back window and was in flight once more with the "seductive young lover."

Comstock was not one to give up easily. He hired all the horses in the town's livery stables and sent riders out in all directions with a promise of one hundred dollars' reward to the one who captured the fleeing lovers. Next day one of the searchers came back into Placerville, walking the runaways in front of his six-shooter. Comstock paid the hundred-dollar reward, and this time he locked his wife up securely. In the meantime, his friends took charge of the young man, placing him under armed guard. As soon as night fell, the young man was told he was to be hanged. A little later a new guard, previously instructed by Comstock, came on duty. He whispered to the prisoner that he was opposed to hangings. "I'm going outside to take a drink," the guard said, "and if I find you here when I return, it will be your own fault." The young lover made good the arranged escape, and he was never seen around Placerville or Carson City again.

As for the wife, she stayed on with Comstock through the winter, but she kept an alert eye out for another chance. In the spring she ran away with "a long-legged miner who, with his blankets on his back, came strolling that way." The last known of the onetime Mrs. H. T. P. Comstock she was working in a beer cellar in Sacramento.[33]

4

In the course of time, the West's dearth of females attracted the attention of a number of ingenious entrepreneurs and social theorists, including knaves, fanatics, and a few sincere philanthropists. One of the first to propose a solution to the problem was Catharine E. Beecher, sister of the famed Harriet and Henry Ward Beecher. As early as 1845, Catharine recognized the great need for schoolteachers in the West, as well as the increasing geographical displacement of the sexes. She wrote a book called *The Duty of American Women to Their Country*, advocating "Go West, Young Woman" long before Horace Greeley thought up the phrase for young men. One of the points she belabored was the vast excess of female population in New England and other eastern areas.

A frontier newspaper editor took note of Miss Beecher's manifesto with this comment: "To supply the bachelors of the West with wives, to furnish the pining maidens of the East with husbands, and to better equalize the present disposition of the sexes in these two sections of our country, has been one of the difficulties of the age. The remedy was simple; it was only for the girls to go West and get married; but to go expressly to get married, offended their ideas of delicacy. Miss Beecher, herself a Yankee girl, has ingeniously got over the whole difficulty. She is engaging the girls to go West as school teachers."[34]

The first money-making schemes for delivering marriageable females to western males appear to have originated in Europe. In Paris—which had been the hatching place for numerous American promotions from the time of John Law's Mississippi Bubble—a project was organized to recruit young girls for shipment to western America. The company's income was to be derived from a percentage of the girls' marriage portions. This Parisian plan failed before it was fully developed, but a different system originating in Germany met with more success.

Upon this German scheme the *Alta California* leveled a scorching editorial blast: "It may hardly seem credible that a system of peonage of Anglo-Saxon flesh and blood is rife in California. The system of importing females from Germany, by contract, has been carried on with great profit to one or two parties in this city. Young girls are bought, sent out here in ships, and have to serve a term of years to their master—no matter what labor may be required." The editor went on to say that dance houses were being supplied with these girls to act as partners to male customers at rates of four dollars per evening up to midnight and seven dollars if retained until morning. "We are informed they are virtuous; though notions of propriety forbid that a female who can be fondled and clasped by every comer, be he drunk or sober, uncouth or comely, can be chaste; yet such a miracle may exist."

As anyone might have guessed, it was a woman who organized the first American effort to supply brides to the California gold miners. She was Elizabeth Farnham, a New York prison matron, whose husband, Thomas J. Farnham, had gone to San Francisco and died there in 1848. Farnham left his business affairs in such confusion that Elizabeth decided to leave New York and journey out by ocean vessel and collect what monies might be due the estate. From her late husband and other sources she had learned of the great demand for marriageable women in the West, and being of a practical turn of mind she decided to organize a company of prospective brides and take them along with her. She also needed money and hoped to profit from the venture.

On February 2, 1849, Mrs. Farnham published a circular to explain her purposes:

> It is proposed that the company shall consist of persons not under twenty-five years of age, who shall bring from their clergyman, or some authority of the town where they reside, satisfactory testimonials of education, character, capacity, etc., and who can contribute the sum of two hundred and fifty dollars, to defray the expenses of the voyage, make suitable provision for their accommodation after reaching San Francisco, until they shall be able to enter upon some occupation for their support, and create a fund to be held in reserve for the relief of any who

may be ill, or otherwise need aid before they are able to provide for themselves.

It is believed that such arrangement, with one hundred or one hundred and thirty persons, would enable the company to purchase or charter a vessel, and fit it up with everything necessary for comfort on the voyage, and that the combination of all for the support of each, would give such security, both as to health, person, and character, as would remove all reasonable hesitation from the minds of those who may be disposed and able to join such a mission. It is intended that the party shall include six or eight respectable married men and their families . . .

The New York built packet ship *Angelique* has been engaged to take out this Association . . . She will be ready to sail from New York about the 12th or 15th of April.[85]

To lend her circular an air of respectability and authority, she appended the endorsements of such leading figures as Horace Greeley, William Cullen Bryant, and Henry Ward Beecher. During the next several weeks, about two hundred women communicated with Mrs. Farnham, but unfortunately she fell ill and was not able to work actively in organizing the expedition. In the end, only three women agreed to go to California with her. Her plan, however, was widely publicized in the West, and the California miners undoubtedly were more disappointed than she was by its failure, as this miner's diary entry of June 10, 1849, suggests: "Went to church 3 times today. A few ladies present, does my eyes good to see a woman once more. Hope Mrs. Farnham will bring 10,000."[36]

5

The most successful project for importing brides was that of Asa Shinn Mercer, a gentleman astute enough to follow the lead of Catharine Beecher and disguise his cargo as "schoolteachers."

Mercer began his western career in Seattle in 1861, at the

age of twenty-two, immediately following his graduation from Franklin University of Ohio. He was soon convinced that the Northwest was the Promised Land and began a campaign to establish a university to educate its young citizens. With the approval of the territorial commissioner, he founded the University of Washington, becoming its first president. The young educator was disappointed, however, in the size of his student body—only a dozen or so enrolled—and he realized his institution was unlikely to grow very rapidly in a territory where men outnumbered women nine to one. What the new country needed most, he decided, was an importation of women to breed future students.

Mercer has been described as a handsome young man, tall and thin, with intense dark eyes and an affable, persuasive manner. His talent for persuasion enabled him to convince the Washington territorial legislature that hundreds of prospective brides could be obtained in New England, where females outnumbered males and the raging Civil War was leaving a number of them fatherless. The territorial authorities gave Mercer's amorphous project their blessings, but no money. He had to raise private contributions from hopeful bachelors to finance the venture.

In the early spring of 1864, Asa Mercer arrived in New England, ready to address all his powers of persuasion to that area's thousands of young single women. His most successful appearance was in Lowell, Massachusetts, where he spoke before a large crowd in Mechanics' Hall, picturing in glowing terms the advantages awaiting any and all young ladies who would leave their New England homes and migrate to Washington Territory to engage in school and music teaching. He carefully avoided all references to matrimonial advantages, stressing the appeal to his listeners' desire for financial improvement.

His brief tour won him eleven converts, ranging in ages

from fifteen to twenty-five. Each paid $225 passage money, and in March 1864 the little party, with Mercer in charge, sailed from New York. After crossing the Panama Isthmus, they reached Seattle on May 16. As Mercer had hoped, most of his "schoolteachers" were soon married; only one, a Miss Ann Murphy, became homesick and returned to Lowell.

Hailed as a local hero, Mercer was soon afterward elected to the territorial legislature. By the next year he was ready to go back east, make a longer and wider canvass, and return to Seattle with an entire shipload of girls. His plans included enlisting the aid of President Abraham Lincoln, but the day he reached New York, April 19, 1865, Lincoln was assassinated.

Shocked but undaunted, Mercer went on to Washington, D. C., waited until the furor surrounding the President's assassination had died down, then sought an audience with President Andrew Johnson. Although Johnson did not oppose the female emigration scheme, he would offer no financial assistance from the Federal Government. In desperation, Mercer turned to General Ulysses Grant, a man who had soldiered in the West and knew how desperately women were needed there. Grant cheerfully wrote out an order authorizing Mercer's use of a troopship for transporting his schoolteachers to Washington Territory.

Elated by this good fortune, Mercer immediately headed for New England to round up his cargo. He traveled through Massachusetts, Connecticut, New Hampshire, and Maine, spreading the good news. He was now in a position to offer bargain rates, only twenty-five dollars per passenger, and those who could not afford that sum could pay later. In his speeches, he asked for female volunteers below the age of twenty-five, guaranteeing employment as soon as they arrived in Washington Territory, "with sufficient remuneration to make them independent." When a newspaper reporter asked him to name the exact amount they would earn, Mercer replied that the minimum would be "four dollars per week in *gold*," more than a living wage in those days.

Both in New York and in New England, Mercer ran into some opposition from the press. One editor accused him of "seeking to carry off young girls for the benefit of miserable old bachelors," and a number of papers attempted to undermine his efforts by publicly ridiculing those who joined the expedition. But in spite of opposition, Mercer signed up about four hundred girls, issuing them contracts guaranteeing the holders passage to Washington Territory.

In July he wrote his friends back in Washington Territory: "I sail from New York about August 19 with upward of 300 war orphans, daughters of those whose lives were given on plain and field in our recent war. I appeal to every true warmhearted family to open wide your door and share your home comforts with these whose lot is about to be cast in your midst. I can cheerfully vouch for the intelligence and moral character of all these persons accompanying me."

On the first day of August, Mercer arrived in New York to prepare for the departure. His first step was to take possession of the promised military transport ship. Armed with the written order from General Grant, he called on Quartermaster General Montgomery Meigs. But Meigs was a stickler for military procedures, and also a bit of a martinet. He declared that Grant had acted without authority, and deliberately refused to permit use of a government vessel for transporting females anywhere. The dismayed Mercer protested that he must have a ship; almost four hundred young women were ready and eager to sail; they had his written promises guaranteeing transportation to Washington Territory. Meigs replied that he would sell the ship at a bargain, $80,000.

Time was pressing, but Mercer tried to raise the money. When that failed, he attempted to contract passage with a shipping line. The best price he could get was $120,000, fare for four hundred passengers. He hurriedly postponed the sailing date, and began sending frantic messages for help to his friends in the West.

On September 30, when the *New York Times* interviewed him about his plans, Mercer confidently announced that his list of applicants had grown to 650 females and 50 male mechanics—also needed in the West—and that they would be sailing within a few weeks. He evidently made careful replies to questions concerning the matrimonial chances for the girls. "Although this is not a matrimonial venture," the newspaper said, "it being expressly stipulated that the wages of the girls shall be adequate for their support without recourse to marriage, there is not the most distant probability that any young woman who desires to marry will be prevented."

It was Ben Holladay, king of the stagecoach and overland mail lines, who saved the day for Asa Mercer. Holladay also owned the California, Oregon & Mexican Steamship Company, and he volunteered to buy one of General Meigs' military ships and transport the girls at low rates.

At last, on January 15, 1866, the steamship *Continental* was ready to clear the port of New York with the Mercer expedition aboard. All the delay and bad publicity, however, had served to cut Mercer's proud cargo to only about one hundred single women, a dozen married couples, and fourteen single men.

When the passengers boarded the *Continental*, they found everything in confusion. No repairs had been made to the vessel's interior fittings since it was last used for transporting soldiers, and the galley was in such condition that no meals could be served the first day. Off Staten Island, the *Continental* anchored to await a pilot boat; as the boat approached, a man standing in the bow began shouting: "Where is Mercer? I want to see Mercer!" Mercer quickly hid in a coalbin, suspecting the caller might be a creditor armed with a legal summons which might further delay the voyage. Actually the man was a Maine farmer who had sold his farm at Mercer's suggestion and wanted to take his family west with the expedition.

As the ship headed south through calm waters, the passengers settled down to the usual routines of ocean voyaging. The food was monotonous; for seventeen days they were served nothing but fried salt beef, parboiled beans, and tea steeped in salt water. The girls were on the point of rebellion because Mercer was dining at the captain's table, where the diet was more varied, but when Mercer heard of their dissatisfaction he deserted the captain and began sharing the poor fare of his charges.

Aboard the *Continental* was a special newspaper correspondent who, after the fashion of the day, signed his dispatches with a cognomen, "Rod." According to Flora Pearson —one of the girls who later recorded her experiences—"Rod of the *New York Times* paid open court to first one and then another of the fair sex, evidently with serious intentions each time, but the ardent wooer failed to make a permanent impression; his charmers suffered his devotions for a brief season and then gave him the cold shoulder."

There were other shipboard flirtations, including four of the vessel's engineers and a grizzled California miner who had booked passage at the last minute. "Around him [the miner] revolved as regularly as the planets in their orbits, five unmarried females, who were known as 'the Constellation.' How the much-sought man escaped entanglement in the matrimonial mesh will never be known—possibly he made haste upon landing to lose himself in the foothills of California."

Asa Mercer himself fell victim to the mood of romantic enchantment which seemed to hover over the *Continental*. In the words of Flora Pearson, "he succumbed to the fascination of one of the most accomplished of our maidens, but she would none of him." However, when he formed a second attachment, to a Miss Annie Stephens of Baltimore, his "passion was reciprocated."

Among the personalities aboard, as described by Miss Pearson, was a dyspeptic young lady nicknamed "Spepsy," an exclusive maid whose mouth always had the "prunes and prisms expression," and who showed deep disdain with all her surroundings until she "grew chummy with the captain's daughter and ate at the table with the royal household." Another interesting member of the party was "the plain spoken Miss S. who was locked in her room at the command of the ship's master." Annoyed by the flirtatious actions of his engineers, the captain ordered them to remain in their quarters and not mingle with the female passengers. Miss S. disliked this order, and to show her contempt for the captain she drew a chalk mark across the deck by the saloon door and lettered a huge sign along it: OFFICERS NOT ALLOWED AFT. The captain retaliated by confining Miss S. to her quarters also.

When the *Continental* reached Rio de Janeiro, the passengers all went happily ashore, and Rod of the *New York Times* was able to send dispatches back by mail boat to his paper. By modern journalistic standards, Rod was a rather inept correspondent. Instead of reporting the activities of "the marriageable young ladies on board," he composed several hundred words of glowing prose describing the buildings and streets of Rio. When the ship moved on around the Horn and anchored for a week off a Chilean port, Rod went ashore with some of the girls to buy souvenirs. He wrote mostly about the local market place, concluding his report with some waspish comments about Chilean officials. "Ever since our arrival at this port, the *Continental* has been completely overrun, night and day, with Chilean officers. So intense has been their admiration for the ladies that every inducement has been held out to persuade them to remain in Chile. Offers of marriage; offers of schools at fabulous prices, and offers of positions as housekeepers flowed in in abundance."

On May 1 the girls landed in San Francisco, where they were hailed by crowds of enthusiastic male Californians. As this was the end of the journey for the *Continental,* Asa Mercer arranged further passage for his party on the brig *Tanner,* and they continued north for Seattle. On June 1, 1866, four months and one week after leaving New York, the celebrated "Mercer girls" reached their destination.

"All the men in Seattle that could get new suits did so," reported a member of the reception committee, "and others got new overalls and were on the dock when the *Tanner* arrived. Mr. Mercer thought they seemed to think they would get a wife immediately, so he made a speech to them before they landed, telling them that the women were all of the best and if the men wanted them for wives they must do it in the good old way. All were well treated when they came ashore, and were taken into homes until they married or got employment as milliners, dress makers, school teachers, etc."

Asa Mercer himself married Annie Stephens six weeks after their arrival, and he made no more journeys east in search of prospective brides. Perhaps he had found what he had been searching for. In the course of time, all of his "girls" except one found husbands. The exception was Elizabeth Ordway, who had signed on to be a schoolteacher, and a schoolteacher she was for many years. "Nothing could induce me," she said in later life, "to relinquish the advantages of single blessedness."

As for Mercer, his later life is worthy of a brief footnote. Whether it was the strain and excitement of his two expeditions, or something else, Mercer was never again able to settle down and fulfill the bright promise of his youthful twenties. He became a drifter, moving first to Oregon to found a periodical, engage in the grain trade, and work as an employee of the state government.

In 1876 he moved on to Texas, operating four newspapers, none too successfully. In 1883 he drifted north to Wyoming, founded a livestock journal, and there met his downfall. During the Johnson County War between the settlers and the big cattlemen, he sided with the settlers and published an exposé of the Johnson County invasion, *The Banditti of the Plains*, in which he named names in bold print. Copies of his book were searched out and burned, the plates were destroyed, and he was thrown into jail. For the remainder of his life, Mercer lived on the verge of poverty, accomplishing nothing of importance, finally dying in 1917 at the age of seventy-eight.[37]

XIII

Wyoming Tea Party

1

ON the evening of September 2, 1869, in a small shack in South Pass City, Wyoming Territory, occurred an event that has since become known as "the Esther Morris tea party." This Wyoming tea party had as much significance in the fight for women's rights as the Boston Tea Party had in the American struggle for independence.

At the time she gave her tea party Esther McQuigg Morris was fifty-five years old, a self-reliant lady of great charm, who enjoyed fierce battles and was accustomed to winning most of them. Orphaned at eleven, she supported herself as a milliner in Oswego, New York, until she married John Slack. Then in her later years she followed her second husband, John Morris, to Wyoming to keep house for him while he tried to make a fortune in the gold diggings.

Because of Esther Morris' air of quiet reserve and her strong personality, South Pass City elected her justice of the peace—the first woman to hold that office anywhere in the world. In the late 1860's, South Pass City was the largest city in Wyoming, a row of miners' shacks stretching along a ledge of the Wind River Mountains, with a population of three thousand, mostly males seeking gold. Soon after her election the rowdies of the place undertook to intimidate her, but of the forty cases she tried during her term of office not one was appealed, and the more respectable males of the community testified that she conducted her office with greater credit than most men, "administering justice with a vigorous and impartial hand."

Esther Morris' unique office naturally attracted considerable publicity around the country. Some of the eastern sporting papers, notably the *Police Gazette* and *Day's Doings*, printed cartoons of Esther Morris, J. P., representing her as being a formidable female who sat with her feet propped on the magistrate's desk, conducting her court with a cigar between her lips and whittling a heap of shavings with a huge jackknife.

These disparaging caricatures barely amused Mrs. Morris, but she wasted no time being annoyed by them. She was too busy with such important matters as seeing that laws were passed giving women the right to vote. On the eve of Wyoming's first territorial elections, September 2, 1869, she invited twenty of the most influential citizens of South Pass City to a tea party in her tidy little miner's shack. Among the guests were Colonel William H. Bright, Democratic candidate for the legislature, and Captain Herman G. Nickerson, Republican candidate. At the proper moment during the convivial evening, Esther Morris dropped what she thought would be a bombshell into the conversation. With quiet seriousness, she suddenly asked each candidate if he would introduce a bill in the new legislature that would give the women of Wyoming the right to vote. At that time, no woman in the world had such a legal right.

If the gentlemen thought Mrs. Morris was joking, she soon made it plain that she was not. Colonel Bright knew her well enough to recognize her sincerity. He had a high regard for her learning, her abilities, and above all her skill as a nurse. Esther Morris had probably saved the life of his wife Betty, nursing her through a difficult childbirth. Colonel Bright replied that he would introduce a women's suffrage bill. And then not to be outdone, the Republican candidate, Herman Nickerson, said he would do the same if elected.

Very likely, neither candidate had any expectation that such a bill would ever reach a vote. In those days, women's suffrage in the United States was considered by males as a subject for humorous remarks or bitter condemnation, depending upon the temperament of the discussant. But they reckoned without Esther Morris' determination.

As soon as the election was over and Colonel William Bright had won, Mrs. Morris took her campaign to Betty Bright. The new legislator's wife was an intelligent woman, and she put up a convincing case for women's suffrage. Her husband has been quoted as saying before going down to Cheyenne for the convening of the legislature: "Betty, it's a shame that I should be a member of the Legislature and make laws for such a woman as you. You are a great deal better than I am; you know a great deal more and you would make a better member of the Assembly than I. I have made up my mind that I will do everything in my power to give you the ballot."[1]

On October 1, 1869, the Wyoming territorial legislature assembled for the first time. It was a body composed entirely of Democrats but with a Republican holding the office of governor and possessing the power of veto. A few days later, William Bright was elected president of the Senate, a position of authority that readily enabled him to sound out opinions of the men who composed the two houses of the legislature. Bright brought up the idea of a women's suffrage bill, arguing that it would give the Democrats a chance to show the Republicans they were a more advanced party, and that it also would advertise Wyoming Territory as nothing else could. None of his fellow members seemed to consider the bill seriously, but only a few spoke out in opposition. Undoubtedly some of those in favor foresaw an opportunity to embarrass the Republican governor, John Campbell, who would be placed in the position of having to veto it.

Bright drew up his bill, "An Act to Grant to the Women of Wyoming Territory the Right of Suffrage and to Hold Office," and introduced it November 9, 1869. The text was brief and to the point:

Be it enacted by the Council and the House of Representatives of the Territory of Wyoming:

Sec. 1. That every woman of the age of eighteen years, residing in this Territory, may, at every election to be holden under the laws thereof, cast her vote. And her rights to the elective franchise and to hold office shall be the same under the elective laws of the territory, as those of electors.

Sec. 2. This act shall take effect and be in force from and after its passage.

A vote was taken, and the result startled all Wyoming—six in favor, two opposed, one absent.

The bill now went to the House, and as the news spread about the Territory males and females alike wondered if Colonel Bright's "Female Suffrage Act" was not some sort of huge practical joke. But Esther Morris and a number of other women saw it as a golden opportunity; they wrote letters and made personal calls upon members of the legislature and the Governor. Sensing a drift in the winds of public opinion, Cheyenne's two newspapers came out heartily in support of the bill.

Bill Nye of the *Laramie Boomerang*, however, quoted a mythical railroad man's remarks on the proposed law: "Gentlemen, this is a pretty important move. It's a kind of a wild train on a single track, and we've got to keep our eye peeled or we'll get into the ditch. It's a new conductor making his first run. He don't know the stations yet, and he feels just as if there were a spotter in every coach besides. Female suffrage changes the management of the whole line, and may put the entire outfit in the hands of a receiver in two years. We can't tell when Wyoming Territory may be sidetracked with a lot of female conductors and superintendents and a posse of giddy girls at the brakes."[2]

When the bill finally was introduced in the House, a formidable opposition group was set to kill it with amendments. Ben Sheek, the principal opponent, moved that the age requirement be changed to thirty years in place of eighteen, on the theory that no woman would vote because none would admit to being thirty. When this failed to pass, he offered a substitute, requiring that the word "woman" be stricken out and the phrase "all colored women and squaws" be inserted. Another legislator proposed that a vote on the bill be postponed until July 4, 1870—a holiday and a year when the legislature ordinarily would not be in session.

Debate was acrimonious, but all amendments failed except one, a change in the age requirement from eighteen to twenty-one being accepted. The vote on the bill was six in favor, four opposed, one absent.

Now the fate of the "Female Suffrage Act" lay in the hands of Governor John Campbell. Several of the Democrats who had voted for the bill were certain the Republican Governor would veto it. But there was something in Campbell's background the legislators were unaware of; as a young man he had lived in Salem, Ohio, one of the first towns to hold a women's suffrage convention. A lover of oratory, he had attended the convention in order to hear Susan B. Anthony speak, and he had been impressed by her arguments in favor of the vote for women. Although caught now in a bitter cross-fire of opinion for and against the territorial suffrage bill, Campbell signed it, on December 10, 1869. And for the first time anywhere on earth, women had won the legal right to vote.

According to a prominent Wyoming male citizen, the most amazed inhabitants of the territory were the women themselves. "If a troop of angels had come down with flaming swords for their vindication," he recalled, "they would not have been much more astounded than they were when that bill became a law." [3] One Wyoming woman, however, probably was not so surprised. She was Esther Morris, whose tea party had set the miracle in motion, a lady who enjoyed a good fight and was accustomed to winning most of the time.

2

Even before they had an opportunity to vote in an election, a few Wyoming females found themselves involved in the second provision of the suffrage act—the right to hold office. During late 1869 and early 1870, thousands of idle railroad laborers collected in Laramie following completion of the Union Pacific, and lawlessness almost got out of hand. Male juries brought in so few convictions that when the grand jury was empaneled in March 1870, someone had the brilliant idea of recognizing the new Wyoming law and naming women to jury duty.

Six women and six men were summoned to sit on the grand jury, the first notice going to Eliza Stewart, Laramie schoolteacher. And for the first time in criminal court history, the presiding justice brought the assembly to order with the words: "Ladies and gentlemen of the Grand Jury."

The justice, John H. Howe, realizing the significance of the event, told the women that "the eyes of the world were upon them as pioneers serving in a movement that was to test the power of being able to protect and defend themselves from the evils of which women were victims . . . You shall not be driven by the sneers, jeers and insults of a laughing crowd from the temple of justice, as your sisters have from some of the medical colleges of the land. The strong hand of the law shall protect you . . . it will be a sorry day for any man who shall so far forget the courtesies due and paid by every American gentleman to every American lady as to even by act of word endeavor to deter you from the exercise of those rights with which the law has invested you."

As soon as news reached the eastern states that a female grand jury had been empaneled in wild Wyoming, a number of illustrated weeklies dispatched reporters, photographers, and artists to record this phenomenal event. Asked to sit for photographs, the women jurors refused, and when they discovered newspaper artists in the courtroom sketching their portraits, they donned heavy veils. The artists resorted to caricature, as in the case of Esther Morris when she was justice of the peace. Some eastern publications printed illustrations showing the women holding babies in their laps while doing jury service, captioned with such couplets as:

> Baby, baby, don't get in a fury;
> Your mamma's gone to sit on the jury.[4]

There were many sly jokes made about locking the two sexes up in one room until they could reach decisions on cases, but the sheriff solved the problem by locking the women in one room with a female bailiff on the door, the men in another room with a male bailiff.

This first mixed grand jury was in session for three weeks, hearing bills brought for consideration for murder cases, cattle and horse stealing, and illegal branding. The women took their duties seriously, indicting almost all the businessmen in Laramie for keeping their places open on Sunday contrary to law. Even Judge Howe was embarrassed. If he convicted all, practically every influential businessman in town would be in jail. He solved that dilemma by paroling the gentlemen on their individual written promises to keep the law thereafter.

3

The first election in which Wyoming's women voted was held September 6, 1870. Early on the morning of that historic day, Louisa Ann Swain, age seventy, of Laramie, Wyoming, fastened a fresh clean apron over her housedress and walked to the polls. She was carrying an empty pail for yeast to be purchased at a bakeshop on her return home. Louisa Swain was the first woman in the world to cast a vote in a public election.

Over in Cheyenne, the *Daily Leader* reported in its evening edition: "At noon today the election was progressing quietly in this city. Many ladies have voted and without molestation or interference . . . The first lady voting in Cheyenne was Mrs. Howe, the wife of the U. S. Marshal. Hers was a straight Republican ticket." [5]

Margaret Thomson Hunter, a Scotch-born housewife, said that on that first election day her neighbor, a Mr. Hellman, stopped by and asked her to go and vote for him. "I was busy making pies and hadn't intended voting, but after all Mr. Hellman was a neighbor, and also a very good friend of my husband's. So I pushed my pies aside, removed my apron, and tidied myself up a bit. Then I got into the buggy with Mr. Hellman and he drove me to the polls. Well, I voted and as we turned to leave we came face to face with my husband. When I explained to him that I had just voted for Mr. Hellman, I thought he would have a fit. You see, my husband was a staunch Democrat, and one of the leaders in his party, and there I had just voted for a Republican. He was never so humiliated in all his life, he told me. Then I said he should have explained those things to me if they were so important, for he knew I had never done any voting in Scotland." [6]

Bill Nye's account of the first election in Laramie was favorable: "No rum was sold, women rode to the polls in carriages furnished by the two parties, and every man was straining himself to be a gentleman because there were votes at stake." [7]

4

Late in the following year, 1871, the women's suffrage law ran into rough weather, mainly because the Democrats lost several seats in the legislative elections. The Democrats blamed these defeats on the very voters they had enfranchised in 1869—the ungrateful women.

Legislators Ben Sheek, C. K. Nuckolls, and W. R. Steele— all Democrats—opened fiery attacks upon the female suffrage law, and a bill was introduced to repeal it. "I think women were made to obey," declared Nuckolls. "They generally promise to obey, at any rate, and I think you had better abolish this female suffrage act or get up a new marriage ceremony to fit it."

His colleague, W. R. Steele, made a strong seconding speech, which has been preserved in this recording: "Women got so degraded as to go to the polls and vote and ask other women to go to the polls. This woman suffrage business will sap the foundations of society. Woman can't engage in politics without losin' her virtue. No woman ain't got no right to sit on a jury, nohow, unless she is a man and every lawyer knows it. They watch the face of the judge too much when the lawyer is addressin' 'em. I don't believe she's fit for it, nohow. If those hev it tuck from 'em now can at least prevent any more of them from gitten it, and thus save the unborn babe and the girl of sixteen." [8]

Although Democrats still controlled the legislature, the pro-suffrage members could not stem the opposition tide. The repeal bill passed both houses and went to Governor Campbell. Campbell vetoed it immediately, and thus a Republican saved a law that was created originally by Democrats and then was repudiated by them. The score was even, and both parties thenceforth could claim credit for enfranchising the female voters of Wyoming.

Again, some eighteen years later, the women's suffrage law was thrust suddenly into a state of jeopardy. In 1889, when Wyoming applied for statehood, opposition developed in the U. S. House of Representatives because of the suffrage article in the territory's constitution. James Carey, who was in Washington, D. C., representing Wyoming's case for statehood, became concerned over the mounting attack, and he telegraphed back to Cheyenne for instructions. Local newspapers published a report of the situation, and rumors spread that Wyoming would not be admitted to the Union as a state unless the suffrage law was abolished. A group of Cheyenne women telegraphed Carey: DROP US IF YOU MUST. WE CAN TRUST THE MEN OF WYOMING TO ENFRANCHISE US AFTER OUR TERRITORY BECOMES A STATE. But the legislature meanwhile had also sent a telegram to the Washington delegate: WE MAY STAY OUT OF THE UNION A HUNDRED YEARS, BUT WE WILL COME IN WITH OUR WOMEN.

Wyoming's bill of admission to statehood barely squeezed through the House committee and then was passed into law by the narrow margins of 139 to 127 in the House, 29 to 18 in the Senate.

From that time forward few male politicians in Wyoming were so bold or so foolish as to make public statements against female suffrage. "It has been weighed and not found wanting," the new state's Chief Justice declared. "It has made our elections quiet and orderly. No rudeness, brawling or disorder appears or would be tolerated at the polling booths. There is no more difficulty or indelicacy in depositing a ballot in the urn than in dropping a letter in the postoffice." [9]

When a Boston newspaper ran a story on the new state, the editor included an interview with "a gentleman from Wyoming" traveling in the East. At that safe distance from Wyoming, the reckless male uttered some disparaging remarks about women's suffrage, not suspecting that he would be quoted in the Cheyenne press a short time later. The mayor of Cheyenne promptly wired the Boston newspaper that the "prominent gentleman was a horse thief convicted by a jury half of whom were women," and that his remarks therefore were biased.

Thus defended by their males, Wyoming's women peacefully cast their ballots for several years, then audaciously began running for office. In 1910, Mary G. Bellamy won the distinction of being the first woman elected to a state legislature. Seven years later, the all-male United States Congress was startled to find a woman in its membership for the first time in history—Jeanette Rankin, Representative from Montana. And on January 5, 1925, the first female state governor in the nation, Nellie Taylor Ross, was installed at Cheyenne.

Because Wyoming was the first place—and for a long time the only place—in the world where women could vote, professional suffragettes of the late nineteenth century journeyed there like Moslems to Mecca. Susan B. Anthony, Dr. Mary Walker, Ann Eliza Young, and Sarah Lippincott were among those making pilgrimages. Mrs. Lippincott, who wrote under the pseudonym Grace Greenwood, was sadly disappointed in Cheyenne of the 1870's. "As the capital of the Territory that has taken the first bold practical step in the matter of woman's civil rights, the place commends itself to my heart, certainly I should rejoice to find it a very Eden, a vale of Cashmere,— which it isn't." [10]

Outside of Wyoming, the fine-mannered eastern suffragettes had a hard time of it in the West. Travel conditions were arduous; the suffragettes found few people of either sex willing to listen to them and often met with active opposition. When Susan B. Anthony and Anna Shaw were making an early western tour, they arrived in a small Dakota town one Sunday morning to discover that the local clergymen had persuaded all the women of the town to stay away from their suffrage meeting. The reason given for the ban was that the meeting was scheduled to be held in a church on a Sabbath day. The two women immediately rented the local theater, roused a printer out of bed, and hired him to run off some handbills which they distributed personally to each dwelling in town. "We had a glorious meeting," said Anna Shaw. "Both Miss Anthony and I were in excellent fighting trim."

Another time, Miss Shaw was snowbound in a western train, the only woman among a crowd of cowboys and cattlemen. "They were an odoriferous lot," she recalled, "who smoked diligently, and played cards without ceasing, but in deference to my presence they swore only mildly, and under their breath. At last they wearied of their game, and one of them rose, and came to me. 'I heard you lecture the other night,' he said awkwardly, 'and I've bin tellin' the fellers about it. We'd like to have a lecture now.'"

Anna Shaw consented to say a few words, and the men went through the snowbound train to bring in the remaining passengers. The meeting began with the singing of a Moody and Sankey hymn, followed by "Where Is My Wandering Boy Tonight?" in which all joined with special zest. Then Anna Shaw delivered one of her lectures on women's suffrage. The men listened politely, and after the meeting ended they made the speaker a bed by taking the bottoms out of two seats, arranging them crosswise, and donating their overcoats for bedding. Anna Shaw crept in between the overcoats and slept peacefully until she was aroused the next morning by the rumble of a snowplow.[11]

Much as it had been a skirmishing ground in the early struggles over Negro slavery, Kansas became a western battlefield in the fight for women's suffrage. Even before the Civil War, advocates of women's rights in Kansas had linked their cause with that of slaves and unenfranchised free Negroes. Kansas diarists of the 1850's indicate that local debating societies frequently argued the question, "Resolved that Women Should Execute the Election Franchise." The negative side usually won.

Clarina Nichols was the most articulate of Kansas' pioneer lecturers on women's rights. In 1859, the Fort Scott *Democrat* reported she had delivered a fiery speech in the local hospital. "Of course the room was crowded, and although the weather was very warm, there was a large number of ladies in attendance. She said if the men didn't give them their rights, they would revolt—wouldn't marry. What a row that would make. They wanted to vote but didn't care about holding office if the men only behaved themselves. Haven't heard of any converts in this region." [12]

When Kansas became a state in 1861, Clarina Nichols fought so hard for women's suffrage that the lawmakers saw fit to compromise and allow Kansas women the small privilege of voting in district school elections. That is why some Kansans claim that their women were voting eight years before the women of Wyoming won that right.

In 1867, professional suffragettes decided the time was ripe to take more ground in Kansas. They invaded the state in force, Elizabeth Stanton, Lucy Stone, Olympia Brown, and Susan B. Anthony combining their efforts for a grand tour. "We had a low, easy carriage, drawn by two mules," said Elizabeth Stanton, "in which we stored about a bushel of tracts, two valises, a pail for watering the mules, a basket of apples, crackers, and other such refreshments as we could purchase on the way. Some things were suspended underneath the carriage, some packed on behind, and some under the seat and at our feet . . . We spoke in log cabins, in depots, unfinished schoolhouses, churches, hotels, barns, and in the open air." [13]

The *Topeka Weekly Leader's* editor wrote most irreverently of this tour and its participants. Female suffrage, he declared, was "a pernicious doctrine." He described Elizabeth Stanton as "a buxom gray haired matron of about fifty" whose speech "was elegant and eloquent—everything but convincing." Susan B. Anthony "seemed only desirous to sell some pamphlet speeches of Parker Pillsbury and other ancient ladies, at the small price of twenty-five cents each. As preliminary thereto, however, she entered into a discursory argument of the right of suffrage for females. She insisted that as men and women were of the same physical formation (with a slight variation), their political rights were the same." [14]

Through the next three decades the suffrage war raged in Kansas, but it was all to no avail. Kansas women did not win the franchise until 1912.

Other western women were victorious, however, long before that date. The women of Colorado, Idaho, and Utah were voting before 1900; indeed, the first dozen states to pass women's suffrage acts were all western states, far to the west of the Mississippi River. The pioneers in petticoats were casting off their shackles in preparation for a final taming of the masculine Wild West.

Casting Off the Shackles

1

IN other ways than winning the right to vote, western
women were casting off their shackles, or were just quietly
leaving them behind in the East when they crossed the Mississippi River. Many were forced by harsh circumstances into
earning their own livings as best they could, ofttimes working
side by side with men at men's work. As they achieved independence of the male, they flaunted their new-found freedom
like a banner. Sometimes their released emotions erupted into
acts of violence unheard of in the old codes of gentle femininity. A few turned against all the symbols of masculinity; if
the male could not be destroyed, then he must be made
powerless, tamed into domesticity.

At first only a handful of women realized that laws and
customs no longer barred them from doing as they pleased.
But the others caught on fairly rapidly, bursting loose from
centuries of law and order, starting a revolution which is still
spreading round the world. Politics, business, the professions,
outlawry—nothing was safe from female invasion in the American West.

Because the work was only an extension of keeping house,
women in great numbers went into the business of operating

boardinghouses and hotels. It was possible for a woman with a stake of only a few dollars to open a boardinghouse in a western boom town and become independent within a year. Cooking and baking were other remunerative occupations for females in predominantly male communities. In 1852, a Boston newspaper printed a letter from a woman in California who reported that in less than a year she had baked and sold $18,000 worth of pies, about one third of which was clear profit. "I dragged my own wood off the mountains and chopped it, and I have never had so much as a child to take a step for me in this country. $11,000 I baked in one little iron skillet, a considerable portion by a campfire, without the shelter of a tree from the broiling sun. But now I have a good many 'Robinson Crusoe' comforts about me. I bake about 1,200 pies per month and clear $200. I intend to leave off work the coming spring and give my business into the hands of my sister-in-law. Not that I am rich, but I need little, and have none to toil for but myself." [1]

In Nevada City, California, during this period, a Mrs. Phelps engaged in a similar business. She had brought a stove across the plains, and began making dried apple pies, selling them at a dollar each. "She drove a wonderful trade, especially on Sundays when the miners came to town, they having played euchre every evening of the week to determine who should pay for the pies when they went to the 'city.' She often found it impossible to supply the demand on that day, notwithstanding her efforts in anticipation of increasing numbers. She soon increased her facilities for business by getting another stove and purchasing a couple of bright-looking cows, which made her place look home-like and were a great attraction. There was such a demand for milk that it readily sold at a dollar a pint, and one-half water at that. I have often seen her place literally thronged with miners waiting for her pies to come out of the oven, and as soon out, devoured." [2]

Even in the wilds of Wyoming, a Mrs. Washington earned ready cash by selling home-cooked meals to soldiers grown weary of Army rations. She lived in a cabin a few yards outside Fort Phil Kearney, and on paydays her home was thronged with hungry soldiers.

During the 1880's a silk-culture movement spread across the West, women everywhere being drawn into it with great hopes of earning enormous fortunes. In California, Mrs. J. H. Hittell organized the Woman's Silk Culture Association, and went about the countryside preaching silk culture with all the optimism of a seller of gold-mining stocks. "One acre planted in mulberry trees will yield 50,000 pounds of leaves, enough to feed one million worms. From these silkworms will come 400 pounds of raw silk. At $7.50 per pound this would equal $3,000; even with accidents and diseases one could expect $2,000 an acre." [3] It was no wonder that silk culture attracted wide interest among women.

Brigham Young was taken in by the silk-culture fad, believing it would be a profitable occupation for Mormon women. He assigned one of his wives to put the scheme into operation, but nothing much ever came of it. Kansas women also were excited for a time over the speculative possibilities of cultivating silk cocoons for sale to others, but the only one who appears to have earned any money at all from the silkgrowing mania was Mary Davidson of Junction City. She wrote a manual for beginners in silk culture and reaped a tidy little sum from its sale.

It took imagination for any emigrant to earn expenses while en route to the West, but a Missouri woman showed that it could be done if one did not mind sharing the covered wagon with a flock of hens. She sold new-laid eggs at two dollars a dozen all the way to California, and arrived there with liquid capital to spare.

Imagination was also required to see that gold could be

found above the ground in California as well as below it. The first commercially produced raisins were packed by some Fresno County women in 1878, and a few years later the first fresh table grapes were shipped east from California by a woman, Minna E. Sherman, who just wanted to prove that it could be done. She also made a profit on the experiment.

Western women soon ventured into fields of activity that males had always thought were secure from weak-muscled females. They built claim shacks on homesteads, plowed, raised crops, broke horses, and drove cattle.

Mary Rosencrance of Washington Territory told of how she hated to see the settlers come in and end the pleasures of roundup times. "I rode in many roundups, but the longest one was when I rode with five hundred cowboys for that last roundup when the Big Bend was thrown open to settlement. Over two thousand head of horses carried our brand, the Bar-X. We were four or five months in the saddle . . . we had to quit raising stock when the settlers came and didn't know how to do anything else." [4]

Mary Meagher, also of Washington Territory, owned one of the largest ranches on the Pacific slope. Interviewed by a Cheyenne newspaperman in 1885, she was described as a tall, majestic woman about thirty years old who liked to play poker; she traveled to markets by train with her cattle, riding in the caboose with ten cowboys. When the reporter asked her how she kept the cowboys within bounds, she replied: "Oh, I suppose it's because they admire pluck. If a man talked to some of them as I have he would have been killed long ago." [5]

A few women earned their livelihoods in transportation activities—notably Arizona Mary, who drove a sixteen-yoke ox team, hauling supplies in the Southwest and accumulating a sizable fortune. And of course there was Charlie Pankhurst, whose name was really not Charlie but something more fem-

inine. Always dressed as a man, Miss Pankhurst drove a stagecoach across some of the West's most dangerous terrain for
twenty years, and nobody knew she was a woman until the
day she died in 1879.

There were also professional female athletes in the West—
baseball players—although one newspaper editor reporting
an exhibition made snide remarks about the girls' skill. He
was impressed only by their advertising poster, depicting a
young woman in a short dress preparing to strike at a ball
which had already passed behind her. After the game the
editor wrote: "The reason they can't play ball is, to use a
stereotyped expression, 'They ain't built that way.'" But he
admitted "they stacked up in great style in their cute uniforms." [6]

2

Maybe they weren't "built that way," but there were times
when women showed more endurance than men under the
worst of conditions in the West. California's first Governor,
Peter Burnett, admitted that the experiences of the Donner
party indicated that women's mental and physical stamina
seemed to be superior to that of men. "I expressed my surprise," he wrote, "that all the women escaped, while eight out
of the ten men perished, saying that I supposed it was owing
to the fact that the men, especially at the beginning of the
journey had performed most of the labor. They said that, at
the start, the men may have performed a little more labor
than the women; but, taken altogether, the women performed
more than the men. After the men had become too weak to
carry the gun, it was carried by the women." [7]

Of all western women none was more durable than Martha
Connarray, better known by her legendary sobriquet, Calamity Jane. There are so many tall tales about Calamity that it
is virtually impossible to differentiate fact from folklore, yet

through them all she persists as the epitome of the free western female who has declared her independence from the male
sex.

A story told by cowboy Teddy Blue reveals this stubborn
streak of self-reliance that was typical of the "new" frontier
female. Blue met Calamity at a stage stop out of Miles City;
he was temporarily without funds and borrowed fifty cents
from her to buy a meal. "I thanked her for the fifty cents and
said: 'Some day I'll pay you.' And she said: 'I don't give a
damn if you never pay me.'"

Not until some years later did Teddy Blue meet Calamity
again, in Gilt Edge, Montana. "I walked up to her and said
'Don't you know me?' and gave her the fifty cents. She recognized me then and said: 'I told you, Blue, that I didn't give
a damn if you never paid me,' and we went and drank it
up." [8]

This independent spirit among western women revealed
itself in other ways. "Guess my husband's got to look after
me, and make himself agreeable to me, if he can," a pretty
young wife remarked to a visiting Englishman, William Dixon,
in 1875. And she added: "If he don't, there's plenty will." This
was shocking stuff to a mid-Victorian Briton, and he offered
the opinion that the cheap, easily obtained divorces in the
West were the result of women's being allowed too much freedom. "The application for divorces mostly comes from the
woman's side, and any allegation is enough to satisfy her
judge." [9]

On the other hand, a young married woman, after looking
over the males in her part of the plains country, had nothing
good to say for any of them, cataloging the lot as follows:
"Broken-down merchants, absconding debtors, escaped crim-
inals, young scamps who dodged a suit for breach of promise
of marriage, scoundrels who avoided a prosecution for something worse, and married men who wished to live apart from

their wives, or with some other man's wife, or who wanted wives by the score." [10]

3

All through contemporary records of early western travel and settlement, one may find signs of a burgeoning female rebellion, but if the males noted the warnings they were either indifferent or helpless to do anything about them. An 1857 account tells the story of a woman who "took a nursing babe, eight months old, from her bosom, and left it with two other children, almost infants, to cross the plains in search of gold." [11]

Another traveler of 1848 reported an incident of a stubborn woman who refused to journey any farther along the trail with her husband. "The woman got mad and would not budge, nor let the children go. Her husband had his cattle hitched on for three hours and coaxing her to go, but she would not stir." Three male members of the wagon company went to the man's assistance. "They each took a young one and crammed them in the wagon and her husband drove off and left her sitting." After a while the woman decided to follow her husband, and taking short cuts down the curving trail, caught up with him. "She set one of his wagons on fire, which was loaded with store goods. The cover burnt off and some valuable articles. He saw the flames and put it out, and then mustered spunk enough to give her a good flogging." [12]

Typical of the unrestrained frontier female was Pamela Mann of Texas, who first came to public notice by defying Sam Houston and getting away with it. Pamela loaned Houston a yoke of oxen for use in his Texan army on the promise they would be returned by a certain time. When they were not returned, she armed herself with a pair of pistols and a long knife and went after them. She rode up to Houston and

declared: "General, you told me a damn lie. I want my oxen."
At the time, Houston's cannon were bogged down in a prairie
wallow, and the General pointed out that he could not move
them without her oxen. "I don't care a damn for your
cannon," replied Pamela, "I want my oxen."

"Madam, don't irritate me," Houston cried angrily.

"Irritate the devil. I am going to have my oxen." She drew
a pistol, rode up to her oxen, unhitched them, and drove them
off. This incident is known in Texas annals as Sam Houston's
Defeat.

After the battle of San Jacinto—a Houston victory—Pamela Mann moved to the town named for the General, and
earned her living by operating a hotel where she provided
"feminine companionship of a robust and none too virtuous
nature." Over a four-year period she was indicted for counter-
feiting, forgery, fornication, larceny, and assault with intent
to kill. She was condemned to death on the forgery charge,
but was given executive clemency by the President of the
Republic of Texas after he considered "the peculiar situation
of the accused, being a female, a mother, and a widow, and
an old settler of the country."

Pamela even managed to patch up her quarrel with Sam
Houston, and when her son was married Houston showed up
to act as best man. Another one of her friends was a Methodist minister, and his description of Pamela Mann is appli-
cable to all the violent women of her time and place: "The
product of life in a new country, with rude surroundings, in
the absence of law and order and the restraints of refined society—a woman, whom, perhaps, under happier environ-
ments, might have proven an honor to her sex, and left her
impress for good upon the sphere in which she moved—a
widow and forced, perhaps from the injustice of others to
step forward in her own defense, and meet lawless men on

their own grounds; it was but natural that she should have developed the rude and free-spoken temper of the times and people among whom she lived." [18]

A different variety of female on the loose was Laura D. Fair, who left a trail of dead and live husbands behind her as she made her way about the West. Adultery for short periods she did not mind, but over the long pull she insisted upon matrimony. When Alexander Crittenden refused to marry her, Laura slipped a Sharps pistol in her handbag, donned a heavy veil, and followed Crittenden, his wife and his daughter aboard a San Francisco ferryboat. At the proper dramatic moment, Laura confronted her lover, shouted "You have ruined me!" and shot him to death.

Laura Fair doubtless expected to be freed in court. All her life in the West she had been idolized merely because she was one of the petticoated few; during the 1850's and 1860's females had shot males down and escaped scot free. But Laura waited until 1870 to commit her murder, and the law insisted upon a lengthy trial.

Out of this trial came the story of an incorrigible western woman, symbolic of a certain class of her sex—unshackled but irresponsible. At sixteen she was married to her first husband, who died mysteriously a year later. Next she became the wife of Thomas Grayson, who in six months' time was coming home drunk every night. "He would shoot over the head of my bed, sir, with a pistol," Laura testified. "Then he would go out and shoot the poultry in the yard, fifty at a time, one after the other." Why he did this Laura did not explain. She divorced Grayson, and then in 1855 set her sights on a prominent California lawyer, Colonel William D. Fair. Fair lived with Laura for five years, then committed suicide because of her unchastity. In 1863 Laura was in Virginia City, operating a boardinghouse, and it was there that she became the mistress of Alexander Crittenden.

At the street level of her boardinghouse was a novelty store, and on July 4 the store owner, a man named Dale, mounted a huge United States flag above her porch. As she was Mississippi-born, Laura objected to the flag; the Civil War was in progress and she was pro-Confederate. She ordered a young man employed as a clerk in her boardinghouse to go out and cut the flag halyards. The clerk refused to do so. "I took a pocketknife," Laura testified during her murder trial, "and went out and cut the flag down. I believe in cutting it I also cut his [Dale's] hand a little, and he had me arrested, but the jury found him guilty of malicious persecution and fined him $75." Alexander Crittenden was her lawyer in the case, and the jury did not even leave their seats to acquit her. From such incidents as this, Laura Fair came to believe that a woman could do as she pleased in the West.

Even while she was still Crittenden's mistress, she married another man, Jesse Snyder, then within a month divorced him on a trumped-up charge of adultery.

But the murder of Alexander Crittenden in 1870 was almost her undoing. Crittenden came from a prominent Kentucky family and was a power in California, and public opinion was against Laura because she had been so unladylike as to shoot her man while he was actually in the presence of his own legal wife. The prosecuting attorney was determined to win the case. He claimed he could bring in a thousand witnesses against Laura Fair's chastity, and he did parade a large number of reticent males through the courtroom.

Throughout the trial, Laura appeared unworried. Crowds of women packed the spectators' benches, applauding her testimony, and whenever the judge ruled these rowdy partisans in contempt, Laura would pay their fines.

At last the lengthy testimony ended, the jury filed out, and when they brought in their verdict Laura Fair and thousands of women throughout the West received the surprise of their lives. The jury found her guilty of murder in the first degree.[14]

The judge's sentence, however, failed to hold. Soon afterward, she was granted a new trial and was acquitted on grounds of emotional insanity. A visitor to California in 1875 reported that Laura Fair was a local heroine. "She lives in style, gives balls, and speculates in stock. Few ladies are so often named at dinner-tables, and the public journals note her doings as the movements of a duchess might be noted in Mayfair." [15]

4

Wars are often blamed for rapid changes in moral and social standards, and it would be easy to theorize that the spectacular acts of outlawry committed by so many border-state women were rooted in the Civil War. Certainly most of the bandit queens and petticoat terrors had their origins in the areas of conflicting loyalties—from Kentucky to "bleeding Kansas"—where bitter guerilla strife involved women and children as well as men.

Official records of the war in the West show active participation by numerous women, especially on the part of those who supported the Confederacy. An exchange of correspondence between General John McNeil of the Missouri State Militia and Provost Marshal W. R. Strachan in December 1862 is indicative. Wrote General McNeil: "The active disloyalty of these two women [Misses Lizzie Powell and Maggie Creath] is notorious, and their beauty, talents and superior education have made many a man a bushwhacker who except for that influence would have been an honest man. They are even openly and persistently disloyal. I regard them each of sufficient importance to either justify a strict surveillance or banishment from the state."

Provost Marshal Strachan replied: "Evidence sent to this

office from Doctor Hueston and several others established that
these young ladies had taken a carriage, driven to Hannibal,
and brought out under the protection of the petticoat flag a
quantity of gun caps, some 50,000, and other essentials to
the guerillas. Miss Creath made quite a sensation in Monroe
County traveling with one Clay Price, a noted captain of
guerillas, dressed in rebel colors and a brace of rebel pistols
ornamenting her taper waist. Their influence, being young
ladies of large talking propensities, was particularly pernicious, they openly declaring that they acknowledge the authority of no Government but that of 'Jeff Davis, the noblest
and wisest man that ever graced a presidential chair.' " [16]

At the close of the war, Federal authorities refused to recognize guerilla bands as official Confederate units. Followers
of such men as William Clarke Quantrill and William
(Bloody Bill) Anderson were posted as outlaws and were not
permitted to surrender as soldiers of a defeated army. Many
of them took to the hills of the border country, drifting into
Indian Territory and down into Texas.

In their ranks were women, some of whom became notorious for one reason or another. Ann Walker, alias Nancy
Slaughter, was Quantrill's raiding mate, though she achieved
more renown for her nymphomaniacal tendencies than for her
freebooting accomplishments. Myra Belle Shirley, later known
as Belle Starr, was the daughter of aristocratic Virginians
settled in Missouri. Myra Belle's brother was killed by Yan-
kees while riding with Jim Lane's Red Leg bushwhackers,
and soon afterward she became a fiery teen-age Rebel. In
1863, conditions became so bad that the Shirleys fled to
Texas, and it was there, immediately following the war, that
she became acquainted with some of Quantrill's former raid-
ers, who were still carrying on the war by robbing banks and
railroad trains and pocketing the money.

After being seduced by Cole Younger, Belle turned to a life

of crime, exchanging one male partner for another through a long line of husbands and paramours that included Jim Reed, Blue Duck, Sam Starr, John Middleton and Jim July—all outlaws. It was while she was married to Sam Starr that she was arrested and received most of her publicity as Belle Starr. The six-month sentence she received on that occasion was the only conviction any court was able to return against her, although she was involved in enough robbings and holdups to fill a large catalog. Only a bullet could stop Belle Starr's blazing career, and that was how she ended—shot in the back, one day in 1889.

Perhaps the Civil War did accentuate the tendency toward violence among certain western women, but it was only one causative force in a much larger revolution. A long roster of female outlaws could be compiled—none of them concerned one way or the other in the War Between the States. Cattle Kate, Rose of the Cimarron, Cattle Annie, Little Britches, Genie Carter, Pearl Hart—all had their various reasons for becoming unshackled outlaws, the common one being that they lost their hearts to some romantic reprobate, and therefore could lay the blame—as their sisters had done for centuries—upon the unregenerate male sex.

5

One of the anomalies of early western society was the marked contrast in the ratio of women to men in Mormon Utah as compared with other parts of the West. To some of the woman-hungry Gentile males who brushed up against the edges of Brigham Young's Kingdom of the Saints, it must have seemed that the Mormons had cornered the market in females. In Utah, a man could have as many wives as he could afford, while in other parts of the West a woman could have as many men as she chose, restricted only by her individual moral code.

A good case for monogamy could be constructed from the personal records of that time. In the predominantly male areas, the men were unhappy under what amounted to a polyandrous system; and in the Mormon country the women were unhappy with the polygynous system.

Anywhere else but in the Wild West, Mormon women probably never would have considered active resistance against plural marriage—no matter how much they disliked it—but the virus of rebellion was in the western air and spread even into this most male-dominated sector.

A number of mutinous women published lurid revelations of life in the Mormon stronghold, often with indifferent regard for veracity. Readers outside the Kingdom were eager for confidential reports on the legendary Saints, and the rebellious women no doubt found both satisfaction and profit in supplying the demand.

Among the rebels who became well known for their pungent writings and lectures were Fanny Stenhouse and Ann Eliza Young, the latter one of Brigham's wives. Both women were tart-tongued and probably would have been a trial to a husband under any system of marriage. They were also quite different in backgrounds and attitudes, yet their stories are representative of those who cast off the peculiar shackles that annoyed them.

Ann Eliza Webb was born into a devout Mormon family at Nauvoo, Illinois, and at the age of three became a member of one of the first migrations to Utah. Her father had several wives. "They did not like a polygamous life, and only endured it because they thought they must. They were not happy women—no women in polygamy are happy, however loudly they may claim to be—and they made no pretense of being. Neither did they quarrel with each other or complain of one another to their husband."

When she was eighteen, Brigham Young took an interest

in Ann Eliza Webb and invited her to become a member of his Salt Lake City theatrical company and to take up residence at the Lion House with the Mormon leader's already enormous family. The Lion House was a long three-storied house with a stone lion crouching over the front portico as a symbol of one of Brigham's titles, "the Lion of the Lord."

While Ann Eliza was training to become an actress she fell in love at first sight with an English convert, James D. Lee. "I surrendered at discretion," she said, "without attempting to remit the hold which the new fancy took on me." Eliza became Mrs. James Lee in 1863, but according to her story he turned out to be a ruffian and a cad. A month before her baby was born, Lee struck her in a fit of passion, and she "fell insensible before him."

With Brigham's help, Ann Eliza got a divorce from Lee in 1865 and went to live with her parents at South Cottonwood. Not long afterward Brigham paid the settlement a visit, being met at the outskirts by a company of cavalry and escorted into the village by a brass band and a procession of the entire population. After church services, he offered to walk Eliza to her home. "You are a very pretty woman," he told her, and after dinner proposed to make her his nineteenth wife. Eliza refused. Brigham, however, was not accustomed to being turned down, and he persisted in his suit until she finally consented.

But when the day of the wedding arrived, Eliza discovered the marriage was to be kept secret because—she said—Brigham was afraid to have his shrewish wife Amelia know he had taken another bride. He gave Eliza some "pretty dresses and a small sum of money," sent her back to her family for a time, then moved her to Salt Lake City into a small rented house. She complained the dwelling was furnished with crockery left over from a bakery, an old carpet discarded from the Lion House, some cheap pine furniture, and sheets for window curtains. As for the busy husband, "he called to see me at my new residence when he could find opportunity, which was not very often."

To earn spending money, Eliza began taking in boarders, most of them non-Mormons, and she said their presence gave her an opportunity to learn for the first time of the world outside. For reasons not clearly explained, she decided to renounce Mormonism. An examination of her celebrated book of revelations, *Life in Mormon Bondage*, indicates that it was Brigham Young she was renouncing, however, and not especially the religion she had been born into. Ann Eliza Young believed herself to be a woman scorned, a low nineteenth on the totem pole of a plural marriage.

On July 17, 1873, she sent her furniture to an auction room, sold it, and moved into a non-Mormon hotel in Salt Lake City. Within a few hours the news spread around the town, and then out into the nation. In an era when any news from polygynous Utah was sensational copy, the fact that one of Brigham Young's wives had left him was better than a nine-day wonder.

"Reporters called on me," said the astonished Eliza, "seeking interviews for the California, Chicago, and New York papers. I had gone to bed a poor, defenceless outraged woman . . . I arose to find that my name had gone the length and breadth of the country and that I was everywhere known as Brigham Young's rebellious wife." Two weeks later, she sued Brigham for divorce, charging neglect and non-support. "I think no one was more astonished than the Prophet himself," she wrote. She was offered $15,000 and her freedom if she would drop the suit, but demanded $200,000. Brigham countered by denying that he was legally married to her, having never been divorced from his first wife. Not until April 1877 was the case ended; the marriage was declared null and void, Brigham paying the court costs but no alimony.

Ann Eliza, meanwhile, had become famous, receiving invitations by the hundreds to lecture around the country. "I did not dare to leave Salt Lake City by rail," she said, and with her flair for dramatics she left her hotel by the back door, walked to a waiting carriage, and drove out of the city much like Marie Antoinette fleeing Paris during the French Revolution. She was sure she was being watched and pursued all the way to Uintah, where she boarded a train for Denver. There, on December 5, she delivered her first lecture and received a rousing send-off from a crowded house of sensation seekers.

As she toured the country, some newspapers began printing what she described as untrue and scandalous articles about her, and she blamed these on Brigham Young's machinations; though she must have been aware that in that day editors often invented salacious stories about prominent persons just to sell their papers. After lecturing in Boston, New York, and Washington, she became daring enough to return to Salt Lake City for a public appearance in August 1874. Brigham did not attend, but he sent all his daughters and daughters-in-law. They sat in the front seats, and throughout the lecture amused themselves by making faces at Ann Eliza.[17]

Unlike Ann Eliza Young, Fanny Stenhouse was born outside the church, in England, where she and her husband, Thomas Stenhouse, were converted to Mormonism and invited to journey to the Promised Land of Utah. En route across America, Mrs. Stenhouse endured the hardships of one of the late handcart emigration parties. Upon her arrival, Salt Lake City looked to her like a beautiful garden, "another Eden in the midst of a desert valley," and her later disillusionments were of the mildest until she suddenly learned one day that her husband, Thomas, was planning to take a second wife.

"The idea that some day another wife would be added to

our household was ever present in my mind, but somehow, when the fact was placed before me in so many unmistakable words, my heart sank within me, and I shrank from the realization that *our* home was at last to be desecrated by the foul presence of Polygamy."

As she explained it, her husband felt that it was his duty, a solemn obligation, to take more wives. When Thomas' first choice fell ill and died, Mrs. Stenhouse was only temporarily relieved; he soon began paying court to another. "Sometimes I shut myself up in my own room and tried to reason with myself; then I would kneel, and pray, and weep with passionate emotion; and again I would pace the floor, my heart overflowing with anger and indignation . . . I longed to die."

In accordance with the church ritual, Fanny had to be present when Thomas Stenhouse took his second wife. It was an ordeal for her. Brigham Young performed the ceremony, and then Thomas and his two wives returned home together. Fanny Stenhouse wrote later—after she withdrew from the church—of how on the way home she made a brave show of being indifferent to this new sharer of her husband's marriage bed. "But how I watched their looks and noticed every word! To me their tender tones were daggers, piercing my heart and filling me with a desire to revenge myself upon the father of my children."

The first night following the wedding she retired alone to her room, the thought of her husband bedding with another wife "a terrible anguish consuming me." After the three had lived together for about a year, Thomas Stenhouse built a separate house for the second wife, a great relief to Fanny, who admitted that "the sight of that other wife constantly before my eyes, sitting at my table, in the midst of my family, walking in the garden with my husband in the evening, or tête-à-tête with him in the parlor was more than I could bear."

Later, when Stenhouse took a third wife, the acute jealousy between the first two vanished almost completely. Ann Eliza Young corroborates this bit of polygynous psychology: "The hurt comes with the first plural wife; no suffering can ever exceed the pain she feels then." It was always the second wife that caused trouble; after that, added women in the household went almost unnoticed.

That is, unless one of them happened to be a strong-minded subversive such as Fanny Stenhouse or Ann Eliza Young.[18]

6

Early one morning in December 1900, a middle-aged woman dressed in a black alpaca dress, a poke bonnet, black cotton stockings, and heavy square-toed shoes, walked into the swanky barroom of the Hotel Carey in Wichita, Kansas. She stood there in the entrance, a six-foot, 180-pound female with broad shoulders and hips. Her thin lips were pursed under a flat round nose, her black piercing eyes were glaring furiously at the scene before her—a scattering of males imbibing at a luxurious curved bar of cherrywood.

Reflected in a huge mirror behind the bar was an enormous nude painting, "Cleopatra at the Bath," an original by artist John Noble. Not only was Cleopatra completely naked; so were her handmaidens, and the two huge eunuchs who fanned her were clad only in loincloths.

The large woman who had entered the barroom was Carry Nation, and she was armed with a cane, an iron rod, and several large stones. She turned suddenly toward the painting and hurled two stones at the naked Cleopatra, shattering the protective glass and ripping the canvas. Then she whirled around and smashed another stone into the $1500 mirror. Before the startled early-morning drinkers and the bartender could recover from their astonishment, she whipped out her cane and rod, drove the drinkers from the room, and smashed all the bottles and glassware upon the bar and sideboard.

At 8:30 A.M., Carry Nation was arrested, her weapons were seized, and she was transported bodily to the Wichita jail. As the cell door closed upon her, she shouted at her jailers: "You put me in here a cub, but I will go out a roaring lion and make all hell howl."

This was the incident that first brought Carry Nation of Kansas into the nation's headlines. Less than a month later she was out roaring like a lion and making all hell howl with the celebrated hatchet which became her trademark.

What were the origins of this woman and her destroying hatchet? It would be easy to conclude from contemporary records that Carry Nation sprang full-blown out of the frontier West, but actually she had been making hell howl for most of her adult life. Also, she had several predecessors. Beginning with the days of the California gold rush, a shrewd observer could have noted numerous signs and portents of Carry Nation's coming.

One of her forerunners was Sarah Pellet, who arrived in California in 1854 wearing a pair of brown bloomers. When asked by a fellow traveler how she expected to earn her living there, she replied that she would do so by delivering lectures on temperance. Soon after her arrival she stirred up a rumbullion in Weaverville by advocating a prohibitory liquor law. Mounted atop a pile of boxes in front of the Weaverville hotel, she stopped the town dead. "The saloons and stores were deserted. No dog fight ever drew together such a crowd." [19]

And Sarah Pellet knew how to draw poison from the opposition's fangs. She promised her male audience that if they would outlaw liquor she would go back to New England, recruit five thousand young girls and bring them back to California to become wives and mothers of teetotaler miners. Nothing came of her promise, however; the miners kept their saloons, and Sarah kept busy lecturing and collecting donations for the cause of temperance.

As early as 1856, temperance unions were developing in hard-drinking Kansas. In July of that year, the Topeka union, dominated by women, engaged in "liquor spilling" on such an extensive scale that Topeka was completely dry for twenty-four hours.[20]

Almost twenty years later, in the midst of Dodge City's trail-town glory, the editor of a local newspaper became alarmed over movements to close saloons in Kansas, and he warned his readers what to expect if the righteous females invaded Dodge. "The ladies form themselves into praying bands, and hold prayer meetings in the barrooms if allowed to do so, and if not, on the sidewalk outside. One band relieves another and the meeting is kept up until the saloon keeper is converted or his business ruined." [21]

A Briton traveling in the West during this period witnessed several of these performances. "Americans are fond of hymns," he declared, "and there are few American males who will not doff their caps and join in singing such pieces as 'Rock of Ages' and 'There Is a Fountain.'" After the hymn singing, he continued, the women would march away to the nearest church, followed by a crowd of repentant drinkers. Some blackhearted barkeepers retaliated by offering free drinks to any male who would join in chanting "jovial and indecent choruses to the hymns." [22]

Most of the tactics and techniques used by Carry Nation had been developed before she joined the battle. It was her violence and her hatchet that focused public attention upon her. Not only did she smash her way out of her personal shackles, she dedicated her life to evening the score with the hated male sex by smashing at his symbols of masculine domination.

In the early pages of her autobiography she reveals more than enough reasons for her later erratic behavior. "I shall not in this book speak much of my love affairs," she begins, "but they were, nevertheless, an important part of my life. I was a great lover." If these great loves were reciprocated, no prying journalist or latter-day biographer has been able to identify any of the other parties. If she ever had a mild flirtation with any male other than her two husbands—neither of whom she could tolerate—Carry Nation must have been the most secretive and discreet woman of modern times.

Born Carry Amelia Moore, she spent her adolescent years on the Missouri frontier. "I would go to the country dances and sometimes to balls. But my native modesty prevented me from ever dancing a round dance with a gentleman. I can not think this hugging school compatible with a true woman."

In the autumn of 1865 when Carry was nineteen, a young physician, Dr. Charles Gloyd, came to board with her family. "I liked him and stood in awe of him because of his superior education, never thinking that he loved me." When Dr. Gloyd surprised Carry one evening by suddenly kissing her, she threw up her hands and cried: "I am ruined! I am ruined!"

But Carry arranged a secret communication system between herself and the young doctor. Using a volume of Shakespeare on the living room table as a post office, they exchanged passionate notes. Two years later they were married. Gloyd was half-drunk on his wedding day, no doubt for some secret reasons of his own. "My mother warned me that the doctor was addicted to drink, but I had no idea of the curse of rum . . . I did not find Dr. Gloyd the lover I expected. He was kind but seemed to want to be away from me; used to sit and read, when I was so hungry for his caresses and love."

As her marriage collapsed, Carry would sit and brood, building up an intense hatred for all the masculine things that seemed to keep her husband away from her—liquor, saloons, tobacco, and the local lodges the doctor used as refuges from a home life he obviously despised. Although Carry became pregnant, she decided to leave her husband.

After her child was born she prayed daily for a new husband, and she was relieved a few months later when she learned of Gloyd's death. She now began an active search for a replacement, and one day while walking along a street in Holden, Missouri, she suddenly saw the man she wanted. He was standing in a doorway with his back to her, a man with flowing whiskers and wearing a high-crowned hat, a man old enough to be her father. "A peculiar thrill passed through my heart which made me start." He was David Nation, lawyer, minister, editor, and veteran of the Union army. He stood no chance against the determined Carry, who had already made up her mind that he was to be her next husband.

Later she wrote: "My married life with Mr. Nation was not a happy one. I found out that he deceived me in so many things." Nevertheless, she went with him to Texas, where they operated an unprofitable hotel for a few years. Then in 1889 they moved to Medicine Lodge, Kansas, a wide-open border town that needed a new minister and was willing to take David Nation on faith.

Now in her early forties, Carry began to have strange visions. She convinced her husband that she had direct revelations from Jesus Christ and began planning the texts for his sermons, violent diatribes against liquor and tobacco. If David deviated from the text, she would rise and correct him from the front pew, and if she thought he was wandering too much, she would order him to stop the sermon for the day.

She also turned her attention to lay matters. "I became very much interested in the prohibition cause." Before moving to Kansas she had heard it was a dry land of no whisky, and was disturbed to find open drinking in the streets of Medicine Lodge. Although there was a state law making the sale of intoxicating beverages illegal except for "medical, scientific, and mechanical purposes," local authorities interpreted these exceptions liberally. "Joints" replaced saloons, and drugstores provided back rooms where male citizens could drink quietly for "medicinal purposes." Occasionally the law would order a violator into court, but the fines were quite mild.

To break up all this masculine frivolity, Carry Nation organized a small group of women into an antiliquor force, and began a carefully planned assault upon the forces of evil. She rose in church one Sunday and called the roll of the local liquor sellers' names. When she would meet one of these unfortunates upon the street she would call out loudly: "Good morning, destroyer of men's souls! Shame on you, you rumsoaked ally of Satan!"

With one of her local supporters, a Mrs. Wesley Cain, she appeared without warning one Saturday afternoon outside Mort Strong's liquor joint. Mrs. Cain played a hand organ until a crowd gathered, and then Carry marched into the bar, singing what was to become her most feared fighting song:

> Who hath sorrow? Who hath woe?
> They who dare not answer no;
> They whose feet to sin incline
> While they tarry at the wine.
> They who tarry at the wine cup,
> They who tarry at the wine cup,
> They who tarry at the wine cup,
> They have sorrow, they have woe.

Mort Strong ordered Carry out, but she refused to leave. "I continued to sing, with tears running down my face."

Strong finally pushed her out the door, setting her down hard on the board sidewalk out front. He asked his customers to leave quietly and locked the door. But within a few hours, local women had spread the story around town that Mort Strong had publicly assaulted a woman. He departed Medicine Lodge a defeated man, leaving the six remaining joint owners to carry on the defense.

They were no match for Carry Nation. Repeating the tactics used against Mort Strong, she soon closed the remaining joints, then concentrated her attacks upon a stubborn druggist; it took her almost a month to drive the druggist out of town. At last, Medicine Lodge was dry.

Although she was now a heroine to most of the town's women, Carry soon discovered a flaw in her triumph. The males of Medicine Lodge were obtaining all the liquor they wanted through bootleggers from Kiowa, twenty miles south on the Oklahoma border. The word "bootlegger" is said to have originated in this very region, the liquor runners concealing whisky bottles in the legs of their heavy boots, and they were a sore trial to Carry. She realized she could not smash these migratory agents of Satan, but perhaps she could cut off the supply.

She worried with the idea of taking her battle to Kiowa, and prayed for a vision to guide her. One afternoon while lying across her bed, she heard voices saying: "Go to Kiowa, Go to Kiowa!" And the voices instructed her: "Take something in your hands, and throw at these places in Kiowa and smash them." She now knew what she had to do. "When no one was looking I would walk out in the yard and pick up brick bats and rocks, would hide them under my kitchen apron, would take them in my room, would wrap them up in newspapers one by one. I did this until I got quite a pile."

She started out in her buggy over the dusty road to Kiowa, and had not gone far when she received another vision. "I saw in the middle of the road perhaps a dozen or so creatures in the forms of men leaning towards the buggy as if against a rope which prevented them from coming nearer. Their faces were those of demons and the gestures of their hands as if they would tear me up. I did not know what to do, but I lifted my hands, and my eyes to God, saying, 'Oh! Lord, help me, help me!' When I looked down these diabolical creatures were not in front of the buggy, but they were off to the right fleeing as if they were terrified." She interpreted them as being devils who knew more of what she was going to do in Kiowa than she did.

Late in the evening she arrived in Kiowa, stabled her horse, and stayed the night in a hotel. Next morning, armed with her packages of brickbats and stones, she went into Dobson's Saloon and informed the proprietor calmly: "I am going to break this place up." She smashed mirrors, bottles and glasses in rapid succession. "My strength was that of a giant. I felt invincible." After wrecking the other Kiowa joints in similar fashion, and before the astounded drinkers, saloonkeepers, and town officials could act, she headed back for Medicine Lodge. The town was boiling with excitement when she arrived, the news of her activities having been telegraphed ahead.

Carry now began wondering if she should not venture into other parts of Kansas, and having heard of the hard drinking that went on in Wichita she decided to go there. And it was in the Carey Bar that she pulled off the magnificent wrecking job that brought her a jail sentence and nationwide publicity. After the adoption of her hatchet and some subsequent adventures in Wichita, there was no stopping Carry Nation.

Meanwhile old David Nation was beginning to lose patience. He went up to Wichita to see her. "You will have to stop and come back to Medicine Lodge," he said mildly, "or I will get a divorce from you." She told him the Lord had given her a mission and she dared not turn back from it. After giving her plenty of time to change her mind, the long-suffering old gentleman sued for divorce. He accused Carry of desertion, cruelty, and taking his feather bed and nine hundred dollars of his bank account. Carry retorted that David never had nine hundred dollars in his life and that the feather bed was hers. David won the divorce, but she was awarded the house in Medicine Lodge. She promptly sold it, using the money as a down payment on a large house in Kansas City which she named the Home for Drunkards' Wives.

She now added tobacco to her list of top hates. "I would as soon kiss a spittoon as to kiss the mouth of a man who uses tobacco." When walking on the streets or riding on trains and boats, she would jerk cigars or cigarettes from the mouths of startled men. "I have the right to take cigars and cigarettes from men's mouths in self-defense."

Although Carry made half-hearted attempts to organize groups of women to back her in local campaigns, she was always suspicious of any who won publicity away from her and considered them as rivals. Among her followers and imitators was a Miss Blanche Boies, who invaded the capitol in Topeka one morning and attacked with an ax the state historical society's framed print of Custer's Last Stand. When a gentleman appeared and remonstrated with her, Miss Boies explained that she was only attempting to remove the brewer's name at the bottom of the picture. She was led away, the broken glass was swept up, and Custer's Last Stand became the leading drawing card in Topeka. After souvenir hunters mutilated it, the historical society ordered another print but cautiously painted out the beer advertisement before exposing it to public view.

Another imitator was Mrs. May Sheriff, who organized a company of fifty women called "The Flying Squadron of Jesus." The flying squadron made several devastating raids upon barrooms along the Oklahoma border. Still another rival was Myra McHenry, who sometimes disguised herself as a man so as to be able to enter saloons unnoticed before beginning her bottle smashing.

As for Carry, she spent the rest of her life at touring, lecturing, smashing saloons, attacking fraternal orders and corsets, knocking cigars and cigarettes out of the mouths of males, and occasionally advocating women's suffrage. She also published two magazines, *The Smasher's Mail* and *The Hatchet*.

Ironically, it was a woman who finally stopped Carry Nation. She was May Maloy, operator of a saloon and dance hall in Butte, Montana. When Carry invaded May's saloon to do a bit of smashing with her hatchet, she spied a nude painting and strode toward it with fire in her eyes. But May Maloy sprang to the defense and chased Carry out upon the street in a disorderly retreat. Carry Nation never smashed up another saloon. She retired to the Arkansas Ozarks to dream of her past glories and died in 1911, almost forgotten.[23]

7

Although Carry Nation announced herself as being in favor of votes for women, the truth is—if we may judge from her autobiography—she rated suffrage about on a par with the cause of abolishing corsets. She preferred physical action rather than the oratorical exertions of nineteenth-century politics.

But there was another woman of Kansas who was deeply interested in breaking the economic and political shackles of her sex through the ballot box; she believed a vote was more powerful than a hatchet. Her name was Mary Elizabeth Lease. About the same time that Carry Nation was beginning to make herself unpopular with the men of Medicine Lodge, some two hundred miles to the northeast on the fairgrounds near Paola Mary Lease was haranguing a large crowd which contained three or four thousand cheering males.

"You farmers were told two years ago to raise a big crop," she cried in her resounding orator's voice. "Well, you did, and what became of it?" She paused, her melancholy blue eyes sweeping the crowd. "Six-cent corn, ten-cent oats, two-cent beef. We want the accursed foreclosure system wiped out. We will stand by our homes and use force if necessary, and we will not pay our debts to the loan sharks until the government pays its debts to us. The people are at bay. Let the bloodhounds of money who have dogged us thus far beware!" Mary Lease waited until the thundering applause died away. She knew her audience, she knew from bitter personal experience what foreclosure meant, and now she raised herself up straight—a long-legged, fair-skinned, dark-haired woman in a high-collared black dress—and delivered the closing line that was to make her the darling of the western plainsmen: "What you farmers need is to *raise less corn and more hell!*"

Mary Lease's history was typical of many a western frontier woman. Her father was a Union soldier who died in Andersonville prison, leaving her an orphan. She had emigrated from Pennsylvania in the early 1870's, an academy graduate who had heard that schoolmarms were needed in the West. She secured a position at the Osage Mission, and there in 1873, when she was twenty, she met a young druggist, Charles Lease. After their marriage Lease persuaded her that farming would soon make them rich, and they settled with bright hopes in Kingman County.

Life on the prairies, however, was not what Mary Lease had dreamed it would be. There was no money to buy the things her growing family needed, and there was no market for the crops her husband raised. At times the drudgery and discomfort were almost unbearable, and she afterward said that she was saved from despair only by constantly rereading Emerson's "Essay on Self-Reliance."

Eventually Charles Lease gave up farming and moved his family to Wichita, where he made a poor living as a druggist. Mary helped out by doing laundry for her neighbors, earning about fifty cents a day. She was an insatiable reader and borrowed books from those who had them, copying passages she liked and fastening the written sheets on the walls of her laundry room so she could reread them as she worked.

After becoming acquainted with a Wichita lawyer, she decided to read for the law and, to the astonishment of the town, was admitted to the bar in 1885. By this time she had made up her mind that only through politics could women achieve economic independence. She joined the Knights of Labor, then the Farmers' Alliance, and was one of the leaders in organizing the People's Party, the fabulous Populists, who came to power in the West as a third party toward the end of the nineteenth century.

During the campaign of 1890 Mary Lease made 161 speeches, and her dramatic oratorical attacks upon Democrats and Republicans alike have been given much of the credit for the surprising political victory of the new third party.

Newspapers attacked her, humorously at first, then with all the bitter venom that was common in political journalism of that day. One editor, for example, described her as "a miserable caricature of womanhood, hideously ugly in features and foul of tongue," and then admitted she had personally attacked him in one of her speeches. "Just what were the old hag's reasons for attacking us, we are not apprised. All we know about her is that she is hired to travel around the country by this great reform People's party, which seems to find a female blackguard a necessity in its business, spouting foul-mouthed vulgarity at $10 a night. No doubt the petticoated smut-mill earns her money, but few women with any regard for their reputation would care to make their living that way . . . Her venomous tongue is the only thing marketable about the old harpy, and we suppose she is justified in selling it where it commands the highest market price. In about a month the lantern-jawed, goggle-eyed nightmare will be out of a job, and nobody will be the worse for the mud with which she has tried to bespatter them."

"I have no newspapers to give me publicity," Mary Lease remarked prophetically early in the campaign, "but my tongue is loose at both ends and hung on a swivel, so I'm likely to have considerable notoriety in the future." Her supporters compared her to Joan of Arc, but her enemies called her the Cyclone of Kansas, and one editor always referred to her as Mary Yellin', a name that spread so widely that she was often introduced on platforms by loyal supporters as Mary Ellen instead of Mary Elizabeth.

After hearing her for the first time, a western farmer recorded in his diary: "Went to town to hear Joint discussion between Mrs. Lease & John M. Brumbaugh. Poor Brumbaugh was not in it."

Mary Lease's principal contribution to the unshackling of western women was to prove to her sex that a female could enter politics and become a heroine to males at the same time. Several women followed her into the political wars—Annie Diggs, Fanny Vickery, Bettie Gay, Sarah Emery, and Eva Valesh—but none was as dynamic and popular as she. At the height of the Populist movement it would have been difficult to find a horny-handed, mortgaged farmer anywhere in the West who did not swear by Mary Elizabeth Lease, and there were many who believed that she alone could save them.

But as women will, she later changed her mind and let her fanatical followers down. When the Populists joined forces with the Democrats and backed William Jennings Bryan for

President, Mary Lease switched sides and joined the Republicans. Although she never repudiated her past, she once admitted that "there were times when I actually made speeches without knowing it, when I was surprised to read in the morning paper that I had spoken the night before."

In her later life she was often asked what she had meant by her famous phrase, "less corn and more hell." To one newspaper interviewer she replied: "When I told the farmers to raise less corn and more hell, I meant they should think less of the material rewards, and more of the spiritual problems of the great experiment in democracy." [24] But it is doubtful, indeed, if the hard-bitten plainsmen of the six-cent-corn, ten-cent-oats, and two-cent-beef days ever interpreted those plain and meaningful words in any such grandiloquent manner.

XV

Schoolmarms and Maternal Forces

1

OFTEN the real movers and shakers of an era go unnoticed during their lifetimes, and this was certainly true of the legions of anonymous schoolmarms who moved westward with the first waves of settlement. Most western schoolmarms married eventually and raised children of their own for other women to teach, living out their lives as busy wives and mothers, bent primarily upon taming their wild environment. They attracted little attention individually as breakers of shackles, but as a mass maternal force their power was unmatched in the domestication process that transformed the wild frontiersmen into ordinary placid citizens.

Until the middle of the nineteenth century, schoolteaching, like all other professions and occupations, was monopolized by the dominant males. In the public mind, woman's place was in the home, and the few females who did venture into teaching were considered incompetent and incapable of governing a classroom. The arrogant males who made these charges conveniently overlooked the fact that very few women had opportunities to attend colleges so that they might become competent.

At mid-century, however, the situation changed rapidly,

largely because of a surging population that was spilling over the Alleghenies and across the Mississippi. In 1845 Catharine Beecher published her widely distributed manifesto, *The Duty of American Women to Their Country*. With an eye cocked on western frontiers, she cried out a warning that population increase was running so far ahead of the supply of school-teachers that children would grow up in ignorance unless women came forth and entered the profession by the thousands. Men, she charged, were deserting teaching for more profitable occupations, and few could be persuaded to return to the "humble, unhonored toils of the schoolroom and its penurious reward . . . It is *woman* who is to come in at this emergency and meet the demand; woman, whom experience and testing has shown to be the best, as well as the cheapest, guardian and teacher of childhood, in the school as well as in the nursery." Miss Beecher argued passionately for school-teaching as a more rewarding way for a woman to earn her living than engaging in the monotonous toil of New England factories and workshops, and as being more satisfying than idling away one's time at "shopping, dressing, calling, and gossiping."[1]

Catharine Beecher found a fertile field for her propaganda in New England, where emigration and seafaring had reduced the number of men well below that of women. J. L. McConnell, a writer on western life, declared in 1853 that New England was the prime source of schoolmarms and that "a competent number of them have been found willing to give up the comforts of home for the benefit of the 'barbarous west.' "[2]

By the late 1850's the western frontier was begging for eastern women to emigrate and become schoolteachers. In 1858, Julia Lovejoy of Kansas published a notice in *Zion's Herald*, a Boston religious magazine: "We want good female teachers, who could obtain constant employment, and the best of wages. Do send on a score from East Greenwich, Wilbraham, or Newbury, Vt.; we want them immediately and they would do much good."[3]

The following year the *Lynn County* (Kansas) *Herald* announced that the school authorities could give employment to "one hundred School Marms, who will pledge themselves not to get married within three years." Commenting on this restriction clause, the editor of the *Kansas Express* of Manhattan made a better offer: "We want one hundred in this county, between the ages of 18 and 21, *who will pledge themselves to get married within one year,* and who are willing to commence school on one scholar."[4]

Certainly it could not have been the income that attracted women to teaching in the West. They must have been possessed by either a missionary fervor or hopeful expectancy of matrimony. Although Julia Lovejoy promised the best of wages, twelve dollars a month and board was average, and many schools paid by the head, one dollar per month per pupil, with no guaranteed minimum. Meals and lodging were usually provided by the families who had children in school, the teacher "boarding around" from one home to another.

A frontier schoolteacher recorded that she changed boarding places every two weeks, walking three to six miles to and from the log schoolhouse in all kinds of weather. She had fourteen pupils and no textbooks except almanacs and hymn books used for practice reading. The homes she stayed in were usually one-room cabins, with bunks at one end partitioned off by a sheet or a blanket. It was the custom for the man of the house to "delicately retire to the barn while we women got to bed, and to disappear again in the morning while we dressed." Her salary was two dollars per week, payable in the spring after the county dog tax was collected.[5]

Another teacher told of how she signed on to teach in one of the wilder cattle- and sheep-ranching areas of the Far West. She was quite young and weighed less than a hundred pounds. When she got off at the rail stop, a large crowd of cattlemen and sheepmen were gathered to see the new school-marm arrive. For a moment, they all stared in astonishment at this tiny female creature, then they broke into shouts of laugh-ter. She discovered afterward that they were laughing at the idea of such a small girl whipping all the big boys in her school. But she made out all right, and showed the stockmen that no male schoolroom bully was a match for a strong-willed female, regardless of size.

The stubborn male school directors also met their match in schoolmarms who were determined to improve standards. A teacher in Washington Territory during the Civil War decided for sanitary reasons to abolish the local practice of having all pupils drink from the same water dipper. When she asked each child to bring his own drinking cup, a delegation of school directors appeared, demanding to know the reason for such nonsense. She won the argument and proceeded to other matters. "There was not the slightest sign of a toilet. When I told the directors that I could not teach if they did not build one, one of them remarked, 'Now you see what comes of hiring someone from the Outside. Never had any trouble before, plenty of trees to get behind.' Several of the pupils were older than I was and many larger. One father came to see me about teaching 'frills' because I taught the boys to take off their hats when they came in the door."[6]

Settlements almost invariably grew faster than the schools, and it was not unusual to find sixty or seventy children crowded into a one-room cabin with only one teacher to in-struct them. Single desks had to be shared by two pupils, with sometimes a small child squeezed in between. Older students were drafted by the teacher to help in "hearing the younger ones read."

A typical western school was described by a teacher of the 1870's as having a puncheon floor, with a rock-stick-and-mud fireplace half filling one end of the room. The walls were papered high and low with copies of the *Christian Advocate* and Horace Greeley's weekly *Tribune*. She added to this decorative ensemble a series of hand-lettered mottoes: HEALTH IS WEALTH, TIME IS MONEY, NEVER SAY FAIL, LOOK BEFORE YOU LEAP, A ROLLING STONE GATHERS NO MOSS, A STITCH IN TIME SAVES NINE. All of these precepts she believed in sincerely, and she drilled them unceasingly into her pupils' heads.

Just as there exists today in the public mind a stereotype of the American schoolteacher, so was there one of the frontier schoolmarm in the nineteenth century. "Her name was invariably Grace, Charity, or Prudence; and, if names had been always a descriptive of the personal qualities of those who bore them, she would have been entitled to all three . . . She was somewhat angular and rather bony. Her eyes were usually blue, and, to speak with accuracy, a little cold and grayish, in their expression—like the sky on a bleak morning in Autumn. Her forehead was very high and prominent, having an *exposed* look, like a shelterless knoll in an open prairie. Her mouth was of that class called 'primped,' but was filled with teeth of respectable dimensions . . . She had, however, almost always one very great attraction—a fine, clear, healthy complexion . . . In manners and bearing, she was brisk, prim, and sometimes a little 'fidgety,' as if she was conscious of sitting on a dusty chair; and she had a way of searching nervously for her pocket, as if to find a handkerchief with which to brush it off . . . Though rigid and austere, I have never heard that she was at all disinclined to being courted; especially if it gave her any prospect of being able to make herself useful as a wife . . . She was careful of three things—her clothes, her money, and her reputation . . . Almost invariably, the western schoolmarm in the course of time became a married woman, but the man who courted her must do so in the most sober, staid, and regulated spirit."[7]

This caricature, like all its kind, was only a half-truth. The Wyoming schoolmarm heroine of Owen Wister's *The Virginian* did not fit into this mold, nor did most of her colleagues of that place and time. A pioneer resident of Mason, Texas, for example, described that community's first schoolmarm as being an "Irish woman who had the strength of a strong man and the typical fighting spirit of her race. She kept a quart of whiskey and a leather quirt in her desk. The whiskey was strictly for her own use, the quirt for use on the kids." [8] But she, of course, was an exception to the rule.

2

In addition to teaching the very young, a few audacious female educators founded seminaries and institutes for the benefit of young ladies interested in higher learning. As early as 1851, a female institute was launched in San Francisco by a Mrs. E. M. Parker, who assured the public that "the morals and manners of her pupils will be carefully attended to and the discipline, though mild, will be firm and steady."[9] She offered courses in English, French, Spanish, music, and drawing. In 1860, a Miss H. K. Clapp opened a seminary in Carson City, Nevada, and according to historian Hubert H. Bancroft she and the school "did much to give tone to Carson society."[10]

It was a New England schoolmarm on the Minnesota frontier, Caroline Arabella Hall, who wormed her way into the sacrosanct inner councils of the secret order, Patrons of Husbandry, and against strong opposition of its male founders forced them to take women as members. With wives and daughters infiltrating the movement in large numbers, the Grange meetings lost their barnyard aroma and became cultural events, the programs including debates, lectures, and group singing from a special songbook compiled by Miss Hall. "A good library, an organ or piano, a microscope, botanical collections &c., are amongst the items with which each Grange is furnished. Ladies become 'patrons of husbandry' in more senses than one."[11]

Profane language was opposed by the schoolmarms on rhetorical as well as moral grounds, and although they never succeeded in completely abolishing its use, nothing was so likely to dry up a barrage of obscenities among miners or cowboys than the sudden appearance of a lady schoolteacher. One old miner, wearied of hearing a continual flow of the same four-letter words from his associates, noticed a change for the better as soon as a schoolmarm arrived in camp, and he sat down and wrote a letter of appreciation to the nearest newspaper: "So far as the improvement of society is concerned, one true, pure woman is worth a volume of sermons."

3

"There is among western women," wrote Hjalmar Boyesen in 1889, "a universal hopefulness and aspiration." This was the maternal force against which the males' brute force could not contend, and which ultimately brought the Wild West under complete domination of the female sex.

Faced with adversity, the male wrote despairingly in his diaries—of no gold found, of the unfriendly land, of failing crops, of economic disasters. Women, on the other hand, did not ignore vicissitudes, but they were determined to endure, to win in the end. "When we got to the new purchase, the land of milk and honey, we were disappointed and homesick, but we were there and had to make the best of it," one woman wrote. Another was struck with the sudden shock of being a stranger in a strange land. "Can it be that I have left my quiet little home and taken this dreary land of solitude in exchange? It is truly so, but I must not let my mind run in this channel long or my happiness is gone." And another, after recording a list of hardships of western life, could say: "Do not think I regret coming. No, far from it. I would not go back for the world. I am contented and happy, notwithstanding I sometimes get very hungry and weary."[12]

It was remarkable how quickly women adapted to the harshest of lands—the empty plains—learning to see beauty where their husbands saw only a bleak, monotonous landscape. "I sometimes long for my trees and hills at home, yet nothing can excel this enchanting, endless view. The sun flattens on the prairie until it looks like a sea of fire as it disappears from the horizon." And many women have written of how at first they hated the southwestern desert country, considering it the dreariest, most desolate face of the earth, yet eventually they learned to see it truly so that they longed passionately for the peaceful loneliness of that unique land when they were away from it.

No one has drawn a better picture of a woman alone than Dame Shirley in her description of a widow determined to endure for the sake of her brood—a raw maternal force pitted against the man's world of the gold rush. "When but two weeks on the journey, she had buried her husband, who died of cholera after about six hours' illness. She had come on; for what else could she do . . . she had eight sons and one daughter. She was immensely tall, and had a hard, weather-beaten face, surmounted by a dreadful horn comb and a heavy twist of haycolored hair, which, before it was cut, and its gloss all destroyed by the alkali, must, from its luxuriance, have been very handsome. But what really interested me so much in her was the dogged and determined way in which she had set that stern, wrinkled face of hers against poverty. She owned nothing in the world but her team, and yet she planned all sorts of successful ways to get food for her small, or rather large, family. She used to wash shirts, and iron them on a chair, in the open air of course, and you can fancy with what success. But the gentlemen were too generous to be critical, and as they paid her three or four times as much as she asked, she accumulated quite a handsome sum in a few days. She made me think of a long-legged very thin hen scratching for dear life to feed her never-to-be-satisfied brood."[13]

There were many like her in the West. They feared God, got their work done, were probably as content as any one has a right to be, and they endured.

XVI

Male Viewpoint

1

IN that sweet, anarchic male society enjoyed by frontiersmen from the time of the Mountain Men and explorers down through the busy fur-trading years and into the gold rush, the only females were squaws, and they were no problem. If that free company of bearded, unwashed gentlemen had any collective vision of an ideal female, she must have been as rough-textured as they—hard-muscled, independent but obedient at proper times, unmindful of discomfort, and capable of preparing a meal from whatever edibles were at hand.

Among the yarns told and retold around western campfires were differing versions of a traveler's experience during an overnight stop at a frontier cabin. The visitor was sitting with the old mother before the fireplace when a barefoot daughter came in out of the weather and stood before the fire to dry her homespun dress. Without changing her half-reclining position, the mother drawled casually: "Sal, there's a live coal under your foot." In the same unhurried tone, the barefoot daughter replied: "Which foot, Ma?"

They admired tough-footed women, those unfettered wanderers of the plains and the Rockies, and they liked them gay and daring, too. "The woman who made the least secret of the color of her garters, and who was the 'flyest of the mob,' was the belle of the place, the leader of the *ton*, the pet of society."[1]

The strong male feeling against artificial femininity persisted well up into the days of later settlement. It was as if the frontiersmen sensed a hint of danger hidden among the fripperies and fancies of womanliness. Male newspaper editors struck out boldly with ridicule and satire; they shamed, scolded, and mocked. "We are sorry to see the girls of the present day have such a tendency to utter worthlessness," complained an editor of 1857. "Years ago it was fun to go a dozen miles afoot, with mud knee deep, to see them, nature instead of art. But now it is different. The dentist supplies the teeth, an artist furnishes the paint, a yankee the hoops, some 'French milliner' gets up artificial maternal founts, and the very devil robs himself to give them a disposition to lie, tattle, gossip, make mischief and kick up all sorts of hobberys among people generally."[2]

An Idaho editor was even more derisive in 1864: "Ye pining, lolling, screwed-up, wasp-waisted, putty-faced, consumption-mortgaged and novel-devouring daughters of fashion and idleness, you are no more fit for matrimony than a pullet is to look after a family of fifteen chickens."[3]

Occasionally the conscience of some male would prickle briefly, and he would utter a private admission of guilt. "Men has got wimmin so corraled that there ain't only about two occupations fer 'em: Prostitution or runnin' a boardin' house. Danged if a feller can tell which on the whole is worst."[4]

And in their bungling way, one or another would make an effort to aid the poor, benighted gentler sex in making their way on the frontier. Benjamin Godfrey, for example, decided that what young women needed before settling in the West was special education and training. On the banks of the Mississippi he constructed a four-story limestone building which he called the Monticello Female Seminary, and he announced that its purpose was "to educate wives for the West." He advertised for eighty young ladies, all over fourteen years of age, who were willing to be taught lessons in setting tables, arranging rooms, sweeping and scrubbing floors, and laundering clothing. Mr. Godfrey's experiment never got off the ground.

2

It was the males themselves, of course, who brought about the destruction of their lusty frontier hegemony. The very nature of their disheveled way of life precluded any organized division of labor among themselves. When they collected in the mining camps to dig for gold, all wanted to dig for gold. No male was willing to hew wood, draw water, cook meals, or wash clothes for the other males. The habitations of these womanless men resembled pigsties and became favored haunts of fleas, rats, and other vermin. Laundry expenses often exceeded the price of new underwear and shirts. One of the curious commercial ventures of the time was the shipping of dirty laundry all the way from California to China to be washed, starched, ironed, and then returned. "Washing is still $8.00 a dozen," wrote a miner of 1849, "and the consequence is, large quantities of soiled linen are sent to China to be purified,— and the practice is now becoming general. A vessel just in from Canton brought 250 doz. which were sent out a few months ago; another from the Sandwich Island brought 100 doz."[5]

Faced with the absurdities and inconveniences of such conditions, the helpless men could think of no solution but to cry out for women. "Oh! for a woman. No clean clothes, ragged shirts, no buttons on, O! the inconvenience of keeping old

Bach! A Kingdom for a woman now. May Kind providence smile upon me soon; for I'm getting in a dilapidated condition, am afraid to see the Rag-man."[6]

And when females at last began arriving, the male newspapermen wrote as if the millennium had dawned upon a darkened world. "It looks civilized and Christianlike to see ladies daily passing along our streets, amusing themselves in that never tiring occupation of shopping . . . During the last few months there has been a most marked increase of the gentler sex into our city. Both during the day and evening the rustling of silks and soft musical voices are quite familiar sounds, and with the silent accompaniment of fresh blooming and pleasant faces, exercises a most pleasurable influence over the minds of the male portion of our citizens."[7]

To be treated like white goddesses was a new experience for members of a sex which the world had long relegated to inferiority. And once they had tasted the privileges of influence, they were not inclined to relinquish them ever again. Many envisioned a petticoat utopia.

"The first woman whose acquaintance I made in the United States was a very pretty western girl," wrote a traveler of 1869. "She took a peculiar pleasure in saying and doing things which she knew would shock my European notions of propriety. She was slangy in her speech, careless in her pronunciation, and bent upon 'having a good time' without reference to the prohibitions which are framed for the special purpose of annoying women. She had about as much idea of propriety as a cat has of mathematics . . . I met this type of young American woman for the first time in 1869, and have been meeting her daily ever since. Though she may object to the name I shall call her the Aspiring Woman."[8]

Many males looked askance at the revolution going on under their noses, but they were unorganized in their opposition. In fact, the females found as many allies as enemies among the opposite sex, so that the hostile male array was always on the defensive, unable to distinguish friend from foe in its own camp.

The Wyoming gentlemen who opposed women's suffrage in that territory were routed—with the odds all in their favor— and the only comfort they received from male allies abroad was verbal sympathy. It must have been galling, indeed, for them to learn that a group of virile cowboys had defected in Oregon, and not only had listened politely to female advocates of the "pernicious doctrine" but had cheered them lustily; one more traitorous than the others even lettered a streamer for the occasion: WOMAN SUFFRAGE—WE ARE ALL FOR IT.

Such straws in the wind were discouraging to the defenders of male superiority. All they could do was view with alarm and make public statements against strong-minded women who were beginning to smoke cigarillos in public and ride horseback astride.

None of them, of course, could read the future, or could have known in that day that women truly are the most conservative of creatures, hating with a passion those three concomitants of the western frontier—poverty, physical hardship, and danger. And to destroy these traditional testers of human endurance was to destroy something male in the race.

None could have dreamed that by the third or fourth generation there would be no more zestful combat with frontier dangers and hardships, and that the Wild West would be tamed by its petticoated pioneers. Yet if any male of the Old West could have foreseen the day that descendants of miner, cowboy and Indian fighter would be reduced to a routine of freeway commuting, do-it-yourself gadgetry, tract-development living, dishwashing, baby-sitting, neighborhood committee meetings, and television viewing—what would he have done differently in that long-ago time?

More than likely he would have shrugged in disbelief and would have agreed with a pioneer named Seth Smith, who took a long look at the big empty western land around him and penned a letter home: "The finest country in the world. Women is all that is needed."[9]

Notes

I. THE SUNBONNET MYTH

1. Emerson Hough, *The Passing of the Frontier* (New Haven, 1921), 93-94.
2. Julia L. Lovejoy, "Letters," *Kansas Historical Quarterly*, XVI (1948), 302.
3. Amelia K. Clappe, *The Shirley Letters* (San Francisco, 1922), 321.
4. Susanna Moodie, *Roughing It in the Bush* (New York, n.d.), 160.
5. Eliza S. Warren, *Memoirs of the West: the Spaldings* (Portland, Oregon, 1916), 55.
6. Lydia M. Waters, "Account of a Trip Across the Plains in 1855," *Society of California Pioneers, Quarterly*, VI (1929), 59.
7. Lodisa Frizzell, *Across the Plains to California* (New York, 1915), 5.
8. Hubert H. Bancroft, *Works*, XXV (San Francisco, 1890), 47.
9. *Ibid*, XXIII, 123-145.
10. Georgia W. Read, "Women and Children on the Oregon-California Trail in the Gold-Rush Years," *Missouri Historical Review*, XXXIX (1944), 6.
11. Bancroft, *op. cit.*, XXV, 371.
12. Read, *op. cit.*, 7.
13. *Ibid.*
14. James F. Meline, *Two Thousand Miles on Horseback* (New York, 1867), 34.

II. "PERIL WAS AT EVERY HAND"

1. Virginia R. Murphy, "Across the Plains in the Donner Party," *Century*, XLII (1891), 409.
2. Lodisa Frizzell, *Across the Plains to California* (New York, 1915), 14-18; Mary A. Maverick, *Memoirs* (San Antonio, 1921), 44.
3. Elizabeth B. Custer, *Following the Guidon* (New York, 1890), 2.
4. Maverick, *op. cit.*, 44.
5. James F. Meline, *Two Thousand Miles on Horseback* (New York, 1867), 267-69.
6. Mrs. N. D. White, "Captivity Among the Sioux," *Minnesota Historical Society, Collections*, IX (1898-1900), 407.
7. Meline, *op. cit.*, 267-69.
8. *Annual Report*, U. S. Commissioner of Indian Affairs (Washington, 1879).
9. *Ibid.*

10. *White River Ute Commission Investigation*, 46th U. S. Congress, 2nd sess., House Exec. Doc. 83 (Washington, 1880), 21.
11. *Ibid.*
12. *Ibid*, 41-42.
13. *Ibid*, 15.
14. *Testimony in Relation to the Ute Indian Outbreak*, 46th U. S. Congress, 2nd sess., House Misc. Doc. 38 (Washington, 1880), 82.
15. House Exec. Doc. 83, *op. cit.*, 42.
16. *Ibid*, 16-17.
17. House Misc. Doc. 38. *op. cit.*, 2.
18. *Ibid*, 89.
19. House Exec. Doc. 83, *op. cit.*, 43-50.
20. *Ibid*, 23-27.
21. M. Wilson Rankin, "The Meeker Massacre," *Annals of Wyoming*, XVI (1944), 131.
22. John Ross Browne, *Adventures in the Apache Country* (New York, 1869), 88-98.
23. Josiah Gregg, *The Commerce of the Prairies* (Chicago, 1926), 207-08.
24. Elizabeth B. Custer, *Tenting on the Plains* (New York, 1887), 668.
25. W. J. Ghent, *The Road to Oregon* (London, 1929), 158.
26. Sarah Royce, *A Frontier Lady* (New Haven, 1932), 19.
27. John H. Clark, "Overland to the Goldfields of California in 1852," *Kansas Historical Quarterly*, XI (1942), 236.
28. *Ibid.*
29. Susan S. Magoffin, *Down the Santa Fe Trail and into Mexico* (New Haven, 1926), 38.
30. Frizzell, *op. cit.*, 13.
31. Clark, *op. cit.*, 237, 400.
32. Mrs. H. A. Ropes, *Six Months in Kansas* (Boston, 1856), 185.
33. Mrs. Orsemus B. Boyd, *Cavalry Life in Tent and Field* (New York, 1894), 136.
34. *Minneapolis* (Kansas) *Messenger*, Oct. 3, 1895.
35. Frances Carrington, *My Army Life* (Philadelphia, 1911), 63.
36. William W. Fowler, *Woman on the American Frontier* (Hartford, 1879), 449.
37. Elizabeth D. S. Geer, "Diary," *Oregon Pioneer Association, Transactions*, XXXV (Portland, 1907), 173.
38. Mrs. Marcus Whitman, "A Journey Across the Plains in 1836," *Oregon Pioneer Association, Transactions*, XIX (Portland, 1891), 46.

III. THE ARMY GIRLS

1. Mrs. Orsemus B. Boyd, *Cavalry Life in Tent and Field* (New York, 1894), 29.
2. Frances M. A. Roe, *Army Letters from an Officer's Wife* (New York, 1909), 161.
3. *Ibid*, 46.
4. Martha Summerhayes, *Vanished Arizona, Recollections of My Army Life* (Chicago, 1939), 54-55, 62, 81.
5. *Ibid*, 12.
6. Boyd, *op. cit.*, 276, 279.
7. Katherine G. Fougera, *With Custer's Cavalry* (Caldwell, Idaho, 1942), 67.
8. Margaret I. Carrington, *Ab-Sa-Ra-Ka, Land of Massacre: Being the Experience of an Officer's Wife on the Plains* (Philadelphia, 1878), 175.

9. Summerhayes, *op. cit.*, 234.
10. Elizabeth B. Custer, *Following the Guidon* (New York, 1890), 239.
11. Fougera, *op. cit.*, 78.
12. Summerhayes, *op. cit.*, 154.
13. Frances Carrington, *My Army Life* (Philadelphia, 1911), 57.
14. *Ibid*, 89-90.
15. *Ibid*, 144; Margaret I. Carrington, *op. cit.*, 201.
16. Frances Carrington, *op. cit.*, 144-46.
17. Margaret I. Carrington, *op. cit.*, 206.
18. *Ibid*, 207; Frances Carrington, *op. cit.*, 153-54.
19. John Guthrie, "The Fetterman Massacre," *Annals of Wyoming*, IX (1932-34), 717.
20. Frances Carrington, *op. cit.*, 155-56.
21. *Ibid*, 180, 186.
22. *Ibid*, 208-09.
23. Case of the U. S. vs. Captain George Sokalski, 2nd U. S. Cavalry, War Dept. Files, National Archives; U. S. War Dept., Adjutant General's Office, General Court Martial Orders No. 177 (Washington, D. C., July 10, 1866).
24. Summerhayes, *op. cit.*, 277.
25. Boyd, *op. cit.*, 61.
26. *Ibid*, 193.
27. Frances Carrington, *op. cit.*, 102.
28. Roe, *op. cit.*, 58.
29. Fougera, *op. cit.*, 264.
30. Summerhayes, *op. cit.*, 217.

IV. BEAU SABREUR AND HIS LADY FAIR

1. Elizabeth B. Custer, *Following the Guidon* (New York, 1890), 230.
2. Katherine G. Fougera, *With Custer's Cavalry* (Caldwell, Idaho, 1942), 149.
3. Custer, *op. cit.*, 119.
4. Elizabeth B. Custer, *Tenting on the Plains* (New York, 1887), 515.
5. *Ibid*, 239.
6. Custer, *Following the Guidon*, 275.
7. *Ibid*, 122.
8. *Ibid*, 204.
9. *Ibid*, 174.
10. Fougera, *op. cit.*, 100, 227.
11. Custer, *Tenting on the Plains*, 411.
12. Charles J. Brill, *Conquest of the Southern Plains* (Oklahoma City, 1938), 45-46.
13. Custer, *Following the Guidon*, 90.

V. SOME LADIES OF EASY VIRTUE

1. Ross Cox, *Adventures on the Columbia River* (London, 1831), 286.
2. *Ibid.*
3. Elliott Coues, *New Light on the Early History of the Greater Northwest: Manuscript Journals of Alexander Henry and of David Thompson* (New York, 1897), 895.
4. *Ibid*, 898.
5. *Ibid*, 909.
6. Cox, *op. cit.*, 286.
7. Kenneth W. Porter, "Jane Barnes, First White Woman in Oregon," *Oregon Historical Quarterly*, XXXI (1930), 129.

8. Cox, *op. cit.*, 290.
9. Coues, *op. cit.*, 908.
10. *Ibid*, 896.
11. *Gold Hill Daily News*, January 21, 1867; *Territorial Enterprise*, January 22, 1867.
12. Lucius Beebe and Charles Clegg, *Legends of the Comstock Lode* (Oakland, Calif., 1950), 17; Oscar Lewis, *Silver Kings* (New York, 1947), 29; George D. Lyman, *Saga of the Comstock Lode* (New York, 1949), 58.
13. Lyman, *op. cit.*, 120.
14. *Ibid*, 107-113; William Wright, *History of the Big Bonanza* (Hartford, 1876), 118-121.
15. Lewis, *op. cit.*, 29; Lyman, *op. cit.*, 90.
16. Flannery Lewis, *Suns Go Down* (N. Y., 1937), 136; Oscar Lewis, *op. cit.*, 28.
17. C. B. Glasscock, *The Big Bonanza* (Indianapolis, 1931), 218-20.
18. Charles L. Martin, *Sketch of Sam Bass, the Bandit* (Norman, Oklahoma, 1956), 20-21.
19. Mrs. D. B. Bates, *Incidents on Land and Water, or Four Years on the Pacific Coast* (Boston, 1860), 315 ff.
20. Joel E. Ferris, "Hiram Gano Ferris of Illinois and California," *California Historical Society, Quarterly*, XXVI (1947), 296.
21. Ernest de Massey, "Some Phases of French Society in San Francisco in the 'Fifties," *California Historical Society, Quarterly*, XXXII (1953), 118.
22. Henry Miller Madden, "California for Hungarian Readers," *California Historical Society, Quarterly*, XXVIII (1949), 129.
23. Mrs. Frank Leslie, *California, A Pleasure Trip from Gotham to the Golden Gate* (New York, 1877), 121.
24. William Perkins, "California Journal, 1849-1852," *Amateur Book Collector*, VI (1955-1956), 17, 19-20.
25. *Sacramento Union*, Sept. 19, 1879.
26. Loreta J. Velazquez, *The Woman in Battle* (Hartford, n.d.), 578.
27. Works Progress Administration, Writers' Program, *Copper Camp* (New York, 1943), 178.
28. *Cheyenne Democratic Leader*, Sept. 27, 1884.
29. Elizabeth B. Custer, *Following the Guidon* (New York, 1890), 168.
30. W.P.A., Writers' Program, *Copper Camp*, 176.

VI. "MANY A WEARY MILE"

1. Virginia R. Murphy, "Across the Plains in the Donner Party," *Century*, XLII (1891), 410.
2. *Ibid*, 411.
3. *Ibid*, 412.
4. Virginia Reed to Mary Gillespie, Edwardsville, Illinois, July 12, 1846 (Southwest Museum, Los Angeles, California).
5. Murphy, *op. cit.*, 415.
6. *Ibid*, 422.
7. Caroll D. Hall, ed., *Donner Miscellany*, (San Francisco, 1947), 66.
8. Louella Dickinson, *A Trip Across the Plains in 1846* (San Francisco, 1904), 96.
9. *New York Daily Tribune*, July 8, 1852.
10. Lydia M. Waters, "Account of a Trip Across the Plains in 1855," *Society of California Pioneers, Quarterly*, VI (1929), 64.
11. Washington Pioneer Project, *Told by the Pioneers*, I (1937), 162.

12. Lodisa Frizzell, *Across the Plains to California* (New York, 1915), 23.
13. Washington Pioneer Project, *op. cit.*, 162.
14. A. W. Harlan, "Journal While Crossing the Plains in 1850," *Annals of Iowa,* XI (1913), 51.
15. Frizzell, *op. cit.*, 20.
16. Mary A. Maverick, *Memoirs* (San Antonio, 1921), 12.
17. Susan Shelby Magoffin, *Down the Santa Fe Trail and Into Mexico* (New Haven, 1926), 4.
18. Mrs. D. B. Bates, *Incidents on Land and Water* (Boston, 1860), 213.
19. Oregon Pioneer Association, 19th Annual Reunion, *Transactions* (Portland, 1891), 42.
20. James Clyman, "Diary of a Journey Through the Far West," May 28, 1844 (Henry E. Huntington Library).
21. Frizzell, *op. cit.*, 15.
22. Oregon Pioneer Association, *op. cit.*, 51.
23. Frizzell, *op. cit.*, 21.
24. Magoffin, *op. cit.*, 7, 37, 75.
25. Oregon Pioneer Association, *op. cit.*, 41, 45.
26. Frizzell, *op. cit.*, 21.
27. Oregon Pioneer Association, *op. cit.*, 42, 45.
28. Walker D. Wyman, "California Emigrant Letters," *California Historical Society, Quarterly,* XXIV (1945), 133.
29. Georgia W. Read, "Women and Children on the Oregon-California Trail in the Gold-Rush Years," *Missouri Historical Review,* XXXIX (1944), 10.
30. Frizzell, *op. cit.*, 16.
31. Jesse Applegate, *A Day with the Cow Column in 1843* (Chicago, 1934), 55.
32. Waters, *op. cit.*, 73.
33. Magoffin, *op. cit.*, 66.
34. Fred Lockley, "Recollections of Benjamin Franklin Bonney," *Oregon Historical Quarterly,* XXIV (1923), 49.
35. Read, *op. cit.*, 9.
36. Oregon Pioneer Association, 35th Annual Reunion, *Transactions* (Portland, 1907), 169.
37. Oregon Pioneer Association, 19th A.R., *op. cit.*, 41-42.
38. Waters, *op. cit.*, 64.
39. Frizzell, *op. cit.*, 17, 19, 23.
40. Oregon Pioneer Association, 35th A.R., *op. cit.*, 161.
41. Oregon Pioneer Association, 19th A.R., *op. cit.*, 54.
42. Magoffin, *op. cit.*, 30.
43. Read, *op. cit.*, 9.
44. Applegate, *op. cit.*, 19.
45. Waters, *op. cit.*, 79.
46. Mrs. Orsemus B. Boyd, *Cavalry Life in Tent and Field* (New York, 1894), 30-35.
47. Mrs. H. A. Ropes, *Six Months in Kansas* (Boston, 1856), 34-36.
48. Bates, *op. cit.*, 225.
49. Loreta J. Velazquez, *The Woman in Battle* (Hartford, n.d.), 577.
50. Montana State University, *Sources of Northwest History,* No. 4, 1937, 3.
51. Elizabeth B. Custer, *Following the Guidon* (New York, 1890), 117.
52. Julia L. Lovejoy, "Letters," *Kansas Historical Quarterly,* XVI (1948), 180-181.
53. Major Sir R. L. Price, *The Two Americas* (London, 1877), 258.

54. Bates, *op. cit.*, 284-85.
55. *Ibid*, 291; Edward A. Sherman, "Sherman Was There," *California Historical Society, Quarterly*, XXIV (1945), 65-69.
56. Atchison (Kansas) *Weekly Free Press*, November 10, 1866.

VII. A LODGING FOR THE NIGHT

1. James F. Meline, *Two Thousand Miles on Horseback* (New York, 1867), 151.
2. Mrs. H. A. Ropes, *Six Months in Kansas* (Boston, 1856), 40-41.
3. Martha Summerhayes, *Vanished Arizona* (Chicago, 1939), 40-41.
4. Elizabeth A. Roe, *Recollections of Frontier Life* (Rockford, 1885), 197.
5. Mrs. Orsemus B. Boyd, *Cavalry Life in Tent and Field* (New York, 1894), 145.
6. Sara T. L. Robinson, *Kansas: Its Interior and Exterior Life* (Boston, 1857), 28.
7. Ropes, *op. cit.*, 51.
8. Eliza W. Farnham, *California Indoors and Out* (New York, 1856), 307.
9. Elizabeth Ellet, *Pioneer Women of the West* (New York, 1852), 412.
10. Boyd, *op. cit.*, 46.
11. Amelia K. Clappe, *The Shirley Letters* (San Francisco, 1922), 321.
12. Loreta J. Velazquez, *The Woman in Battle* (Hartford, n.d.), 578.
13. Farnham, *op. cit.*, 348.
14. Mrs. D. B. Bates, *Incidents on Land and Water* (Boston, 1860), 218.
15. Julia L. Lovejoy, "Letters," *Kansas Historical Quarterly*, XV (1947), 369.

VIII. VANITY CONQUERS ALL

1. *Kansas Historical Quarterly*, XVI (1948), 100.
2. Mrs. George H. Gilland, "Pioneer Patchwork," *Annals of Wyoming*, XI (1939), 255.
3. Elizabeth Gedney, "Cross Section of Pioneer Life at Fourth Plain," *Oregon Historical Quarterly*, XLIII (1942), 14.
4. Howard County (Missouri) *Advertiser*, May 1, 1884.
5. Clinton (Missouri) *Daily Advocate*, September 3, 1883.
6. Washington Pioneer Project, *Told by the Pioneers*, III (1938), 162.
7. Gedney, *op. cit.*, 14.
8. Elizabeth B. Custer, *Following the Guidon* (New York, 1890), 257.
9. Mrs. Orsemus B. Boyd, *Cavalry Life in Tent and Field* (New York, 1894), 225.
10. Alice M. Shields, "Army Life on the Wyoming Frontier," *Annals of Wyoming*, XIII (1941), 332.
11. Mary A. Maverick, *Memoirs* (San Antonio, 1921), 56.
12. *Larned* (Kansas) *Optic*, July 30, 1880.
13. *Alta California*, July 14, 1851.
14. Bradford R. Alden, "Oregon and California Letters," *California Historical Society, Quarterly*, XXVIII (1949), 199-232.
15. Edward A. Sherman, "Sherman Was There," *California Historical Society, Quarterly*, XXIV (1945), 67-69, 165.
16. Amelia K. Clappe, *The Shirley Letters* (San Francisco, 1922), 143, 330.
17. Albert D. Richardson, "Letters on the Pike's Peak Gold Region," edited by Louise Barry, *Kansas Historical Quarterly*, XII (1943), 17.
18. Theodore G. Blegen, ed., *Land of Their Choice; the Immigrants Write Home* (University of Minnesota Press, Minneapolis, 1955), 306-07.
19. Gilland, *op. cit.*, 257.

20. Emily Faithfull, *Three Visits to America* (Edinburgh, 1884), 216.
21. Martha Summerhayes, *Vanished Arizona* (Chicago, 1939), 172.
22. Lydia M. Waters, "Account of a Trip Across the Plains in 1855," *Society of California Pioneers, Quarterly*, VI (1929), 76.
23. Elizabeth B. Custer, *Tenting on the Plains* (New York, 1887), 133, 238.
24. Mrs. H. A. Ropes, *Six Months in Kansas* (Boston, 1856), 24.
25. *Idaho World*, December 10, 1864.
26. William H. Dixon, *White Conquest*, I (London, 1876), 213.

IX. "A LITTLE LIGHT DIVERSION"

1. Angie B. Bowden, *Early Schools of Washington Territory* (Seattle, 1935), 389.
2. Lydia M. Waters, "Account of a Trip Across the Plains in 1855," *Society of California Pioneers, Quarterly*, VI (1929), 76.
3. Mrs. Orsemus B. Boyd, *Cavalry Life in Tent and Field* (New York, 1894), 172.
4. Alice M. Risley, "Pioneer Days in West Plains and Howell County," *Missouri Historical Review*, XXIII (1929), 580.
5. Percy G. Ebbutt, *Emigrant Life in Kansas* (London, 1886), 58.
6. *White Cloud* (Kansas) *Chief*, January 6, 1859.
7. Mrs. T. B. H. Stenhouse, *An Englishwoman in Utah* (London, 1882), 209.
8. William Wright (Dan De Quille), *History of the Big Bonanza* (Hartford, 1876), 29.
9. Amelia K. Clappe, *The Shirley Letters* (San Francisco, 1922), 330.
10. Hjalmar H. Boyesen, "Types of American Women," *Forum*, VIII (1889), 343.
11. Ebbutt, *op. cit.*, 56-57.
12. *Dickinson County Chronicle*, Abilene, Kansas, June 28, 1878.
13. *Topeka* (Kansas) *Daily Commonwealth*, January 25, 1873.
14. Washington Pioneer Project, *Told by the Pioneers*, III (1938), 185.
15. Edward A. Sherman, "Sherman Was There," *California Historical Society, Quarterly*, XXIV (1945), 61.
16. *White Cloud* (Kansas) *Chief*, January 5, 1860.
17. Harriet K. Orr, "A Pioneer Bride," *Annals of Wyoming*, IX (1934), 666-67.
18. Frances M. A. Roe, *Army Letters from an Officer's Wife* (New York, 1909), 26-27.
19. Sara T. L. Robinson, *Kansas: Its Interior and Exterior Life* (Boston, 1857), 72-73.
20. Eliza S. Warren, *Memoir of the West: The Spaldings* (Portland, Oregon, 1916), 58.
21. Julia L. Lovejoy, "Letters," *Kansas Historical Quarterly*, XV (1947), 312.
22. Timothy Flint, *Recollections* (Boston, 1826), 258-61.
23. Charles A. Johnson, *The Frontier Camp Meeting* (Dallas, 1955), 94, 265, 282.
24. Mary D. Taylor, "A Farmers' Wives' Society in Pioneer Days," *Annals of Iowa*, XIII, Ser. 3 (1921), 23.
25. *Missouri Register*, Boonville, July 23, 1840.
26. Martha Summerhayes, *Vanished Arizona* (Chicago, 1939), 161.
27. Oregon Pioneer Association, 19th Annual Reunion, *Transactions* (Portland, 1891), 50.
28. Washington Pioneer Project, *op. cit.*, 182.
29. Montana State University, *Sources of Northwest History*, No. 24, 1937, 2.
30. Mary Dodge Woodward, *The Checkered Years*. Published by the Caxton

Printers, Ltd., Caldwell, Idaho, 1937. Used by special permission of the copyright owners.
31. Washington Pioneer Project, *op. cit.*, I, 79; III, 65.
32. Boyd, *op. cit.*, 65.
33. Mrs. George H. Gilland, "Pioneer Patchwork," *Annals of Wyoming*, XI (1939), 274.
34. Washington Pioneer Project, *op. cit.*, I, 101.
35. Christiana Holmes Tillson, *A Woman's Story of Pioneer Illinois* (Chicago, 1919), 82.
36. Boyd, *op. cit.*, 182.
37. *Missouri Statesman*, December 14, 1849.
38. Sarah J. Lippincott, *New Life in New Lands* (London, 1873), 27.

X. PINK TIGHTS AND RED VELVET SKIRTS

1. H. H. Bancroft, *Works*, XXIII (San Francisco, 1888), 245.
2. Sarah J. Lippincott, *New Life in New Lands* (London, 1873), 43, 115.
3. David R. Cobb, "Letters," edited by David G. Cobb, *Kansas Historical Quarterly*, XI (1942), 65-71.
4. Edwin F. Morse, "Story of a Gold Miner," *California Historical Society, Quarterly*, VI (1927), 339.
5. Constance Rourke, *Troupers of the Gold Coast* (New York, 1928).
6. *Ibid*, 174.
7. Edgar M. Branch, *Literary Apprenticeship of Mark Twain* (Urbana, Illinois, 1950), 288.
8. George D. Lyman, *The Saga of the Comstock Lode* (New York, 1949), 280.
9. Mrs. Charles Ellis, "Robert Foote," *Annals of Wyoming*, XV (1943), 84.
10. *Missouri Historical Review*, XLV (1951), 75.
11. Mrs. D. B. Dyer, *Fort Reno* (New York, 1896), 22.
12. *Atchison* (Kansas) *Globe*, March 2, 1881.
13. *Frank Leslie's Weekly*, October 13, 1877, 85.
14. *Kansas Daily Commonwealth*, Topeka, July 1, 1873.
15. Louella Dickenson, *A Trip Across the Plains in 1846* (San Francisco, 1904), 84.
16. Lippincott, *op. cit.*, 43.
17. Warren Richardson, "History of First Frontier Days Celebrations," *Annals of Wyoming*, XIX (1947), 42-43.

XI. A HOME IN THE WEST

1. Sarah Royce, *A Frontier Lady* (New Haven, 1932), 80-84.
2. Mrs. H. A. Ropes, *Six Months in Kansas* (Boston, 1856), 49.
3. Washington Pioneer Project, *Told by the Pioneers*, III (1938), 48.
4. Mrs. D. B. Bates, *Incidents on Land and Water* (Boston, 1860), 131.
5. Howard Ruede, *Sod-House Days, Letters from a Kansas Homesteader*, edited by John Ise (New York, 1937), 29.
6. Louise Barry, "New England Emigrant Aid Company Parties of 1855," *Kansas Historical Quarterly*, XII (1943), 247.
7. Julia L. Lovejoy, "Letters," *Kansas Historical Quarterly*, XV (1947), 314.
8. Mrs. John Berry, "A Letter from the Mines," *California Historical Society, Quarterly*, VI (1927), 293.
9. Margaret W. Sackett, "Pioneer Ranch Life in Wyoming," *Annals of Wyoming*, XIV (1942), 172.
10. Virginia H. Asbury and Albert N. Doerschuk, "The Boone, Hays and Berry

Families of Jackson County," *Missouri Historical Review*, XXIII (1929), 537.
11. Sarah Welch Nossaman, "Pioneering at Bonaparte and Near Pello," *Annals of Iowa*, XIII, Ser. 3 (1921), 450.
12. Oregon Pioneer Association, 19th Annual Reunion, *Transactions* (Portland, 1891), 54.
13. Bates, *op. cit.*, 152.
14. Washington Pioneer Project, *op. cit.*, 156.
15. Frances C. Carrington, *My Army Life* (Philadelphia, 1911), 56.
16. Mary Osborn Douthit, ed., *Souvenir of Western Women* (Portland, Oregon, 1905), 91.
17. Ropes, *op. cit.*, 154.
18. *Liberty* (Missouri) *Weekly Tribune*, February 5, 1858.
19. Elizabeth Gedney, "Cross Section of Pioneer Life at Fourth Plain," *Oregon Historical Quarterly*, XLIII (1942), 15.
20. Mrs. Orsemus B. Boyd, *Cavalry Life in Tent and Field* (New York, 1894), 38.
21. Mrs. D. B. Dyer, *Fort Reno* (New York, 1896), 37.
22. Mrs. George H. Gilland, "Pioneer Patchwork," *Annals of Wyoming*, XI (1939), 271.
23. Jesse Applegate, *A Day With the Cow Column in 1843* (Chicago, 1934), 156.
24. Carrington, *op. cit.*, 99.
25. Frank Haucke, "The Kaw or Kansa Indians," *Kansas Historical Quarterly*, XX (1952), 51.
26. Washington Pioneer Project, *op. cit.*, I, 112.
27. Susan Shelby Magoffin, *Down the Santa Fe Trail and Into Mexico* (New Haven, 1926), 245.
28. Christiana Holmes Tillson, *A Woman's Story of Pioneer Illinois* (Chicago, 1919), 120.
29. Eliza W. Farnham, *California Indoors and Out* (New York, 1856), 357.
30. Applegate, *op. cit.*, 28.
31. Oregon Pioneer Association, 35th Annual Reunion, *Transactions* (Portland, 1907), 155.
32. Boyd, *op. cit.*, 299.
33. Oregon Pioneer Association, 19th A.R., *op. cit.*, 108-09.
34. Mary Dodge Woodward, *The Checkered Years* (Caldwell, Idaho, 1937), 84.
35. Frances M. A. Roe, *Army Letters from an Officer's Wife* (New York, 1909), 58.
36. Elizabeth A. Roe, *Recollections of Frontier Life* (Rockford, 1885), 109.
37. Boyd, *op. cit.*, 179.
38. Washington Pioneer Project, *op. cit.*, I, 166-69.
39. Sara T. L. Robinson, *Kansas: Its Interior and Exterior Life* (Boston, 1857), 5.
40. *Dodge City Times*, March 24, 1877.
41. Woodward, *op. cit.*, 73, 207.

XII. THE GREAT FEMALE SHORTAGE

1. William H. Dixon, *White Conquest*, I (London, 1876), 25, 29.
2. Elliott Coues, ed., *New Light on the Early History of the Greater Northwest; the Manuscript Journals of Alexander Henry and of David Thompson* (New York, 1897), 735, 898.
3. Alice H. Finckh, "Gottfried Duden Views Missouri, 1824-1827," *Missouri Historical Review*, XLIV (1949), 22.

4. *Fort Scott* (Kansas) *Democrat*, March 29, 1860.
5. Frances Fuller Victor, *River of the West* (Hartford, 1870), 175-76.
6. Charles D. Ferguson, *Experiences of a Forty-Niner* (Cleveland, 1888), 62.
7. George Gary, "Diary," annotated by Charles H. Carey, *Oregon Historical Quarterly*, XXIV (1923), 269-331.
8. Lewis H. Garrard, *Wah-To-Yah and the Taos Trail* (Norman, Oklahoma, 1955), 54.
9. Colonel William H. Emory, *Notes of a Military Reconnaissance* (Washington, 1848), 73.
10. Ernest De Massey, "A Frenchman in the Gold Rush," translated by Mrs. Van Rensselaer Wilbur, *California Historical Society, Quarterly*, VI (1927), 150.
11. Coues, *op. cit.*, 849.
12. Alex J. Rosborough, "A. M. Rosborough, Special Indian Agent," *California Historical Society, Quarterly*, XXVI (1947), 205.
13. Fred Lockly, "Recollections of Benjamin Franklin Bonney," *Oregon Historical Society Quarterly*, XXIV (1923), 50.
14. Coues, *op. cit.*, 849, 911.
15. Walter Colton, *Three Years in California* (New York, 1860).
16. Caspar T. Hopkins, "California Recollections," *California Historical Society, Quarterly*, XXVI (1947), 68.
17. Peter H. Burnett, *Recollections and Opinions of an Old Pioneer* (New York, 1880), 302.
18. Albert D. Richardson, "Letters on the Pike's Peak Gold Region," edited by Louise Barry, *Kansas Historical Quarterly*, XII (1943), 17.
19. Clappe, Amelia K., *The Shirley Letters* (San Francisco, 1922), 136.
20. Ferguson, *op. cit.*, 153.
21. Caroline C. Leighton, *Life at Puget Sound* (Boston, 1884), 106.
22. H. H. Bancroft, *Works*, XXIII (San Francisco, 1888), 235-36.
23. Washington Pioneer Project, *Told by the Pioneers*, III (1938), 168.
24. Edward C. Abbott and Helena Huntington Smith, *We Pointed Them North* (University of Oklahoma Press, Oklahoma, 1955), 111.
25. Alice McCreery and Tacetta B. Walker, "Wyoming's Fourth Governor—William A. Richards," *Annals of Wyoming*, XX (1948), 99-130.
26. Henry M. Madden, "California for Hungarian Readers," letters of Janos Xantus, *California Historical Society, Quarterly*, XXVIII (1949), 129.
27. Mrs. Orsemus B. Boyd, *Cavalry Life in Tent and Field* (New York, 1894), 196-99.
28. Katherine G. Fougera, *With Custer's Cavalry* (Caldwell, Idaho, 1942), 96.
29. Elizabeth Ellet, *Pioneer Women of the West* (New York, 1852), 384.
30. Bancroft, *op. cit.*, 233.
31. Levi Stowell, "Bound for the Land of Canaan, Ho!" with introduction and notes by Marco G. Thorne, *California Historical Society Quarterly*, XXVII (1948), 365, 368.
32. De Massey, *op. cit.*, 365.
33. William Wright (Dan De Quille), *History of the Big Bonanza* (Hartford, 1876), 77 ff.
34. *Boonville* (Missouri) *Observer*, August 12, 1847.
35. Eliza W. Farnham, *California Indoors and Out* (New York, 1856), 25.
36. Stowell, *op. cit.*, 261.
37. *New York Times*, September 30, November 6, October 24, 1865; January 16, 26, May 6, 1866; Angie B. Bowden, *Early Schools of Washington Territory* (Seattle, 1935), 519; Mary O. Douthit, ed., *The Souvenir of Western*

Women (Portland, Oregon, 1905), 135-36, 190-92; Flora A. P. Engle, "The Story of the Mercer Expedition," *Washington Historical Quarterly*, VI (1915), 225-237; Washington Pioneer Project, *op. cit.*, 207.

XIII. WYOMING TEA PARTY

1. Carrie Chapman Catt and Nettie R. Shuler, *Woman Suffrage and Politics* (New York, 1923), 75; Robert B. David, *Finn Burnett* (Glendale, 1937), 234; Grace R. Hebard, "The First Woman Jury," *Journal of American History*, VII (1913), 1301; Anna H. Shaw, *The Story of a Pioneer* (New York, 1915), 243; Katharine A. Morton, "A Historical Review of Woman Suffrage," *Annals of Wyoming*, XII (1940), 23.
2. Bill Nye, "Bill Nye's Experience; Tells What He Knows About Woman Suffrage," *Annals of Wyoming*, XVI (1944), 66.
3. Catt and Shuler, *op. cit.*, 78-79.
4. Hebard, *op. cit.*, 1302-1304.
5. *Cheyenne Daily Leader*, September 6, 1870.
6. Nora G. Dunn, "Reminiscences of Fourscore Years and Eight," *Annals of Wyoming*, XIX (1947), 133.
7. Nye, *op. cit.*, 66.
8. Morton, *op. cit.*, 24.
9. Hebard, *op. cit.*, 1340.
10. Sarah J. Lippincott, *New Life in New Lands* (London, 1873), 35.
11. Shaw, *op. cit.*, 161, 203.
12. *Fort Scott Democrat*, September 22, 1859.
13. Elizabeth Cady Stanton, *Eighty Years and More* (New York, 1898), 245.
14. *Topeka Weekly Leader*, September 12, 1867.

XIV. CASTING OFF THE SHACKLES

1. Walker D. Wyman, "California Emigrant Letters," *California Historical Society, Quarterly*, XXIV (1945), 348.
2. Charles D. Ferguson, *Experiences of a Forty-Niner* (Cleveland, 1888), 148.
3. Emily Faithfull, *Three Visits to America* (Edinburgh, 1884), 226.
4. Washington Pioneer Project, *Told by the Pioneers* (Portland, 1938), 135.
5. *Cheyenne Democratic Leader*, April 23, 1885.
6. *Howard County* (Missouri) *Advertiser*, December 1, 1886.
7. Peter H. Burnett, *Recollections and Opinions of an Old Pioneer* (New York, 1880), 282.
8. Edward C. Abbott and Helena Huntington Smith, *We Pointed Them North* (University of Oklahoma Press, Oklahoma, 1955), 74.
9. William H. Dixon, *White Conquest*, I (London, 1876), 166.
10. Mrs. D. B. Dyer, *Fort Reno* (New York, 1896), 13-14.
11. Amelia K. Clappe, *The Shirley Letters* (San Francisco, 1922), 39.
12. Oregon Pioneer Association, 35th Annual Reunion, *Transactions* (Portland, 1907), 165.
13. William R. Hogan, "Pamela Mann: Texas Frontierswoman," *Southwest Review*, XX (1935), 360-70.
14. *Official Report of the Trial of Laura D. Fair for the Murder of Alex. P. Crittenden*, from the short-hand notes of Marsh & Osbourne (San Francisco, 1871).
15. Dixon, *op. cit.*, 168.
16. War of the Rebellion, *Official Records*, Series II, Vol. V, 78.
17. Ann Eliza Young, *Life in Mormon Bondage* (Philadelphia, 1908).
18. Mrs. T. B. H. Stenhouse, *An Englishwoman in Utah* (London, 1882).

19. William Hanchett, "The Question of Religion and the Taming of California," *California Historical Society, Quarterly*, XXXII (1953), 286.
20. Russell K. Hickman, "Lewis Bodwell, Frontier Preacher: The Early Years," *Kansas Historical Quarterly*, XII (1943), 286.
21. *Dodge City Messenger*, February 26, 1874.
22. Dixon, *op. cit.*, 317.
23. George A. Root, "Reminiscences of the Historical Society," *Kansas Historical Quarterly*, XI (1942), 82-89; Carry A. Nation, *The Use and Need of the Life of Carry A. Nation* (Topeka, 1909); Herbert Asbury, *Carry Nation* (New York, 1929).
24. Harry Levinson, "Mary Elizabeth Lease," *Kansas Magazine* (1948), 18-24; Martin F. Schmitt and Dee Brown, *The Settlers' West* (New York, 1955), 221-22.

XV. SCHOOLMARMS AND MATERNAL FORCES

1. Catharine E. Beecher, *The Duty of American Women to Their Country* (New York, 1845), 72, 113.
2. J. L. McConnell, *Western Characters* (New York, 1853), 321.
3. Julia L. Lovejoy, "Letters," *Kansas Historical Quarterly*, XV (1947), 318.
4. *Leavenworth Daily Times*, June 10, 1859.
5. Anna H. Shaw, *Story of a Pioneer* (New York, 1915), 46.
6. Angie B. Bowden, *Early Schools of Washington Territory* (Seattle, 1935), 164.
7. McConnell, *op. cit.*, 324-35.
8. Roy Holt, "The Pioneer Teacher," *Sheep and Goat Raiser*, XXXVI (November, 1955), 28-32.
9. *Alta California*, June 19, 1851.
10. H. H. Bancroft, *Works*, XXV (San Francisco, 1890), 171.
11. J. W. Boddam-Whetham, *Western Wanderings* (London, 1874), 43.
12. Sarah W. Nossaman, "Pioneering at Bonaparte and Near Pella," *Annals of Iowa*, XIII, Ser. 3 (1923), 441; Joseph W. Ellison, "Diary of Maria Parsons Belshaw," *Oregon Historical Quarterly*, XXXIII (1932), 330; Oregon Pioneer Association, 19th Annual Reunion, *Transactions* (Portland, 1891), 45.
13. Amelia K. Clappe, *The Shirley Letters* (San Francisco, 1922), 326.

XVI. MALE VIEWPOINT

1. Charles L. Martin, *Sketch of Sam Bass, the Bandit* (Norman, Oklahoma), 20.
2. *Kansas City Enterprise*, August 22, 1857.
3. *Idaho News*, Boise, February 6, 1864.
4. Stuart Henry, *Conquering Our Great American Plains* (New York, 1930), 248.
5. *Western Democrat*, Andrew, Iowa, November 23, 1849.
6. Levi Stowell, "Bound for the Land of Canaan, Ho!" with introduction and notes by Marco G. Thorne, *California Historical Society, Quarterly*, XXVII (1948), 361-62.
7. *Alta California*, February 4 and June 27, 1851.
8. Hjalmar H. Boyesen, "Types of American Women," *Forum*, VIII (1889), 339-40.
9. William Hanchett, "The Question of Religion and the Taming of California," *California Historical Society, Quarterly*, XXXII (1953), 125-26.

Index

311

The author wishes to express gratitude to the societies, university libraries and organizations listed below for permission to include the following valuable photographic prints:

The California Historical Society for Caroline Chapman and Laura Fair.

The Denver Public Library Western Collection for Josephine Meeker (A White Squaw); photo by Bates & Nye.

The F. Hal Higgins Collection for "Mama in her new bustle" inspecting the wheat combine.

The Kansas State Historical Society, Topeka for Clarina Irene Nichols, Carry Nation, Mary E. Lease, and the scene of the dance hall girls on the roof of a Wichita saloon.

The Library of Congress for the cartoon depicting the first female jurists.

The Missouri Historical Society for Susan Shelby Magoffin.

The Nebraska State Historical Society for the family group in front of the sod house, the Chataqua tent, and the schoolmarm surrounded by her charges. (All from the S. D. Butcher Collection)

The Nevada State Historical Society for Julia Bulette.

The Newberry Library, Chicago, for Brown's "ranche-stop." (Ayer Collection)

The New York Public Library for Lotta Crabtree, Lola Montez, Adah Isaacs Menken and Mrs. Brigham Young #19.

The Oklahoma Historical Society for "the reliable sunbonnet" on horseback, and Rose of Cimarron.

The Title Insurance and Trust Company, Los Angeles, for Arizona Mary. (Collection of Historical Photographs)

The University of Illinois Library for the print of the handcart pioneers, pictures of Virginia Reed and Loretta Velasquez, the square dancing scene, and the caricature of the frontier schoolmarm (FAO Darley).

The University of Kansas Library for the Sunday school picnic scene. (Pennell Collection)

The University of Oregon Library for the cook wagons at harvest time and the two young students between lessons (the latter from the Roy Andrews Collection).

The University of Wyoming Library for Elizabeth Custer, Martha Summerhayes, Frances Grummond, Asa Mercer, Esther McQuigg Morris, Louisa Ann Swain, the imposing hall of justice in Laramie, the contemporary impression of local ladies casting their votes (Leslie's Weekly, Nov. 24, 1888), Martha Conneray, and Calamity Jane "in uniform." (Archives and Western History Department)